EMPRESS DOWAGER CIXI

CHINA'S LAST DYNASTY AND THE LONG REIGN OF A FORMIDABLE CONCUBINE

—

Legends and Lives During the
Declining Days of the Qing Dynasty.

X. L. Woo

Algora Publishing
New York

Library of Congress Card Number: 2002006367

Woo, X. L.
Empress dowager Cixi / X. L. Woo.
    p. cm.
ISBN 1-892941-88-0
1. Cixi, Empress dowager of China, 1835-1908. 2.
Empresses—China—Biography. 3. China—History--Guangxu, 1875-1908. I.
Title.
DS763.63.C58 W66 2002
951'.035'092—dc21

2002006367

Printed in the United States

To Beili Cheng, my beloved wife.

TABLE OF CONTENTS

INTRODUCTION

In all the history of China, only two women ever conquered and held the heights of power. Both enjoyed long reigns characterized by ruthless intrigue; they maintained an iron grip at the center while the vast country was torn by rebellions and caught up in foreign wars. Through their policy decisions as well as their personal foibles, both left a deep imprint in history and in the minds of the Chinese people, fueling literature and legend.

Fighting to maintain her power base, Empress Cixi struggled with the need to modernize the painfully backward empire she had inherited while honoring age-old traditions. She studied previous rulers' failures and achievements, and especially followed the example of Wu-Hou, who had elevated herself from concubine to empress some 1200 years earlier.

The stories that follow, some legenday, offer a glimpse of life during the declining days of the last Chinese dynasty. Popular rebellions, foreign wars, devastating floods and drought-induced famines killed tens of millions in the 19th century.

Cixi learned her lessons well. She fended off every adversary, prolonging her reign for 48 years. But all her craft and guile were not enough to repair the internal divisions and preserve traditional China against the onslaught of modernity, of Europe, and of her Asian neighbors.

TIMEFRAMES

Han Dynasty — 206 BC – AD 220.

Three Kingdoms — AD 220 – 280. The wisest strategist during this period was Zhuge Liang (AD 181 – 234), who became a symbol of wisdom (see page 120).

Sui Dynasty — AD 181 – 518. The Grand Canal was dug during this dynasty.

Tang Dynasty — AD 618 – 907. The government exam system was established at the beginning of this dynasty to select government officials.

Song Dynasty — AD 960 – 1279.

Yuan Dynasty — 1271 – 1368. When the Yuan Dynasty was founded to the north of the Yangtze River, the southern Song Dynasty was still active, south of the Yangtze River, till 1279. The Yuan Dynasty, like the Qing Dynasty during which these stories take place, was founded by the minority Manchu Clan.

Ming Dynasty — 1368 – 1644. Emperor Yongle of the Ming Dynasty had the Forbidden City built; it was completed in 1420.

Qing Dynasty — 1644 – 1911.

Rulers

Emperor Kangxi — Succeeded to throne at the age of 8 and handled state affairs at the age of 14 (1654 – 1722).

Emperor Xianfeng — Succeeded to the throne in 1850 (1831-1861).

Empress Dowager CiAn — Queen of Emperor Xianfeng. Presumed poisoned by Empress Dowager Cixi (1836 – 1881).

Empress Dowager Cixi — Imperial concubine of Emperor Xianfeng, mother of Emperor Tongzhi. Made Empress Dowager in 1861, she stayed in power for 48 years till her death (1835 – 1908).

Emperor Tongzhi — Son of Empress Dowager Cixi and Emperor Xianfeng, succeeded to throne in 1861 at the age of 6 (1856 –1875).

Emperor Guangxu — Son of Yihuan, the seventh brother of Emperor Xianfeng, and the sister of Empress Dowager Cixi. Adopted by Cixi after her own son died. Succeeded to throne in 1875 at the age of 4. Presumed poisoned by Empress Dowager Cixi (1871 – 1908).

Emperor Xiantong — Succeeded to throne at the age of 3; abdicated in 1911. (1905 – 1967)

Principal Events

1840 – 1842 — The first Opium War. China loses Hong Kong to the British, is forced to open five ports to foreign trade, and pays $21 million in indemnities.

1851 – 1864 — Anti-Manchu factions under Hong Xiuquan (the "Heavenly King," 1813 – 1864) found the Peaceful Heavenly Kingdom. This is known in the West as the Taiping Rebellion.

1856 – 1860 — The Second Opium War. British and French troops occupy Peking (now Beijing). Emperor Xianfeng escapes to Rehe, and dies there.

1857 — The Nian Rebellion begins, and together with the Taiping Rebellion wreaks havoc. In part due to the chaos they caused and cost of quelling the uprisings, the country is unable to prepare against the periodic floods, droughts and famines. Tens of millions die.

1874 – 1885 — Japan attacks Taiwan; and the Sino-French War begins. China loses Vietnam to France.

1894 — The Sino-Japanese War. Korea starts paying tribute to Japan instead of to China.

1900 — Seeking to fend off further foreign encroachments, Empress Dowager Cixi encourages the Yihetuan uprising, known in the West as the Boxer Rebellion. It spins out of control. The imperial family flees to Xi An City.

1908 — Emperor Guangxu dies, presumably poisoned.

PART ONE
RISING TO THE TOP

CHAPTER 1

However powerful you may be, you cannot pull back the chariot of Time; however powerful, you cannot refuse the visit of Death. However wealthy you may be, you cannot bribe the king of Hades; however wealthy, you cannot buy immortality.

She was so beautiful when she was young. She hated aging. She hated having gray hair, but the silver threads stealthily crept onto her head. Whenever Li Lianying saw a gossamer hint of snow among her silky sable hair, he would bury it under the black ones. If by any chance a white hair came off and entwined itself on the comb, he would hide it in his sleeve. Li Lianying did Empress Dowager Cixi's hair. He knew how she would feel if she saw this painful evidence. He knew what she liked and what she did not. He was her favorite eunuch. In a very short time, he had gotten himself promoted to head eunuch.

Sometimes when Empress Dowager Cixi noticed him putting his fingers into his sleeve, she would ask what he was doing. "Just itching. Scratching a bit, my respected Old Buddha." Later in her life, everyone in the Forbidden City called the Empress "Old Buddha" (the word "old," here, was a respectful epithet), and she liked it. Li Lianying had to please her if he wanted to stay in her favor forever. Everyone wanted to please her. No doubt about that. Even the emperor, who was afraid of her, sometimes tried to please her. No wonder people feel a desire to gain power and hold onto it — for just as long as possible.

Today, West Empress Dowager would have a new hairstyle. Li Lianying called it "A Butterfly Among Flowers." He always invented new hairstyles and gave them fanciful names. And while combing her hair, he would tell jokes (often vulgar), which set her laughing. He knew a lot of such jokes, and sometimes he made up new ones to suit the occasion.

Eunuchs all came from poor families, or no families at all. Who wanted to be a eunuch, if he could live otherwise? It was no fun, not to mention the pain, and a lot of blood. The genitals, once removed, were dried and kept in a jar and hung from the beam in the eunuch's bedroom. It was the custom to bury these missing parts with the body when a eunuch died, to make the corpse whole. That was the best that could be done.

When her hair was arranged and breakfast was finished, Empress Dowager Cixi was helped into her formal dress. She donned a heavy headdress, with an ornament on top that looked somewhat like a fan, with fringes hanging down from both ends. On her natural feet (women of the Manchu Clan never bound their feet.) were special shoes, with something like short stilts in the shape of an upside-down flowerpot attached under the middle of the soles. Thus attired, she went to hold court, sitting behind a pearl screen. Emperor Guangxu, still under age, sat on the huge throne before the screen; he said nothing, but he heard everything. He saw everything. He was a clever boy, ambitious, and anxious to make the weakened empire strong and prosperous again.

* * *

Empress Dowager Cixi and Emperor Guangxu lived in the magnificent and awe-inspiring Forbidden City, the imperial compound in the center of the capital. Sometimes called the Purple Forbidden City, it was built between 1406 and 1420 during the Ming Dynasty. It had been home to 24 emperors of the Ming Dynasty and the Qing Dynasty, and served as the seat of imperial power during all that time. From their throne, the emperors governed the country through their courtiers, secretaries and ministers, issuing imperial edicts and initiating military expeditions.

The Forbidden City is the largest[1] and best-preserved palatial complex in the world. It is surrounded by a moat, and by a wall with four gates, with towers above them. On the four corners of the city walls stand four turrets, each with three roofs and 72 roof ridges — masterpieces of ancient Chinese architecture.

---

1. 720,000 square meters (750 meters from east to west and 960 meters from north to south). The moat is 52 meters wide and six meters deep, and the wall is three kilometers long and ten meters high.

The southern part of the Forbidden City served as the emperors' administrative area, while the northern part was their living quarters.[1] The Forbidden City is a city within a city and it was off limits to the common people.

Nine was regarded as the largest number, and its name, when spoken in the Chinese language, has the same sound as "everlasting" — so its use was restricted and in some cases only emperors were entitled to use it. There were 9,999 houses in the Forbidden City, and the nails on every door were arranged in lines of nine.

The predominant color in the Forbidden City is yellow. Nearly all the roofs were of yellow-glazed tiles. According to the ancient Chinese, the universe was made up of five elements: metal, wood, water, fire and earth, with earth the most basic of them all. Yellow, the color of earth, and the emperors were deemed the supreme rulers on Earth. Only Wenyuan Pavilion had a roof of black tiles; it was the imperial library.[2] Black represents water, and water can overcome fire: a constant threat to the collection inside. The names of places within the Forbidden City reflect the essence of Confucianism, in words such as "Benevolence," "Harmony" and "Peace."

Emperor Yongle of the Ming Dynasty began building the Forbidden City in 1406. Records show that it took one million laborers and 100,000 craftsmen fifteen years to complete the project. Everything was built of wood and brick.[3] A special adhesive, made from steamed glutinous rice and egg white, was used to cement the bricks and stone slabs. Timber came from mountains in the outskirts of Fangshan Town as well as from the remote Sichuan and Yunnan provinces.

---

1. The main structures are arranged symmetrically along a central axis. The most imposing building in the work area is the Hall of Supreme Harmony, where the most important ceremonies of the feudal dynasties were held, including the ascension of the emperors to the throne, their marriages, and their conferring of titles on officials. The Hall of Medium Harmony, standing behind it, was where the emperors rested before holding ceremonies and receiving officials. In the Hall of Protective Harmony, the emperors gave banquets and interviewed in person successful candidates of imperial exams for the selection of government officials. In the living quarters are nine separate housing complexes where the emperors and their families lived. North of the living quarters is a small imperial garden. The Mind Cultivation Hall in the living quarters was where most Qing emperors lived and handled state affairs; it was here that Empress Dowager Cixi attended to state affairs.

2. The Wenyuan Pavilion, or the Imperial Library, stores more than 10 million official documents drawn up over 500 years by central and local governments of the Ming and Qing dynasties. This is the largest and most valuable collection of historical records in the country. It holds a complete collection of all the books published, including an encyclopedia and a 79,337-volume compendium of historical records and feudal rites compiled over ten years (1772-1781) by the nation's most accomplished scholars.

3. Three billion bricks were used.

Tens of thousands of huge stone slabs were transported to the capital from faraway provinces.[1]

The best artists and most skillful craftsmen of the day brought their talents to bear, and today the Forbidden City is a treasury of the finest examples of Chinese frescos, carvings and other traditional crafts.

CHAPTER 2

Empress Dowager Cixi was born into a government official's family. Her father was appointed to the rank of a general, though he had never fought any battles. It was said that when his daughter was born, there was a scent of orchids in the room; so her given name was Lan Er (meaning Orchid Child). She had two brothers and a younger sister, but she was her parents' favorite, the apple of their eye. She was beautiful, clever and talented. When she was eleven, her father was transferred to Wuwu, a large city situated near the Yangtze River, and later to Canton, an even bigger city facing the sea.

"Opium's ready, Dad." Lan Er called to her father, who stood at the window, gazing into the yard where a cock was bullying some hens. He was proud of her. She could load opium for him now. Since China had been defeated in the Opium War in 1840, the opium trade had become open and many government officials and officers had formed the habit of smoking it. Even Empress Dowager Cixi herself smoked while she was in power. Someone had recommended opium to her when she had a stomachache; and it was said that when she smoked, her stomachache ceased.

"Um." Her father grunted his reply. In China, at that time, parents never said "thank you" to children. It was taken for granted that children should do things for parents. Filial duty.

Many aristocrats of the Manchu Clan loved to watch operas. So did her father. And her father often brought along Lan Er. Later on, when she ruled the empire, she had operas performed especially for her in the Forbidden City.

By the age of sixteen, Lan Er had an oval face, a straight nose, crescent-shaped eyebrows, almond-shaped eyes as clear as crystal, peach-flushed cheeks

---

1. The largest piece, which lies behind the Hall of Protective Harmony, weighs 250 tons. It is 16 meters long, 3 meters wide and almost 2 meters thick. The slab was hauled 50 kilometers from the outskirts of Fangshan Town to the site by 20,000 laborers. The hauling was done in winter, on man-made ice, and took 28 days.

that dimpled when she smiled, and ebony-black hair in a tress so oily and smooth that it seemed as though any fly that might have the temerity to halt upon it would slide right down. Now she sat at the table in the center of the room, sipping tea and looking at her father lying on the bed and smoking opium, and sighing deeply at intervals.

"What's wrong?" Lan Er asked. Her father put down the long-stemmed opium pipe on the lacquer tray, and looked up from the bed.

"The situation in Guangxi Province is getting worse. The rebellion."

"Yes, they are fighting their way eastward and will soon reach here." She didn't look worried. Hers was a worriless age.

"They will kill us. Everyone of our clan." Her father could not suppress the anxiety in his voice. He had been appointed a general because of his destiny, not because of his talent as a fighter. He was really no fighter.

"What shall we do?"

"I don't know. Wait to be killed."

"Why not ask for a sick leave? We can go back to Peking."[1]

"Good idea."

* * *

Lan Er's family left Canton City in a boat they had hired, with the crew on board. At that time, such ferryboats belonged to a family or an individual who served as the crew. This particular boat belonged to a family, a husband and wife with a teenage boy. The man and the boy rowed. The wife cooked for the passengers, who were just like lodgers in an inn. Only this was a mobile inn.

The boat had a cabin in the middle of the deck, which was divided into two sections with a partition. The larger, front section was for the passengers; and the back was for the owner's family, including a cooking space. There were no railings around the boat, which was none too big. There was a mast, and when the wind was favorable, the husband would put up the sails and man the rudder — a lot of energy saved. When they reached a village or a town, he would go ashore for provisions. The passengers would also step ashore, for sightseeing.

Everything was all right, along the route, until one night while the boat was at anchor. It was already deep into the night when robbers came on board with swords in hand, reflecting the moonlight. Everyone in the cabin woke up in a

1. In recent years, the accepted spelling of Chinese names and cities in English has been changed. Peking is now Beijing; but for the most part, we will stick with the traditional usage.

panic. They begged the intruders to spare their lives. The robbers took all the valuables from the passenger family, but didn't touch anything that belonged to the boat owner — it was the unwritten rule among outlaws. After the thugs left, no one could go back to sleep. The boat owner's family was hiding in their back cabin while the passenger family was crying bitterly. How could they pay for their lodging and food, when they had just been robbed of almost everything? Lan Er's father collapsed and fell seriously ill.

The family used to be rich. Rich people generally married their daughters off early, to keep them from being selected to work as palace maids in the Forbidden City. Life as a maid in the Forbidden City was not so desirable as might be imagined by someone who had never been there. The slightest mistake or offense would bring a severe punishment; many girls were beaten to death. It all depended on the mood of the emperor or the queen at the time of the offense. Only the emperor or the queen had the right to inflict such penalties in the Forbidden City. Lan Er would have been married already, if her family hadn't lost its wealth.

When her father held his position in Canton City, an officer working under him had offended a critique official. (A critique official was someone who, by law, could file an official criticism of anyone, including the emperor. The ancestors of the Qing Dynasty had made that law in hopes that their descendents, the future emperors, would have someone to look over their shoulders and urge them to do what was good and suitable, befitting them as emperors.) The officer working under Lan Er's father detained a boat that the critique official was on, and blackmailed him for 3,000 taels of silver. The official was very angry and as soon as he reached the capital, he wrote a critique report to the emperor, who sent someone down to investigate. The investigation revealed that Lan Er's father had taken bribes, too. To make his superiors go easy on him, he scraped together everything he had, and bribed them, in turn. He was actually removed from his post before he could send in the planned request for a sick leave — at least they hadn't sent him to jail. He sold some of his estates and paid off the governor of Anhui Province, in the hope that he would appoint him to another position there. But as a Chinese saying goes, misfortunes never come singly. The governor fell sick and died, so the father's money was like pebbles thrown in water, without even ripples to be seen.

Now he was really sick, himself, so off he went with his family back to the capital where he still had at least a house and some farms to live on. The boat got under way at dawn. While the wife served breakfast, Lan Er's mother promised her that they would pay her when they arrived in Peking. The old man was a government official, at least. He could surely afford the fare. The boat owner was not worried about that.

One day, they arrived at the Town of Qinghe. Their boat anchored at the third berth along the wharf. The boat at the second berth, in front, was a little bigger than theirs. The passengers on board that boat were escorting the coffin of an old friend of the mayor of this town to be returned to their hometown. The Mayor, by the name of Wu Tang, was a scholar.

In the late Qing Dynasty, anyone who wanted to serve in the government had two ways to achieve his goal. One was to buy a title and wait for a vacancy corresponding to the title. For instance, if someone bought a title of mayor, he would be eligible for a mayoral vacancy. So-called donations could certainly facilitate the process. The other method was to pass the government tests, at the local and then the provincial levels. Successful candidates could then go to the capital for the final examination, which was held every three years. This examination was very strict, because the top finishers would be made government officials. The system had originally begun in the Tang Dynasty and had been used ever since. Several examiners were chosen by the emperor himself from among the high officials of the central government; they would read and score the test papers.

The examination site had been built long ago. There were rows of bungalows, partitioned into booths. Every candidate was assigned a booth, and the door was locked. He could leave only after he had finished the entire examination, which would take a couple of days. The testee would bring his own food in a basket, and also the brush, the ink and the blank paper to write on; all these things were inspected before he could enter the booth, to prevent cheating. If he wanted to go to the toilet, an attendant would escort him there and back, and lock him in again; he slept inside the booth.

The test consisted of two parts. First, one had to write a composition, under a given title, in a certain fixed style which translates literally as "8-Legged Style." In preparation for this kind of test, the candidates had to learn how to open, carry on and close end an 8-paragraph composition, according to very strict stylistic rules. Second, each candidate had to express his opinions about certain political ideas or about how to handle political affairs. His opinions carried great weight in his score.

When the examiners were reading and scoring the papers, the names of the testees on the papers were covered. When the ten best had been selected, the names were uncovered. Then the papers were handed in for the emperor to read and decide the order of the winners. But before he made any decision, the emperor would give the top ten an additional test, called the imperial exam, in his palace. The title of Zhuangyuan was conferred on the best candidate (in the opinion of the emperor). The next day, the Zhuangyuan would ride on horseback through the main streets in the capital, a special honor. In the evening, the emperor would give a banquet to all those who had passed the final test. Generally, the first three would be given jobs in the Forbidden City, close at hand — where they would have good opportunities to qualify for fast promotion. Others would be appointed to various official posts, some working in the central government, some sent away to be mayors of small towns if there were vacancies.

CHAPTER 3

A scholar should always care for a scholar friend, or his family, when life ran out. It was required by old Chinese customs and etiquette. Mayor Wu knew that his late friend was not a wealthy man. Therefore, he sent a servant to give the family 300 taels of silver. The servant was told where the late friend's boat would be, at the second berth along the wharf. But before the servant arrived, that boat had left and the next boat had moved up one berth. At fate would have it, just as Lan Er's family was in dire need, an unknown mayor sent an unknown former friend 300 taels of silver. The servant didn't know the difference. He only did his job, delivering the silver to the boat at the second berth. Lan Er's family didn't know whether the father had had such a friend at one time. And indeed, with a dead man on board, they had urgent needs to cover. The father had died just the night before. Lucky to have money for a coffin. Also lucky for Mayor Wu, for Lan Er remembered to ask the servant the name of his master. Lan Er had a long memory. And Mayor Wu had a bright future.

* * *

Once back home, they buried the old master's coffin. Now it should have fallen to the sons to shoulder life's burdens for the family. But Lan Er's two brothers were a feckless lot. They idled away their time, lounging about in teahouses, and strolling around town toting cages of their favorite birds. That was the common lifestyle of the sons of the wealthy families of the ruling clan, but they were not wealthy anymore. Now Lan Er had to look after the family's interests.

What could Empress Dowager Cixi remember about her girlhood, living with her parents? Almost everything. She had a distant cousin by the name of Ronglu, a few years younger. They were playmates. She liked Ronglu better than her brothers and sister. Ronglu was clever and talented, while her brothers were undistinguished and her sister mediocre at best, both in looks and in brains. Do birds of a feather flock together? Normally, yes. Still, these siblings would be with her even when she made it to the top. You can't choose your family.

"If you'll be the queen, I'll be your bodyguard," Ronglu often said to Lan Er. (Her family thought she was special, since she was born with the scent of the orchid. And she loved it that way.) He even went so far as to go down on his knees before her to make it look real, or feel real. All this served to rouse in her the ambition for power.

* * *

At three-year intervals, the selection of young ladies for the emperor would begin. It lasted for several months. First, every family of the ruling clan would report their unmarried daughters between the ages thirteen and seventeen to the Clan Affairs Administration. The Administration would send officials and eunuchs to check out the girls on the list. Many names on the long list would be crossed out. Those still remaining would be sent into the Forbidden City for further sifting. Among those selected, some would be sent to the princes. With luck, they would become the princes' concubines. Some of those selected would become imperial maids-in-waiting in the palaces. Only a handful of the luckiest girls would be brought before the emperor.

Most girls longed to be selected and live in the Forbidden City, either as imperial maids or as imperial concubines. Even as an imperial maid, if she took the emperor's fancy she might become an imperial concubine. But as an imperial concubine, if the emperor was never interested in her, she would live alone, forever, until death released her from "solitary confinement." Just try your luck, if you get selected. Getting selected depended on the emperor himself. The girl herself had little hope of affecting that decision — although a girl who was lovely enough, well-born enough, talented enough and ambitious enough might conceivably find ways to tip the scales in her favor.

As destiny would have it, Lan Er was selected as an imperial concubine. She was sent to live in the Round-Bright Garden, the Garden of All Gardens, as the foreigners called it. But getting onto the game board was only the first step. If the emperor never looked at her, her fate would be miserable. Actually, the emperor lived in the Forbidden City, not in the Garden, anyway. So Lan Er was disappointed. But, not to worry. A lucky star was shining over her.

The rebels in the southern provinces had founded their own regime. It was named "The Peaceful Heavenly Kingdom." The Qing Government armies had been defeated. Reports came in from these provinces, bearing bad news. These reports gave the emperor a headache, so he moved into the Round-Bright Garden, with the queen, hoping that a better environment would assuage his dismay when he had to read those reports. Now Lan Er had her chance. She wanted to approach the emperor, but strict rules of etiquette governed every move in the palace. One false step, a whole life of regrets. If she could not go to the emperor, why not let the emperor come to her? Good idea. She always had good ideas.

Emperor Xianfeng came out from the queen's chamber. The queen was of the Nugulu family. Her father was one of the prime ministers. The queen was kind, benevolent and demure. She never showed her teeth, even when grinning. Well, that's right: she never actually grinned, only smiled gently. A real lady.

The emperor sauntered through the imperial garden towards his study. Suddenly, he heard the lilting notes of a woman's voice in song. The voice was so sweet that it drew him toward it, like the song of the sirens. No resistance did he offer. Indeed, the emperor never even thought of resisting. He was quite willing to give in to the magnetic force of so melodious a voice, a female voice. He was a man. How can a man resist a woman? Besides, he could tell that she must be a beautiful young girl. Never was there an ugly female with such a lovely voice. Was there? Ugly, but with a lovely voice? He'd better take a look, and find the answer for himself.

Behind the grove there was a pavilion, and inside the pavilion sat a girl, leaning on the railing. From her attire it was clear that she was an imperial concubine, but a new one he had never set eyes on before.

Lan Er sat in the pavilion, singing for all she was worth. A bait she threw out. She had studied the location well. It lay near the route the emperor would take every day as he went to the queen's chamber and back. Now, from the corner of her eye, she saw him coming. The fish to her hook. The biggest fish.

She knelt down to welcome the emperor, who helped her back to her feet. He studied the new concubine. Beautiful. Really beautiful. The most beautiful of all his concubines. The queen didn't look like this. But an emperor chooses a queen for her modesty and decency, not for her beauty; whereas a concubine is chosen for her beauty. The emperor couldn't take his eyes away from the oval face, the straight nose, crescent-shaped eyebrows, almond-shaped eyes clear as crystal, peach-blushed cheeks that dimpled when she smiled, and ebony-black hair in a tress — a pretty contrast to her fair skin. She was dressed in a red brocade gown of the Mandarin style. The emperor touched her hand, jade-white, with red nails. He felt his heart beating against his rib cage. The emperor was only in his early twenties. His hormones danced.

So that night the emperor slept with Lan Er. She became known later as Imperial Concubine Yan, the emperor's favorite. Before long, Concubine Yan became pregnant. The queen did not have any children and Yan was the only one pregnant among all the concubines at the time, so she received very special treatment. Andehai (known later as Little An), the emperor's favorite eunuch, was sent to wait on her and then became her favorite eunuch. Andehai was a young eunuch with a handsome face and fair complexion. And the most important thing was that he knew how to flatter and to please. If he were to open a school to teach the skills of flattery, he would have had a lot of students.

Emperor Xianfeng was expecting a son, an heir, a successor. If Concubine Yan gave birth to a girl, her side of the scales would tip up; she would lose that precious balance that gave her such an advantage; she would lose her importance in the eyes of the emperor, and with it all her ambitions. But as fate would have it, she bore a son. Now her side of the scales was well weighted indeed. Her position in the palace was unshakable. Even the queen sometimes would yield to her wishes. How did all this come to pass?

CHAPTER 4

Emperor Xianfeng was a young man, and he saw no reason to sleep alone. He had nineteen concubines. Every night before the emperor went to bed, a eunuch brought in a tray on which lay many small rectangular wooden pieces with the names of all the concubines inscribed on them. The eunuch would hold the tray high above his head, and kneel before the emperor. The emperor would make his selection, and would turn upside down the wooden piece with the name on it. Then the eunuch would go to the chamber of the concubine the emperor had chosen. She was stripped naked, bundled into a blanket and deposited at the foot of the emperor's bed — a process that may have dented her dignity, but one that prevented her from damaging the dignity of the emperor by bringing a weapon into his chambers. In the morning, the two eunuchs would come back, wrap the concubine in the blanket, and carry her off to her own chamber. Dates and names were recorded so that if she got pregnant, they could count the days to make sure the child was the emperor's flesh and blood. Since the emperor was so fond of Imperial Concubine Yan, he sent for her almost every night.

They were happy together. Sometimes, the emperor slept so late that he missed holding court.

His courtiers came early and waited in the resting room, but the emperor never showed up to meet them, to hear their reports or discuss all the national affairs. The written instructions set up and handed down by the ancestors did not allow such negligence of state affairs. But the courtiers could do nothing about it. They could hardly go to the emperor's chamber to rouse him. However, the queen could. When she learned from the eunuchs (very gossipy, those eunuchs), she sent her head eunuch to the chamber where the emperor slept. The head eunuch carried on his head the book in which the instructions of the ancestors were written. He knelt before the chamber door and began to recite the instructions aloud. When the emperor heard this, he was obliged to get down from the bed and listen to the recitation, on his knees. If the emperor was sound asleep and didn't hear it, his head eunuch would go to wake him up. Of course, the emperor would be annoyed; but he couldn't ignore the instructions of his ancestors. He had to dress and go to meet his courtiers.

This was happening all too often, lately, for the queen's liking. So one day, the queen went there herself, with the book on her head. The emperor's head eunuch saw the queen coming and dashed into the chamber to report to the emperor, who jumped out of bed and had barely time to put on his shoes. He opened the door and found himself face to face with the queen. He said hastily, "Enough, enough. I'll go now." The queen waited at the door until the emperor left for his court session.

Then she ordered Imperial Concubine Yan to follow her to Kunning Palace. (Each of the buildings in the residential section was called a palace.) Kunning Palace was where the queen held her "court," generally when she wanted to punish someone. The queen was the second in power.

"You mustn't let the emperor sleep so late and neglect state affairs. Do you know it's your fault?" The queen accused Concubine Yan.

In the Forbidden City, if anyone's superior accused him (or her) of anything, no matter whose fault it was, he or she was obliged to say, "It's my fault." And then he or she had to beg to be punished. Once the punishment was inflicted, when it was over, he or she must thank his or her superiors for the punishment. Likewise, if anyone was to be executed by the order of the emperor or the queen, he or she would have to thank the emperor or the queen for the execution. That's feudal China.

So Imperial Concubine Yan said, "Yes, it's my fault." But she pleaded, "I can't refuse to be carried to the emperor's chamber. (Implied, "What's the use of being jealous?") And I can't tell the emperor what to do, if he wants to sleep late." (Implied, "Don't blame me.")

The queen flared up and ordered her eunuchs to beat Concubine Yan. Two eunuchs held her down on the floor. A third eunuch went to fetch a wooden stick. Just as the stick was being brought down, the emperor dashed in and made them stop. While he was meeting with his courtiers, one of his eunuchs had come running to whisper in his ear that the queen had taken Concubine Yan to Kunning Palace. No question what would happen next. He hastily adjourned the meeting and hurried to Kunning Palace, just in time.

"Oh, my dear Queen," the emperor said sweetly, "though Queen has the right to beat her, Queen cannot beat her today." (In the Qing Dynasty, "Emperor" and "Queen" were used to address those august personages; or Empress Dowager, if that were the case.)

"Why not?"

"Concubine Yan is pregnant."

The emperor had no son as yet. If an emperor had no heir, it was deemed a sin to his ancestors. So pregnancy in the palace was very significant in the eyes of the queen. Concubine Yan was spared and sent back to her own chamber.

"Since Concubine Yan is pregnant, Emperor should let her have more rest. Emperor should no longer sleep with her until her child is born," the queen warned him.

* * *

Sushun and Duanhua were brothers. Since Duanhua was the elder, he inherited the title of Prince Zheng when their father died. But the younger brother was a man of ability and determination. The brothers, especially the younger, had won the emperor's favor. They often suggested new ways to have fun and provided him with every possible diversion and pastime. And the pastime that gave the emperor the most pleasure involved women.

The younger brother, Sushun, knew that the emperor could not sleep with Concubine Yan at present. Therefore, he rounded up some very beautiful women belonging to the Han Clan (the majority in the country, although the Manchus were the ruling class during the Qing Dynasty) and slipped them into the Round-Bright Garden, where the emperor lived most of the year — while he should have been living in the Forbidden City. The Round-Bright Garden was located outside the capital, Peking. The garden had hills and lakes, trees and flowers that covered almost every inch of the ground, with footpaths zigzagging among them. And in winter, graced with snow, the scene was as beautiful as ever. All the buildings, the pavilions and the arbors, were architectural copies of famous structures from all over the country. The emperor liked to live in the Round-Bright Garden, not just because of its beautiful scenery, but mostly because when he was in the Forbidden City he had to do almost everything in accordance with a certain etiquette established by his ancestors; when he dwelled in the Garden, there were not so many rules to observe. Life was a bit easier for him there.

But his ancestors had made a rule that women with bound feet — Han women — were prohibited from entering any of the emperor's residences. As a minority, the ruling Manchu had to maintain their identity or be absorbed into the multitude of their subjects. The emperor broke the rule to accept them. Among these women, one was a widow and some were whores from brothels. All were stunningly good looking. One of the whores was originally the mistress of a courtier who, when he heard of this new arrangement, sent in a note of "advice" noting that the emperor ought not to keep Han women in the Garden. The emperor wrote one sentence on the report and gave it back to the courtier. It said, "You are jealous." Among all this new group of women, there were four whom the emperor liked best. He named them "Apricot Spring," "Peach Spring," "Peony Spring" and "Crabapple Spring." (Crabapple, here, means the Chinese flowering crabapple.) The maids and eunuchs called them the "Four Springs."

After giving birth to a son, Concubine Yan expected the emperor's visit every day, but for a long time he seemed to have forgotten her. At length she came to the knowledge that the emperor was keeping a lot of Han women in the Garden; but she could do nothing about it. Only the queen could produce the book containing the ancestral instructions. She must seek an alliance with the queen. So, containing her pride for the sake of the cause, she went to pay her respects. She knelt before the queen and kowtowed. The queen bade her to stand up, after the ritual.

"Queen," she began, "Does Queen know why the emperor looks thinner day by day?"

"No idea," replied the queen. "What have you heard?"

"The emperor has many Han women hidden somewhere in the Garden."

"That's against the rules."

"So. That is why I must report to Queen. Queen must intervene. I'm not jealous. I'm only concerned for the emperor's health."

The queen decided to search the garden. Early one morning, with maids and eunuchs in tow, the queen set off for the Round-Bright Garden. Concubine Yan accompanied her there. They searched every building, every corner, but couldn't find any of the women supposed to be there. The emperor had got wind of the approaching search party, and he had ordered them to be removed to a secret place.

***

It was said that the emperor liked to have fun outside the Forbidden City. He would go out disguised as a commoner. Once he stole out of the Forbidden City, strolling the streets, followed by a eunuch and some bodyguards, also in plain clothes. He looked this way and that at all the interesting things he had never seen before.

One time when the emperor was sauntering along a narrow street, he saw a lovely young woman standing in the doorway of a dye shop. She was the owner's wife. When he made for the door, the woman stepped aside to let him in. He walked in as if he was a customer and talked to the woman, since the husband was in the back of the shop. He said that he could make her husband rich, if she was willing to be his concubine. The woman was at a loss — what to say to such an indecent proposition? Just then, the husband came out. The emperor left, with his attendants. The next day a stranger came into the shop. His servants carried in two boxes, a big heavy box which they left on the floor and a small one which they put on the table. The visitor announced that the emperor wanted his wife. If the shopkeeper refused, he must drink the poisonous wine in the cup in the small box. If he agreed, he could keep the trunk full of gold; and the emperor would make him a government official. Choose. The man had to give up his wife, much as he loved her, and she was sent to live with the Han women. Sushun had done another favor to the emperor.

CHAPTER 5

Unfortunately for Emperor Xianfeng, in the second year of his reign, 1851, a great rebellion broke out in the south of China, a widespread uprising, and it wore a religious cloak. There had been other rebellions cloaked in religion, too, and they had lasted a long time. There were two main groups of rebels. The White Lotus Taoists had originally formed to fight the Manchu Clan that had galloped down from the Mongolian frontier in the far north in the 13th century and, after occupying China, had established the Yuan Dynasty. When they were driven back, after a reign of a little less than 100 years, the White Lotus Taoists went dormant because the next dynasty, the Ming Dynasty, was founded by the Han Clan, their own people. Sometimes, they killed corrupt officials. When the Manchu Clan established the Qing Dynasty, the White Lotus Taoists rose up again like an awakened lion, like a phoenix rising from the ashes. From 1793 to 1802, they waged a particularly intense fight against the Manchus in five provinces in the middle western sections of China. The other main rebellious organization was Heaven and Earth Society, first organized in 1786 in Taiwan. After 1793, they set foot on the mainland and their branches spread over many provinces; but they battled separately, never united.

* * *

Since early in the Qing Dynasty, clergymen and priests had poured into China, where an infinity of souls awaited salvation. Missionaries had left their footprints everywhere, even in the remote villages. The God-Worshipper Society, the largest and longest-lived rebellious organization, was formed in 1850, and took Western religious theory as its basic creed. Since the Manchu Clan had crossed the Great Wall and conquered the Han Clan, there had been quite a few rebellions; and they all were really political organizations cloaked in religion. So was the God-Worshipper Society.

The leader of the God-Worshipper Society was then a young man, Hong Xiuquan by name, born in 1813 in Guangdong Province, a poor region in the

24

south. His father was a peasant who tilled the fields, growing vegetables and raising poultry. Hong had two older brothers who helped their father. At that time, cows were used to plough the ground. Though the family was not rich, they had two cows and enough to live on, so the father sent his youngest son to a local tutor to get an education. Perhaps the son would be a good student who might some day pass the government examinations and become an official. But destiny had prepared for him another road in life. He failed. In 1836, after he had failed again, he ran into a man who was distributing books in the streets of Canton City. Hong was given a copy, but he took it home and never read it. His failures had left him so downhearted that he had given up on the exams. He became a tutor, giving classes to children in his village.

One day in May of 1843, he found time heavy on his hands. Looking for something to read, to pass the time, he came across the long-forgotten volume. It was a gospel book written by a Chinese Christian. The book charmed him so much that he wanted to tell people what he had read. He quit tutoring and started preaching. He believed in Buddha no longer. Nor in Confucius, whom the scholars revered. He believed in God, now, and created the God-Worshipper Society. He headed west to Guangxi Province, and turned over a new leaf. He preached in village after village, sowing his seeds. His following rapidly grew. He set up his headquarters in Jintian, a village that was like a keg of gunpowder.

In 1850, there were droughts in Guangxi Province. Food was scarce. Food merchants raised prices. Starving people began to attack the rich people's residences, looking for food. The rich people organized their own guards to resist. The God-Worshipper Society had its believers in many places all over the province. The believers consisted of all kinds of people, from wealthy landowners to poor tramps, from charcoal burners to peasants. In 1851, a match was applied to the gunpowder.

A small-town police officer who had been sent to arrest a thief came across the charcoal burners in the woods near Jintian Village. He was as corrupt as any officer, and demanded payoffs whenever he could. The charcoal burners, who made charcoals from the tree branches and lived from hand to mouth, refused. They greatly outnumbered his policemen, so he had to leave empty-handed; but he threatened to come back with a larger contingent to arrest them as rebels. The charcoal burners were afraid, and gathered in a rich believer's yard to discuss what to do. In the meantime, the police officer happened to meet another rich believer, and took his concubine away from him as vengeance on the believers. Boom! Believers flooded into Jintian Village and the leader, Hong, declared that God was the Heavenly Father and Jesus Christ was the Heavenly Brother, and that he was the Heavenly Son sent down to save the world. Then he organized them. They called themselves the Peaceful Army, because their purpose was to bring peace to this world. The uprising began on January 11, 1851, smashed its way through 600 cities, and nearly brought down the Qing Dynasty.

The emperor received a report seven days later and immediately sent government armies to squelch the rebellion. The Peaceful Army marched eastward. They defeated the armies of the Qing Government and took over quite a few towns, but they didn't stop anywhere for long. They continued their eastward advance until they came to Yong An City. The word "Yong An" means "long safety"; a good name for a city. So they founded a kingdom there, called Peaceful Heavenly Kingdom. Hong made himself the Heavenly King and gave titles to his chief followers, who were also the leaders of the troops. There were so many kings in this kingdom: East King, North King, West King, South King, Shrewdness King, Swallow King, Protection King, Assistant King and Wing King — lofting upward, raising the entire enterprise heavenward.

They put up slogans so that people could know what were their goals: "If there's land, plough together; if there's food, eat together; if there's clothes, use them together; if there's money, spend together." And "Absolute equality everywhere. Enough food and clothes for everyone." These slogans fascinated and attracted a vast number of poor people, and hence swelled the Peaceful Army. And an order stated that anyone in the Peaceful Army who came into possession of anything must hand it in to the Heavenly Treasury; and everyone could get a share, when needed. Therefore, unlike the armies of the Qing Government, the Peaceful Army had good discipline and was supported by the people. Many young beggars and vagabonds joined it.

Their sublime aim was to overthrow the Qing Dynasty and drive the Manchu Clan out beyond the Great Wall, back to where they had come from. Another edict was given: that men adopt the hairstyle of the Han Clan by allowing the hair to grow in on the front part of their scalps. Men of the Manchu Clan shaved clean the front part of the scalp and braided the back of the hair into a long pigtail or queue. When the Manchu Clan established the Qing Dynasty, they had ordered all the Han men to wear their hair in the same style. Anyone who refused would be beheaded. "Your hair, or your head." So when the Peaceful Army grew their hair, the Qing Government called them Long-Hairs.

While the Peaceful Army was celebrating its victory and newly-founded regime, the Qing Government gathered large troops and encircled Yong An City.

In March, 1852, the Peaceful Army concentrated its forces and drove a wedge through the government forces. The government army pursued them, but was put to rout. The Peaceful Army headed for Guilin City, the capital of Guangxi Province. They surrounded the City for a month, but could not take it. So they quit and marched northward.

The emperor sent three detachments to attack the Peaceful Army, but these, too, were beaten. Then the government troops gathered in Wuchang City to prevent the Peaceful Army from going further north. The emperor issued an order to allow cities, towns and even villages to organize and train their own men for self-defense.

On December 7, 1852, the Peaceful Army split in two. One section went on land and the other by water. They captured ships from the government army. Their goal was the Wu-Han area, which included Wuchang City, Hanyang City and Hankou City. The Three Cities were a strategically important area on the upper Yangtze River. Within ten days, the Peaceful Army had occupied the three cities, one after another. The Heavenly King and all his other kings stayed in Wuchang City to celebrate and recruit, while the emperor ordered his commanders to set up defensive lines in Hunan Province, Hubei Province and Anhui Province, to block the advance of the Peaceful Army towards Nanking City (now known as Nanjing).

On February 9, 1853, after the Chinese New Year, the Peaceful Army left Wuchang City, dividing itself again into two sections. One group went by water, on the Yangtze River; the rest paralleled their course, on land. They were aiming for Nanking City. They took over many cities and towns along the way, including Jiujiang City, Anqing City — a very important spot from the military point of view, and Wuwu City. On March 18, the Peaceful Army entered Nanking City. They changed the name to Tianking City (Tianking means the Heavenly Capital).

The Peaceful Army established renewed law and order in the City. It was very simple. "Those who kill others will be executed." There was no robbery or theft, because any excess was already being taken to the warehouses of the Heavenly Treasury. Every 25 families formed a social unit, to work and live together. A unit leader was elected. A strong male adult was chosen from every family to form the basic military unit. There was a treasury warehouse in every unit; everything they got was stored there and everything necessary for their living was supplied from there. It was said that foreign governments, surprised at all this, sent their representatives to Nanking City to have a look. They considered it a revolutionary army and therefore maintained strict neutrality in the matter.

When this news reached the Forbidden City, the emperor was so anxious he lost his appetite. He appointed new commanders to organize two detachments. One set up camp in the area of Purple Golden Mountain, not far from Nanking City on the southern side of the Yangtze River. It was called the South River Camp. The other was billeted in Yangzhou City on the northern side of the Yangtze River, hence called the North River Camp.

CHAPTER 6

Historians have discussed why the Qing Government armies were so easily defeated; and they offer three conclusions.

First, after almost 200 years of peace, lack of training and practice had rendered the central government's Eight-Flag Army incapable of fighting. The old warriors were long since dead. The new generation of soldiers all came from rich or well-to-do families; they joined the Army as an honor, since there was no likelihood of battle at that time. There were days fixed for training, but most of the "soldiers" just hired some poor young man to show up for roll-call and go through the drills. No one even knew the faces of those who were supposed to have been there. Now the time had come for real combat, but no one knew how to fight. The other available "fighting force," the one belonging to the local government, was the Green-Standard Army. Their sole duty was to defend their city or town against small groups of outlaws; they had no battlefield training.

Second, every commander wanted to be independent; they fought separately, not as a strategic whole. Especially in the Green-Standard Army. Once they chased the rebels out of their own jurisdiction, they felt their job was done: the fleeing rebels were now someone else's problem.

And, third, officials and officers of the Manchu Clan held different ideas and interests from those of the Han Clan. The officers of the Han Clan looked down upon the "barbarian" Manchu, and wouldn't obey them. The commanders were all from the Manchu Clan — and all were no good.

We might also observe that, in the Qing Dynasty, officials were above officers in status and rank, but they had no military knowledge. Why would the officers obey them? Sometimes they just ran away at the start of a battle. It is also true that government officers and soldiers often took advantage of the common people, shaking them down at every opportunity, and therefore could hardly expect universal support.

When the Peaceful Army assaulted Nanking City, there were only 5,000 government soldiers to defend it. This was a big city with a circumference of 48 kilometers and more than 15,000 battlements. Every soldier would have had to safeguard three battlements. The Peaceful Army just walked in.

After the Heavenly King settled in Nanking City and made it his capital, he issued two orders. His Heavenly General and Earthly General (their positions equivalent to that of a commander) would march to the north with a force 20,000 strong, detouring Yangzhou City where the government army was encamped. His Spring General would start from Pukou Town northward. They were instructed to advance towards Peking to overthrow Qing Dynasty. They easily fought their way through Anhui Province, and met some resistance in Hunan Province. But they penetrated the defensive line of the government army and approached Kaifeng City, the capital of Hunan Province. They assailed the city, but couldn't break through. So they went by a roundabout way and ferried across the Yellow River at Yixin Town. They encircled Huaiqing Town and conquered the government army there, headed by the governor of Zhidi Province (now Hebei Province). And on they marched towards Baoding City, close to Peking.

The emperor was shocked. He scraped up all his available forces, even the regiment of his bodyguards, 150,000 in all. By this time, detachments of the Peaceful Army had reached Tianjin City. The Mayor, a little cleverer than some, apparently, had a section of the dike dug open. Water from the Grand Canal deluged the area and blocked the Peaceful Army. It was winter. The soldiers of the Peaceful Army were all from the south of China, where the climate is warm. They began to retreat, and were assaulted by the government army. The Qing Government used Mongolian cavalry to attack. Four hooves are much quicker than two feet. Spring General of the Peaceful Army was killed in the battle. Heavenly General was surrounded, waiting for rescue. The Heavenly King did send reinforcements, twice, but they could not get through. The Mongolian cavalry had trapped Heavenly General by breaking through the dike of a nearby river, and the flood soaked the Peaceful Army's provisions and gunpowder. Heavenly General was captured and executed. Earthly General escaped with 2,000 soldiers, but was ambushed, captured and executed, too. The goal to seize

Peking failed. 40,000 men of the Peaceful Army could not fight against 150,000 of the government army. This all took place in 1855.

However, the war went on, on both sides of the Yangtze River. In April 1856, Swallow King of the Peaceful Army vanquished the North River Camp of the government army. In July of the same year, Swallow King and Wing King together beat the South River Camp. The Peaceful Army had control of the entire area of the Yangtze River. The revolutionary cause had reached its apex.

Emperor Xianfeng ordered some of his courtiers to organize new troops in the southern provinces. One of the courtiers was Zeng Kuofan, of the Han Clan. Zeng was born in 1811, into a family of the land-owning class. He passed all the government exams in 1838 and was promoted to be the Right Deputy Minister of the Etiquette Ministry. When Emperor Xianfeng succeeded to the throne, he was given another title — the Left Deputy Minister of Judicial Ministry.

Zeng exercised the self-education of his own character. He believed in patience, perseverance, honesty and hidden wisdom (outwardly indicating that one is not clever, or may even be stupid). These were his principles in everything he undertook.

There are various ways to organize troops. The way the Qing Government had adopted was to allow all men of suitable age join the troops, with officers (mostly Manchu) appointed by the government. The officers and soldiers did not know each other; there were no other ties between them. Zeng took a different approach; in fact, it was the same approach used by the rebel forces. He appointed those he knew well as his officers and he let his officers recruit their own soldiers, mostly from the same village or from the same neighborhood. Thus they knew each other and cared about each other. The ties between them were based on more than mere military discipline, and morale was better. Furthermore, most of his officers were literate, and some were even learned, while many officers in the government army were illiterate — some couldn't even write their own names, or recognize them on paper. High-ranking government officers, if they were illiterate, had secretaries to do the writing for them when needed. Coincidentally, this meant a gradual transfer of military control into the hands of the Han, which would have repercussions much later.

Zeng named his army the Xiang Army. (Xiang was telegramese for Hunan Province: one word that stands for a whole province can save money). In 1853, when the Xiang Army was just a newborn, it wiped out a group of outlaws — as a little test of its mettle, like testing the edge of a new sword. Then it beat a division of the Peaceful Army. This was while two detachments of the Peaceful Army were fighting in the area of the Yellow River, trying to reach Peking. Other detachments went back westward and took Anqing City and Wuchang City again. They met with the Xiang Army in the district between the Xiang River and the Puyang Lake, and defeated the young and inexperienced Xiang forces there.

Zeng gathered up his beaten troops, and reorganized and trained them, both on land and on the Yangtze River. After that, the Xiang Army marched eastward and conquered the detachments of the Peaceful Army and took back the beleaguered Wuchang City once more. But the defeated detachments were not the Peaceful Army's main forces. Now the Xiang Army advanced further eastward, by land and by water, and suddenly they faced Wing King of the Peaceful Army at Jiujiang City. This was one of the main forces of the Peaceful Army and so the Xiang Army was subdued again. Wing King proceeded towards the upper Yangtze River and reoccupied Wuchang City. Now the Peaceful Army controlled a vast stretch of the Yangtze River, from Wuchang City in the west to Nanking City in the east, like the sun clambering toward the zenith. This all took place in 1856.

The Peaceful Army reached a turning point in that same year. Victory shifted into failure, due to internecine strife. When the Peaceful Army had just been formed, Heavenly King had placed East King in charge of everything, as his prime minister, in effect. Later, South King and West King were killed in battle. Therefore, when they settled in Nanking City there were only three powerful kings left, besides Heavenly King: East King, North King and Wing King. The other kings were not so powerful. East King was very arrogant and bullied the others, even Heavenly King, who began to suspect that East King had ambitions to usurp his position. Other kings, especially North King, harbored a grudge against East King (unbeknownst to him). When they were fighting the government army, they had enjoyed a feeling of unity and solidarity. But when they had won the day, victory had turned their heads. Heavenly King and North King commenced to plot against East King, who never thought that such lethal danger could be in store.

One day, Heavenly King and North King sent their faithful men to assail the residence of East King. His bodyguards were unable to withstand the onslaught, and he was slain. Then the massacre began. His family, his relatives and his faithful supporters were hunted down and put to death. It was said that 20,000 people were butchered.

All that time, Wing King was in Anqing City. When he learned of the bloody incident, he hurried back to the capital and blamed North King for the slaughter. North King flared up in rage and schemed to assassinate him; Wing King was tipped off and escaped under cover of night back to Anqing City. North King had Wing King's family murdered. Back in Anqing City, Wing King gathered his troops. He had many supporters among the Peaceful Army, because he was always trustworthy and considerate. When Heavenly King learned that Wing King was bringing his troops to the capital, he panicked — and executed North King. Then he had the severed head of North King sent to Wing King to mollify him. When Wing King arrived in the capital, many other kings suggested that Wing King should take charge, as East King had done before. But Heavenly King feared that Wing King would become a threat to him one day, and so he made his two brothers kings, so they could help him. His eldest brother was made Security King and his second brother became Fortune King. The two often interfered with Wing King's affairs. This made him uneasy. Not wishing to follow East King and North King to an unnecessarily early grave, Wing King left the capital with his own troops and headed westward, to develop his own interests. From then on, he dropped contact with Heavenly King.

Four kings were dead and one had been forced to flee. This greatly weakened the Peaceful Army. The government army seized the opportunity to counterattack. The Xiang Army occupied Wuchang City once and for all. Another government army took Hanyang City. A detachment of the Xiang Army was controlling Jiujiang City. Therefore, the banners of the Peaceful Army were no longer seen in Hunan Province and Jiangxi Province. The Wing King fought his way from Zhejiang Province through Jiangxi Province and Fujian Province, then across Hunan and back to Guangxi, where he had taken up arms in revolt five years before. The Qing Government reorganized its North River Camp and South River Camp, and approached Nanking City again.

With five kings gone, two of the other kings became powerful. One was Shrewdness King, who was in Anqing City, and the other was Loyalty King, who stayed in the capital to defend it.

In spring of 1857, in the provinces between the Yellow River and the Yangtze River, there arose another rebellion, in the form of the Nian Army, 100,000 strong. They often allied with the Peaceful Army. The Qing Government had to divide its forces to combat both simultaneously. The Nian Army also called its leaders kings. Every king led a detachment, but they did not have a head king. They fought separately, never unified as a whole. They never established a capital. They never stayed long at one place. The leader of the largest detachment was called Fertility King, and he had 80,000 fighters. In 1858, he took control of Fengyang Town and set out for Peking. In September of 1858, the Peaceful Army, led by Swallow King and Loyalty King, subjugated North River Camp again at Pukou Town, and then annihilated a Xiang Army detachment of 6,000 soldiers in Anhui Province. A brother of Zeng was killed in the action. No more threat to Nanking City from the north.

Then Action King and Loyalty King of the Peaceful Army worked out a stratagem. Loyalty King marched toward Hangzhou City, the capital of Zhejiang Province, feigning an attack. This area was an important supply source for the government army. The government army's South River Camp maneuvered east-ward to defend the city. A tiger, once out of its lair, is vulnerable. Now Loyalty King turned around to meet the advancing South River Camp while Shrewdness King, Action King, Service King, Assistant King and five generals attacked the rear and flanks of South River Camp, which couldn't resist the blows of ten fists and were scattered on May 5, 1860. Its commander committed suicide. Besides Jiangsu Province (Nanking City is its capital), the Peaceful Army now possessed Zhejiang Province and Fujian Province, though they lost all the provinces west to Anqing City, which had been attacked since spring of 1860 by the Xiang Army under the command of another brother of Zeng (Younger Zeng).

When the shocking reports of the defeats of the two camps lay on the emperor's desk, he was too downhearted even to meet with his courtiers. He had had ambitions, when he had succeeded to the throne many years before. He had wanted to restore his empire to its former glory and prosperity. But contrary to his hopes and wishes, the situation had turned from bad to worse. He was too tired and depressed to prod the staggering empire again as it stumbled to its knees. He gave up all his hopes. He didn't want to read any more sad reports. Like an ostrich, he buried his head in the sands. Or, to be more literal, he buried his head under the bedclothes, diverting himself with women.

In the Qing Dynasty, an imperial maid serving in the Forbidden City would either be released to her parents' home or be married off at the emperor's whim when she reached the age of 25, unless she had become the emperor's concubine before that age. Almost every year, the emperor would select new girls to replace those who had been released. This event took place even in the heat of warfare. Girls from thirteen to seventeen years of age had to be reported to the Clan Affairs Administration, which would sift among girls on the list. After the preliminary cut, a small group of the most suitable girls were presented to the emperor, who would choose from them himself. This time, the happy day arrived but along with it came many urgent reports from the war districts, demanding the emperor's immediate attention. He had to read them discuss the military situation with his court, and decide how to instruct his commanders. It was late when he made it back to his palace.

All this time, the girls were standing in the emperor's receiving room, waiting for him. They were not permitted to sit down. Young, in formal dress, standing for hours: how did they feel? Hungry. Exhausted. Bored. Irritated, maybe. Dare not complain. Wish you were dead, then and there. One of the girls was bold enough to protest out loud, "It's war time. The emperor is still selecting girls." The eunuch in charge panicked. If the emperor heard about this, not only would the girl be executed but he too would be punished. He bellowed at her, "Shut up! You'll be beaten, if you complain again." He heard that the emperor was on his way. But the girl went on. "I'm not afraid of death, let alone a beating." The eunuch was really piqued. He raised his right hand to slap her face.

"Let her speak." The emperor entered the room. All the girls sank to the floor and kowtowed to the emperor, and were bidden to stand up. "Now," the emperor said to the girl, "you can say what you have to say. I won't take offence." The girl went on: "emperor must know there's war in the southern provinces and people are dying, hundreds upon hundreds every day. There's a devastating flood south of the Yellow River. So many people have lost their homes and all their possessions. In this critical time, emperor should spend his precious hours and energy on these important matters, not on the selection of maids." Cold sweat soaked the clothes of everyone in the room. They thought he would have her beheaded, but to everybody's astonishment, the emperor did not seem angry. He ordered that the girls be sent back to their respective homes. He heard a huge roomful of flattering words every day, and was bored with them. Now, such a young girl told him the hard truth, to his face. He was surprised and fascinated, so he pardoned her.

CHAPTER 7

The hunting season was already over, but Emperor Xianfeng declared that he would go to the Summer Palace in Rehe. Emperors in Qing Dynasty used to go there in the hunting season (generally from May to September), actually for the purpose of training their armies. But this time Emperor Xianfeng used it as a different sort of pretext, because the joint armies of foreign invaders had occupied Tianjin City in July 1860, and would soon reach the capital, Peking. This came to be called "The Second Opium War."

Some courtiers tried to dissuade the emperor from flight, but in vain. On September 21, the combined foreign troops were very close to the capital. He could hear the sound of cannons in the Forbidden City. On September 22, in the late morning, the emperor left Peking with his family, followed by a few courtiers and 2,000 bodyguards.

The autumn scenes along the escape route, the yellow leaves on the trees and on the ground, the chilly winds blowing, the melancholy cawing of the crow, all added to his sorrow at having to flee the warm luxury of the Forbidden City. And he felt he was sinning against his ancestors.

Now the imperial family was in the Summer Palace: the emperor, the queen, Concubine Yan and her son, and Concubine Li and her daughter. The other concubines didn't have time to follow. He left his brother, Prince Yixin, in Peking to negotiate with the foreigners, who entered the Round-Bright Garden on October 6 to pillage and then set fire to it. (Charred ruins can still be seen, even at the time of this writing.)

The emperor was weary; he was sick of dealing with all the troubles. He left the state affairs to his favorite courtier, Sushun, who was not yet even a secretary of state. The emperors of the Qing Dynasty had established a secretarial bureau and they appointed five or sometimes six courtiers as secretaries of state, with one as the head secretary. The bureau handled all state affairs, and military affairs as well, working under the emperor. That left the prime ministers with less to do; but they still had some unspecified duties to perform.

There were six ministries. Every ministry had two ministers, one from the Manchu Clan and the other from the Han Clan, and four deputy ministers, two Manchu and two Han. Politically balanced.

The Personnel Ministry took care of the appointments and the removals of all the officials and officers in the central and local governments all over the country, and their promotions and demotions, based on their own self-evaluations and criticisms from others. For that matter, a critique official could weigh in with a report on any official or officer. There were good critique officials and bad ones. Corrupt officials and officers were afraid of the good ones, since they wouldn't take money or even gifts; but all officials and officers dreaded the bad ones, who would always have a hand out — or else, a critique report would appear on the emperor's desk, based on hearsay. And this was allowed by law. If no critique came in for an official or officer, it meant that he was good; if there were praise, even better. Some mayors forced the people in their districts to give them something as evidence of praise when they left office, such as an umbrella with as many signatures on it as possible. It was called a "People's Petition Umbrella," and signified that the people there wanted him to remain in office: the highest form of praise for a mayor.

The Internal Revenue Ministry kept population statistics and, based on them, decided how much tax the local governments should collect and what percentage of the local tax collections should be sent to the central government. It also set special taxes, like the salt tax. (Salt smuggling became common in an effort to avoid the tax; so an officer was stationed in the area where salt was obtained. He headed an army to enforce the tax collection.) This ministry also controlled the expenditures of the central government; and it controlled the national finances. The local governments had their own departments for that purpose. This ministry often had the toughest job. If there was a war, provisions and arms had to be provided for armies, and money, too. If the emperor needed more money for his personal use, money had to be found. If the emperor was dissatisfied with the minister's performance, he would be removed from office or even imprisoned. On the other hand, the Ministry was a bit like Ali Baba's cave. The minister and his subordinates were buried in treasure and if they were discreet enough, they could help themselves to the hoard, bit by bit. No one would know.

The Etiquette Ministry was poor, albeit respected; it would make rules for the rituals for certain occasions, in reference to the rules used by the previous dynasties, and would act as master of ceremony when needed. Any new rules had to be discussed among the high-ranking officials, the "mandarins," and then approved by the emperor. The job was easy; only, there was no way to make extra money. People could bribe the Personnel Minister for a better position. But why would anyone bribe the Etiquette Minister?

The Military Ministry would make preparations for a war, including suggesting officer candidates and battle strategies (these would be discussed among all the higher officials and officers and then be approved by the emperor). The Military Ministry in a joint effort with the Internal Revenue Ministry was supposed to supply the armies with equipment and provisions. In peacetime, it would oversee the workings of the local garrisons and would train recruits to replace those who were no longer fit to fight.

The Judicial Ministry made laws, which would be discussed among all the mandarins and then be submitted for the emperor's approval. It would interpret laws and try cases concerning government officials and officers. The ministry didn't accept commoners' lawsuits against other commoners. If a commoner wanted to bring suit against an official to the Judicial Ministry, he or she had to go through a certain intimidating procedure by which the validity of the complaint was tested: A plank of wood was placed before the gate of the ministry building, with long, sharp nails sticking up. The plaintiff had to throw himself or herself onto it. If he or she lived to tell the tale, the judicial minister would accept the lawsuit. Fat chance? If he knew what he was doing, the plaintiff would wear thick, quilted clothes, even in summertime. This was allowed. And it worked.

The Construction Ministry built new structures within the capital and repaired old ones belonging to the central government. Although its power was limited, it did have good cash flow. The approved budget for a building was always much higher than the real cost. This seems to be a permanent characteristic in the world of construction. The government is like a gigantic cake and everyone around it has the impression that he has been invited to take a slice. Or two.

Besides these six ministries, there were several departments. The Critique Department, as mentioned, was responsible for overseeing the probity of the officials and officers. Positions in that department could not be bought. Only those who had passed the final examination in the capital were entitled to such appointments. Everyone in that department was deemed a scholar, and each critique report was written as a great literary endeavor. Each scribe would strive for that beautiful, compelling wording that sometimes made a deep impression, even if one didn't agree with the views expressed. This would indelibly imprint the writer's name in the mind of the emperor, and later, when the emperor needed somebody to fill a certain post, his name would pop up. Besides that advantage, those who could write the best-worded reports were more esteemed among scholars and therefore had more influence. These so-called scholars would not condescend to mingle with the officials who had bought their titles; and that created ill feelings among the latter.

There was a Supreme Court, which would try any case that came its way. The head judge was lower in rank than the ministers and the head critique official. If there were an especially important case, such as treason by a high official or officer, it would be tried by the three heads: the judicial minister, the head critique official and the head judge. A long, imposing table was positioned near the rear wall of the main hall. The judge, or the three heads, sat behind the table. Sometimes three smaller tables were placed there instead of one big one. Torture implements were displayed along both side walls and the prison police stood in two rows, on either side, before the long table. When a prisoner was being brought in, the policemen, standing at attention, would make a threatening sound in unison: "Huuuuuuuuuuu—weiiiiiiiiii —" until the terrified prisoner was on his knees, before the table. Then the trial began.

Usually the prisoner would proclaim his innocence, and sometimes he really had not committed the alleged crime. But in either case, since the judge couldn't be sure that the prisoner was innocent or guilty, he invariably ordered the torture equipment used. The first torture, for a man, was to be beaten on his bare buttocks with a thick wooden stick. How many beatings he would get depended on the mood of the judge or the gravity of the offense. Generally 30 to 100. Often, the prisoner would be left bleeding. The first torment for a woman was slaps on the face with a piece of leather, shaped like a hand. If the judge was not satisfied with the prisoner's confession, if any, a second torment would be administered. A male prisoner's forelegs would be put between two pieces of wood with ropes on both ends. The ropes would be tightened, applying unbearable pressure and perhaps breaking the shins. For a woman, the same treatment was performed but on her fingers, with smaller wooden pieces; in either case, the pain was excruciating and the person could be permanently crippled. Under such treatment, even the innocent would repeat whatever the judge wanted to hear. If the prisoner was a high official or officer, torture was prohibited and the judge would have to come up with some evidence. The judge gave the verdict, but it had to be approved by the emperor, who could change even a death sentence as a special favor.

Since many foreign countries had established legations in Peking, the Qing Government also had to set up a ministry to deal with foreign governments. On January 13, 1861, Prince Yixin sent in a report from Peking to the Summer Palace in Rehe, requesting the establishment of the Foreign Affairs Yamen. On January 20, the emperor approved it. Prince Yixin was its head.

CHAPTER 8

Once the Secretarial Bureau had been established, many decisions were made by the secretaries instead of the members of the Cabinet, who were supposed to issue all the orders or statements. The Secretarial Bureau acted only as the emperor's private council and it was not part of the central government. This emperor gave power to the Secretarial Bureau, not to the Cabinet; but a secretary might be simultaneously a prime minister, a minister or even one ranking lower in the official hierarchy than a minister. And now, only four secretaries had followed the emperor to the Summer Palace in Rehe.

The emperor still had to read all the reports sent in by the courtiers in Peking and the governors of all the provinces (of which there were 23 at that time). He had to make decisions and give written orders. Tuberculosis wore at his lungs and as his health deteriorated, he coughed blood and was easily tired. He let Concubine Yan read the reports for him, and in minor affairs even let her make the decisions. Concubine Yan was smart ambitious, and she liked power. This new setup gave her an excellent opportunity to familiarize herself with procedures and learn how to handle state affairs. Just what she needed.

The ancestors of the Qing Dynasty had left written instructions to forbid women from interfering in politics. But Emperor Xianfeng developed a headache whenever he was constrained to read those hideous reports. He had to have someone read them, and who better than Concubine Yan? When he felt a little better, he would sit up on the bed with a stack of pillows behind him and watch her reading. In such peaceful moments, he would eat a bit of fruit, prepared for him by Concubine Li. If it were not for his bad health, if it were not for the rebellion in the south, if it were not for the foreigners who had driven him out of his Forbidden City in the capital — he would enjoy life, with one beauty relieving him of his tedious reports and another beauty serving him his food.

After a while, the emperor began to notice that Concubine Yan showed great interest and zeal in political affairs. She sometimes even suggested solutions, which might be a good thing, but it was not appropriate from a woman. It was becoming very clear that this was no mediocre woman, like the queen. He suspected that she might seize power, after his death, as an empress dowager, because her son would succeed to the throne. (The rule in the Qing Dynasty was that when the son became the emperor, the natural mother must be elevated to the status of empress dowager, regardless of birth or status.) He considered having her put to death for the safety of the empire; but his son was only six years old. Such a small child should have a mother to look after him. Besides, he knew by then that the younger brother Sushun was also ambitious, and might well do his son in. He would let Concubine Yan contend with him and defend their son. If only he could think of a way to restrain her. And now he had thought of something.

* * *

Except for the emperor, Sushun had become the most powerful man in the empire, even before the Second Opium War. The emperor always listened to him, and what the emperor did was really what Sushun wanted done. But Sushun sought to enhance his "authority": he wanted the other courtiers to fear him. How did he pursue this goal? By killing.

Sushun handed in a report saying that Qinying must be executed immediately. In 1856, the joint foreign armies had occupied the Bay of Dagukou and commenced to attack Tianjin City. The emperor had sent Qinying to negotiate with the foreigners, but he had come back to the capital without fulfilling the task, not even asking for the emperor's approval to return. The emperor was outraged. Prince Yixin, his brother, proposed to have Qinying hanged the next autumn. (The Qing Dynasty often executed prisoners in autumn.) But Sushun insisted that Qinying should be executed at once, to set an example for other courtiers. The emperor commanded Qinying to die by his own hand (generally, this was achieved by hanging or by drinking poison, and was deemed better than being beheaded publicly).

Next came another courtier, Paijun, who had offended Sushun before. In 1858, Paijun was appointed the chief examiner in charge of the government exam. This was a very important event. It happened that an actor passed the exam, and came in seventh place. Actors were prohibited from taking the exams because they were considered among the lowest social caste. The emperor was furious, and ordered Sushun to investigate. Now he had found his chance to take revenge. The investigation revealed that many officials handling this examination had accepted bribes, though no evidence implicated Paijun directly. The actor had gotten in through a servant to Paijun's concubine, who persuaded Paijun to let the actor pass. Paijun was guilty of breaking the rules. Every one of the officials was punished according to the degree of his offense. Paijun, as the head examiner, was executed. Many such things occurred. Sushun made a lot of enemies.

* * *

Sons of an emperor were habitually called Brother. If the emperor had quite a few sons, they would be called by seniority: First Brother, Second Brother, etc. If one of them was made the successor to the throne, he would be called Big Brother. It didn't matter if he was the oldest one or not. Emperor Xianfeng had only one son. The son would definitely be the successor, so he was called Big Brother. Six years old was the right age to start learning. If the emperor had more than one son, all the sons would form a class to study; but Big Brother was alone. It was very important to choose suitable tutors for the future emperor, particularly to choose the head tutor, who would greatly influence the young boy. He must be a great scholar, known to be of impeccable character, with a spotless record. Generally, the head tutor was selected from among the Zhuangyuans, those who had finished first in the examinations. At length, the emperor decided on Li Hongzao, who met all the requirements; he sent for Li Hongzao, and assigned him the honorable task.

After Li Hongzao left, the emperor wanted to send him some gifts, as tradition required. Two scrolls of silk, ten brushes, etc. Since they were at the Summer Palace, there were not many courtiers who could be chosen as proper tutors; for now, the boy had only one tutor. When he got back in the Forbidden City, he would have more.

Then the emperor sent for his son and told him to study hard, and other such things. The boy just nodded and blinked. It seemed as if his father's instructions were quite beyond him. When the boy went to see the queen, she told him simply, "Don't be naughty. Respect and listen to your tutor."

Early the next morning, Zhang Wenliang, the eunuch who was assigned to look after the boy, woke him up and dressed him formally. He took the boy first to see the emperor, then to see the queen. Then Jingshou, the emperor's brother-in-law, came and took the boy by hand to the study, followed by the eunuch. The brother-in-law was in charge of the boy's education as a whole and would watch over every step of his progress.

When they arrived, Tutor Li was already there, standing before the door of the study. As they entered, first, Tutor Li kowtowed to the boy, the future emperor. Then Jingshou told the boy to kowtow to the tutor (the traditional ritual). But Tutor Li refused to accept it, saying, "A prince can't kowtow to a courtier." At that, Jingshou told the boy to make a bow instead. So the boy bowed to Tutor Li and Tutor Li accepted it. There were two desks in the room, one for the boy and the other for the tutor. Jingshou sat on a chair at one side of the room and several assistant tutors stood in a row at the other side.

Both taking the seat, Tutor Li said to the boy, "I've made a schedule for you. If you finish it early, you can leave early. Is that all right with you?" The boy said, "Okay." Tutor Li said, "Good. You must come early in the morning. We will begin with learning how to use a bow and arrow, then we will study the Manchu language. Finally, we'll read a book and practice writing Chinese characters (learning the Han language was the biggest challenge, but necessary in order to rule the nation)." He turned to the assistant tutors, "Now, take him to see what you will teach him."

The assistant tutors were from the Manchu Clan. They would teach the boy archery and the Manchu language, the language of the ruling class. Other tutors would instruct the new emperor in Han, the language of the majority of the population. Lessons were based on a book by Confucius; in the olden days, they didn't care whether the pupils understood or not — they just had to learn the text by heart and recite it at the next lesson. Maybe the pupils would understand the text later, when they grew up.

The books, either hand-copied or printed, were difficult to read. There was no punctuation. The tutor had to read first, to show the pupils where to stop. Then he let the pupils read the texts themselves. It would take a while to learn where to mark the full stops of the sentences, so, at first, the learning process was slow. On the first day, Tutor Li only taught the boy how to read a couple of sentences and how to write a couple of Chinese characters with a brush. It's not easy to handle a calligraphy brush, either. A pupil must sit straight and hold the brush upright at a distance of a foot and a half, straight under his nose. He must copy the examples on the tablets written by famous ancient calligraphers. If a student aimed to be an excellent calligrapher, he must practice the brush strokes with a small cup of water placed between the thumb and the forefinger of the hand holding the brush. When he moved the brush, the water in the small cup was not allowed to spill. Digital acrobatics. But the son of the emperor was only taught the basic skills, given that he would never need to be an expert calligrapher.

CHAPTER 9

Concubine Yan would need allies if she were to get any further with the power game. First, she sent someone to make a discreet approach to Sushun, but he despised women. Her doe-eyed looks and her emissary were ignored. Concubine Yan was infuriated. He had created a terrible foe for himself, without even knowing it.

Then she approached Prince Yixin, the emperor's smartest brother. The emperor was afraid that Yixin would some day usurp his throne. Yixin's mother had been a concubine of the late emperor. Xianfeng, the current emperor, was his fourth son and Yixin was the sixth. The queen, Xianfeng's own mother, had died not long after his birth, so Xianfeng had been raised by Yixin's mother. The boys had studied together, played together and grown up together. Their relationship was closer than that among the other siblings. Among the imperial family members Yixin was called Old Six, but his younger brothers called him Sixth Brother.

When the former emperor died, Xianfeng had succeeded to the throne and Yixin's mother became Imperial Concubine Dowager. Several times Yixin had asked the new Emperor to confer on his mother the title of empress dowager, but he had declined, saying that it was against the rules of etiquette (although it is true that such rules had always been found to bend, throughout history). When Yixin's mother was taken ill, Xianfeng often went to visit her. On her deathbed, in her final moments, she mistook him for her own son Yixin, and said, "Take care of yourself when I'm gone. The throne should have been yours." Hearing those words, the emperor was stricken. From then on he felt estranged from Yixin; his fears were heightened. He always kept his brother far from the reins of power. The thought of usurpation never crossed Yixin's mind, but he was talented and wished to use his abilities to serve the empire, to perform great deeds.

Now, with the empire facing a further invasion, Yixin was at last placed in charge of negotiations with the foreign aggressors. After much bargaining, a treaty was signed. The invading armies withdrew from the capital. Yixin sent a report to his half-brother requesting that he return to Peking now that peace had been restored. But the emperor excused himself, saying that he was too sick to travel in the cold weather. At least, there was some truth to that.

* * *

Yixin was the only person Sushun feared. He had had a hand in the emperor's alienation from his brother. Sushun knew that if the emperor had trusted Yixin, he wouldn't have had the power he had now. So the rumor started to spread that Yixin wanted to usurp the throne. Even another brother of Emperor Xianfeng, the fifth son of the late emperor, believed it and mentioned it to Emperor Xianfeng. Therefore, every time Yixin asked to come to the Summer Palace in Rehe for a visit, the emperor declined, saying that it was more impor-tant for Yixin to stay in the capital.

Now a rumor about the emperor's health was going around. Everyone had to re-think his interests, his future, and his fate. Officialdom was a dangerous realm. Ups and downs, life and death, were determined in just a few moments. Yixin had two faithful supporters, like his own two hands. Wenqiang was a secretary of state, the only secretary who had not followed the emperor to the Summer Palace in Rehe. He had stayed in the capital to assist Yixin in dealing with the foreign aggressors. Baojun was head of the Imperial Household Depart-ment. The emperor didn't like him, for two reasons. First, as he was in charge of the imperial residences, he should have submitted a report of self-criticism and asked for punishment when the Round-Bright Garden was burnt, but he had merely reported the conflagration, nothing else. The emperor had already ordered him to give up the keys to the Round-Bright Garden to another head of the Imperial Household Department. Therefore, he hadn't begged for punish-ment, thinking that it was no longer his responsibility. The emperor gave him a demotion; but, a while later, Baojun had to be restored to his former position when Yixin mentioned to the emperor that he had done something to deserve a reward. He was so intimate with Yixin that he could even joke with him. The second reason the emperor disliked Baojun was that as soon as the emperor had reached the Summer Palace in Rehe, he had ordered Baojun to send over 200,000 taels of silver for repairs, but somehow Baojun hadn't sent the money — perhaps because there wasn't any money left. And Sushun disliked him, too, because of his closeness to Yixin.

In the Secretarial Bureau, there were clerical officials to help the secretaries with tasks like drafting an order for the emperor, a report to the emperor, a reply to any official who had sent a report, or copying an emperor's order in a formal writing style and then getting it dispatched to wherever it should go. They did not make any decisions, but they had all the inside information. This made them popular with the rest of the officials. The clerical officials were divided into two shifts because if an emergency arose, clerical assistance would be needed even in the middle of the night. Zao Yueying was the head clerical official in the daytime shift. And he was secretly loyal to Yixin. So Yixin knew everything that happened in the Summer Palace in Rehe.

Wenqiang, the secretary of state who had remained in Peking, was a man of ability and patience. Based on the information sent by Zao, the head clerical official, he came up with a strategy for Yixin. Yixin must not do anything obvious and arouse Sushun's suspicion, but he had better make the necessary preparations. The most important thing in politics, in power struggles, was to have the support of the armies. Sushun had the command of 2,000 emperor's bodyguards in the Summer Palace. Yixin had better get some of the army commanders on his side. The ideal candidate was Commander Shengbao. When the joint foreign troops had advanced toward Peking, Commander Shengbao had been assigned to defend the capital. He had fought the foreign troops but had been defeated. Accordingly to martial law, he should have been severely punished. But the emperor had already fled to the Summer Palace and Yixin had been placed in charge of everything in the capital, and Commander Shengbao got away with only a slap on the wrist. He knew how much he owed to Yixin. Besides, he hated Sushun for his arrogance and hauteur. Now, in Yixin's name, Wenqiang had a letter sent to Shengbao, hinting lightly at the emperor's poor health and Sushun's greed for power. The letter burned before Commander Shengbao's eyes like a red rag before a bull. But he was a scholar-commander. He had brains, though he had also a quick temper. Commander Shengbao was proud that he could write beautifully and could fight, too.

CHAPTER 10

What was the emperor doing at the Summer Palace in Rehe? Mostly, watching performances of Peking operas which, in the Forbidden City, he could do only on certain festive occasions.

There were three stages in the Summer Palace. The one most frequently used was close to his living quarters. He liked to have people with him when he was watching the operas. The queen disapproved of some of the shows, especially the one where a young nun steals out of the nunnery and a young monk climbs over the wall of the temple. They meet at the foot of the mountain and flirt with each other. The emperor particularly enjoyed the absurdity of the flirting scenes (at that time, there were no actresses. Female parts were acted by actors in female costumes); the queen thought it was immoral, but she had her own favorite opera, which was acted by young boys about the age of ten. Concubine Yan preferred a different opera, featuring the owner of an inn and a lodger. Since the man had taken up lodging in the inn, he had fallen ill and spent all his money on medicine and rent and food. Though he was recovered, now, he could not leave the inn without paying his debt. The owner started harassing him and insulting him. He had to swallow the bitter fruit of humiliation. At long last, he had to pawn his weapon and sell his horse. He had been on his way to join the army. Concubine Yan thought that Sushun was very much like the innkeeper: always nasty to people. Perhaps the man's plight also reminded her of a moment in her own family history.

The emperor was happy these days because the military reports said that all the rebellious troops were surrounded and the final victory was soon to come. Besides, his birthday was coming. To please him, Sushun was preparing a celebration in the Summer Palace. The celebration would last for three days, with the birthday falling on the second day. The day before was to "warm up the celebration," and the third day was to cool things down a little. If it weren't for the rebellion in the southern provinces and the foreign invasion, the celebration might last for ten days.

On the day before the big event, only the imperial family watched the operas in the daytime, and a feast was given in the evening for all to attend — the imperial family as well as the courtiers. On the birthday itself, the emperor got up early. After he had breakfast and was garbed in his full court attire, he went to the building where the portraits of his ancestors were hung on the wall opposite the double doors and he kowtowed to the portraits. Then he made his way to another building to receive his male family members and the courtiers. On this formal occasion, the emperor was escorted everywhere by a procession. Before him walked two files of bodyguards, side by side, each carrying a yellow flag embroidered with a writhing dragon, and a long-handled halberd reflecting the sunshine — the symbols of power. The emperor sat on a big, wide sedan-chair, with a yellow canopy over his head to shield him from the sun, carried by eight eunuchs. After the emperor walked two files of eunuchs carrying everything the emperor might need — a change of clothes, towels, teacups, etc. More bodyguards brought up the rear.

When the emperor reached the building, his family and all the courtiers were already outside. They were all in full formal dress, wearing blue gowns with various birds embroidered on the front and the back. The different birds indicated different ranks. A strand of beads hung from each one's neck, almost reaching the knees. The beads were made from different materials for different ranks, and sized between a pigeon's egg and a hen's egg. The hats were decorated on the top with a bead of the same material and the same size. Quite a few courtiers received from the emperor a peacock's tail feather as an honor and ornament, and they stuck it in the hole of the bead on their hats.

At the sound of the approaching procession, they all went down on their knees and prostrated themselves until the emperor entered the building. Then they followed him in. When the emperor was settled on his throne, they arrayed themselves according to rank (the highest in the front), and kowtowed nine times while shouting in unison, "Long live the emperor, long live the emperor, long live the emperor!" Music accompanied the whole ritual. It was almost noon when the ceremony ended. Then the feast began, with every dainty imaginable: bear's paws, shark's fins, swallow's nests and sea cucumbers.

After the banquet the operas began, and lasted late into the night. Before they left, each guest was given a gift. But the emperor didn't stay long with them. He had gone back to the palace, to his queen and concubines, with whom the emperor had his feast and watched operas on another stage. The evening operas were different, especially the first one, which had no scenario. Instead, all characters imaginable, from legends, myths, folk songs and fairytales, stood on stage in costume. The actors sang in unison a chorus of praise for the emperor. The accompanying music was loud with gongs and drums. When the music stopped, ears were ringing. The silence was deep.

During the three feast days, ignoring the doctors' advice, the emperor overate and got too tired; so that on the evening of the last day, he felt really ill while watching an opera. This threw everyone into a panic. After rest and treatment, he felt a little better.

Then came the queen's birthday. The emperor remembered her 20th birthday in 1856. By Chinese tradition, every ten year birthday is more important and should be celebrated on a larger scale. A grand banquet had been held. They both had had the time of their lives. But now, as the emperor was sick, the queen didn't want to celebrate her birthday. The emperor insisted. The queen gave in, but tried to keep it down to done day. On that day, when the celebration began, the queen kowtowed to the emperor for making her the queen. Then the queen sat down and all the concubines came to kowtow to the queen and then all the eunuchs and maids followed suit. All the relatives and courtiers kowtowed outside the queen's chamber. Operas were performed and a feast was held. They ate while watching the shows. Since it was the queen's birthday, the emperor let her decide which operas she wanted to watch. All the operas the queen chose were those of moral instruction or of the good being rewarded and the bad being punished. The queen was always deemed a saintly lady in the Forbidden City.

* * *

The emperor's illness became serious. He coughed blood more often. Although Concubine Yan helped him to read the daily reports, he still needed someone else to wait on him, to console him. He sent for Concubine Li. But when Concubine Yan learned of it, she was smitten with jealousy. She could do nothing and say nothing; but the queen could, she thought. How could she persuade the queen to put a stop to it?

After a sleepless night, she went to the queen's chamber. After the ritual of kowtowing before the queen, she began. "Does Queen know . . ." She trailed off for emphasis.

"What should I know?" The queen was curious.

"The emperor is coughing blood again." She raised her handkerchief to her eyes, and in a faltering voice, added: "I always think that Emperor should have more rest. But how can he, when Concubine Li is with him day and night?" That again? Not good for a man in poor health.

The queen was concerned, too. "Leave it to me." After Concubine Yan left, she sent for Concubine Li, but the queen was weak and she didn't scold Concubine Li as Concubine Yan would have expected.

"How is Emperor's health, these days?" she asked.

"Not good."

" Emperor must have more rest." ("You should leave him alone.")

"I know, but how can I refuse whatever Emperor wants me to do?" Some truth to that, yes.

* * *

When the emperor was well, almost every day he had given out written orders about this and that, however trivial. Now, since the emperor was sick, he could not do that. Rumors were rife; some said that the emperor was on his deathbed. Some even had it that the emperor was already dead and that Sushun was keeping it a secret while he completed his arrangements for seizing power.

The rumors spawned inflation. The value of the currency and the prices of goods were running in opposite directions. This was Sushun's responsibility, as he was still the Minister of Internal Revenue Ministry, in addition to having been made a secretary of state. Sushun planned to clean up the four government money shops (i.e. banks) run by the Internal Revenue Ministry and cast new coins, which should be heavier than the old ones, and issue new money-shop notes.

Before Sushun was appointed Minister of the Internal Revenue Ministry, the corruption in the Ministry had been obvious and public. Some officials in the Ministry and some clerks in the money shops worked hand in glove to chip away at the money supply. The minister at that time was an old man, and not particularly adept. Sushun had asked the emperor to remove him and make him the new minister. Then Sushun had made his fame as a man of great competence by uprooting many of the perpetrators. But the corruption was still there; only the names had changed. Now Sushun wanted to sweep the place clean again, but the emperor was so sick that he couldn't get his approval, and had to wait.

CHAPTER 11

The imperial doctors knew that the emperor was suffering from a terminal disease, but they could not tell the truth about it. No one likes to hear that he will soon die. Rulers are certainly no exception.

One day after the head imperial doctor had examined the emperor, he asked, in a weak voice, "How am I? What's wrong?"

"Nothing serious," was the answer.

"What is my sickness? Does it have a name?"

"Emperor is too tired, needs a lot of rest." He didn't dare to add, "Leave the women alone." After he wrote the prescription, he was summoned into the presence of the secretaries of state.

"What is really the emperor's sickness?" asked Tu Han. "You must tell us the truth."

The doctor hesitated, but he knew that if he didn't tell the truth and the emperor died, he would be accused, at least, of being unable to cure the emperor and of allowing the emperor to die. So he decided to tell the truth. "The case is hopeless. Tuberculosis," he confessed.

"Then, why did you say 'Not serious' to the emperor? Liar!" a newly-promoted secretary of state shouted, indignant.

"What else can a doctor say to his patients?" he pleaded. Some truth to that, too. They couldn't blame him for it. So he was dismissed.

* * *

In Chinese history, when an emperor was too young to rule the country, one of two systems could be adopted: the counselor system, or the empress dowager system. It was a question of who would "help" the young emperor, that is, make decisions for him, give edicts in his name: the counselors, or the empress dowager? Sushun wanted the former; Concubine Yan, of course, wanted the latter. Sushun called a secret meeting, at his house. Only four people were present: his brother Duanhua, Zaihuan, Tu Han and himself. They were in a pavilion, on a tiny island, with only a small footbridge for access. No possible eavesdroppers. They even left the windows open so that no one could approach without being seen. They discussed what they should do, while there was still time to maneuver.

Sushun began, "The last moment for the emperor will soon come. What do we want him to say as his last words?"

"We should have the emperor appoint us to be counselors. But Old Six can't be included," suggested Zaihuan.

"Good," said Sushun. Then to Tu Han, "What do you think?"

Tu Han was a scholar and often had another way of looking at things. He observed, "The appointment of the counselors must come from the emperor. What we do can't be too obvious and incite criticism."

"Don't worry. I'll take care of it," said Sushun

"Good. Let's write down the names," said Duanhua.

"All the secretaries," suggested Zaihuan.

"No, no. Not Wenqiang," Sushun said.

"Okay. Got it," said Zaihuan. "We are four secretaries, here. And another three. Seven in all."

"Not enough," said Sushun. "It's better to add someone closer to the emperor in genealogy, to make eight counselors." In old China, family relationships were very important. It would be highly inappropriate and they would surely be faulted if no one from the emperor's family were included among the counselors. The best candidate was his good-for-nothing brother-in-law, who would not dare to stand up against them. They put his name on the list.

Then they made another list of names to form a group to handle the funeral arrangements. They put Yixin's name on it, but they planned to state that all those who were in the capital, although their names were on the list, need not come to the Summer Palace.

Sushun went to see the emperor almost every day. Today, the emperor felt better, and got up to sit on a chair by the windows. When Sushun saw him, he said, "Congratulations. Emperor will soon be well."

"I wish," said the emperor. Then he bade the eunuchs and maids leave the room. Sushun knew that he had important things to say to him. Sushun got down on his knees, so that the emperor could look at him at a comfortable angle when he spoke.

"I know you have always respected the queen," commenced the emperor. "You must still respect her when I'm gone." He stopped to draw a breath. Cold sweat broke out on Sushun's forehead. Did the emperor suspect him of anything?

Sushun said, "I'm the queen's slave. I'll serve the queen all my life."

"But you must protect her from any harm," said the emperor.

Sushun heaved a sigh of relief. "I will defend the queen with my life."

The emperor nodded his approbation. Sushun thought, it's time to mention the counselor system; but he tried another tactic first.

"What shall I do if someone wants to implement the empress dowager system when Emperor's in Heaven?"

"No such precedent in our dynasty. No one will suggest it."

"Can Emperor appoint some courtiers to help Big Brother? I can't help Big Brother alone."

"Do you mean, counselors?" It was not proper for Sushun to say anything in the affirmative. He just kowtowed on the floor. The emperor didn't say anything. He just looked tired. Sushun begged the emperor to get back in bed.

The emperor knew that his days were numbered. He wanted to make arrangements for his son. He wanted to appoint counselors to help him; and that just suited Sushun and his supporters. When the emperor asked Sushun to suggest some names, Sushun mentioned several, but not his own. The emperor listened, and didn't say anything.

Then he bade Sushun leave and sent for the queen, who came to sit at the emperor's sick bed, weeping. "No time for weeping now, my queen. Look under my pillow. There's a seal and a written will for you."

"What for?" The queen took out the two things and put them into her inner pocket.

"If Concubine Yan does anything terribly wrong, to the detriment of the empire, you can produce this will publicly and execute her." His voice was quite weak.

"Buddha help us!"

"Now you may leave, and tell Concubine Yan to come," said the emperor.

Concubine Yan came and took her seat where the queen had sat, weeping too. The emperor told her to be good to the queen, and after giving her another seal, he bade her go.

He fell into a swoon. When he came to, he was served ginseng soup. It was said that ginseng could prolong a person's life, even on the deathbed. Then he sent for his son and all the courtiers that had come there with him. He encouraged his son to be a good emperor, but his son was too young to understand.

Then the emperor wanted to write formal wills to be declared after his death to the entire empire. Tradition. But he was too feeble to write, so one of the courtiers wrote for him, while he dictated. The first will said that his son would be the emperor when he died. The second will appointed eight courtiers to be counselors to the young emperor; among them were Sushun (the younger brother), Duanhua (the elder brother), and Zaihuan, their nephew who had inherited the title of prince, though he was older than the brothers: just those Sushun wished, and had suggested to the emperor. But many courtiers felt it not fair that the emperor didn't include Yixin, his own brother, as a counselor.

Word came out that when the courtier drafted the will, he added some words, such as, "to help the young emperor to handle state affairs," and this was later deemed false. Anyway, the wills were read to the emperor and he didn't say anything, which, in the opinion of the counselors, meant that he approved them.

* * *

Everyone in the room was watching the emperor, who lay motionless. It was dawn. After a long while, Sushun burned a stick of incense and put it before the emperor's nostrils to see whether he was breathing. The smoke rose straight into the air. The emperor had gone to the Heavens, as they say. Everyone in the room began to wail in mourning. That was also a tradition. While the queen was mourning, her favorite maid brought her the sorrowful news that Concubine Li had committed suicide. She didn't die, because the opium she had swallowed was not enough. The queen had to summon Concubine Li into her presence and console her. It was not an unusual event in the history of China that a concubine should wish to end her own life to follow the emperor to the Heavens. But Concubine Li had her own reason for doing so. She was very much afraid of Concubine Yan who, in her opinion, was both shrewd and cruel. She feared that since Concubine Yan would become an empress dowager she would mistreat her some day out of old jealousy, which would easily turn into abhorrence. And murder. And it was not a stretch to think that when Concubine Yan wanted to get rid of her, she would accuse her of something — something she hadn't even done, to impair her good reputation. By dying now for the emperor, at least she would leave a good reputation behind her. The queen knew why she wanted to die; she promised to protect her from any imaginable harm, and bade her to live on. Concubine Li promised to do no more such foolish things.

* * *

After Emperor Xianfeng died on August 22, 1861, his son succeeded to the throne, becoming Emperor Tongzhi (1856-1875), at the age of six years. The queen became Empress Dowager Xi An. She lived in a chamber on the east side, so she was habitually called East Empress Dowager. According to tradition, the young emperor's biological mother, Concubine Yan, was made Empress Dowager Cixi. She lived in a west chamber, and so was known as West Empress Dowager. The courtiers and maids and eunuchs addressed them as Mother Queen Empress Dowager and Holy Mother Empress Dowager, or, privately, East Side and West Side.

Who would make decisions for Emperor Tongzhi until he came of age? Different people had different opinions, of course. The counselors thought the counselors should make the decisions (especially Sushun). The late emperor had appointed them to help his son to rule the empire. But the empress dowagers, especially West Empress Dowager, had the concept that they should make the decisions for him, since they were his mothers. (By tradition, the queen was treated as his mother, too.) Before Emperor Xianfeng died, two groups used to assist him in handling state affairs: one headed by Sushun, in the Summer Palace, the other headed by Yixin, his brother, in the capital. Now a third group appeared in this political game: the two empress dowagers. The late emperor had made a vague statement on his deathbed, that whenever any written orders were to be issued in the name of the new emperor, the queen should use the seal he had given her at the beginning and Concubine Yan should use the other seal at the end. His intent was to prevent the counselors from taking power from his son. This decision was not accompanied by recognized, detailed procedures, so there was a dispute between the empress dowagers and the counselors. The counselors argued that as the emperor was too young to read, no more reports would be turned in. The counselors would read them all, make their decisions and send the written orders to the two empress dowagers to mark with their seals, and the empress dowagers would not be able to make any changes on the written orders. But the empress dowagers insisted that they should read all the reports for the young emperor and, if they didn't agree with any decision the counselors had made, they would have the right to change it. Otherwise, they would not apply their seals, and the orders would be invalid. The counselors had to give in. The empress dowagers won the first round.

CHAPTER 12

Before Emperor Xianfeng died, he had heard the rumors about his brother Yixin and he tried to keep him at arm's length, so that he could not harm him directly. And in his appointment of counselors, he excluded Yixin for fear that he might harm his son. Flesh and blood holds nothing in politics, though blood is always shed for it. Yixin didn't care about the rumor. Time tells all. Sometimes attempted explanations only persuade people of the opposite. However, the courtiers who remained in Peking were greatly dissatisfied with the late emperor's second will. In their opinion, the late emperor's brother should help his young nephew as a counselor. And they questioned the will's authenticity, since it was not written in the late emperor's handwriting.

* * *

Sushun still wanted to mint heavy new coins and bring the inflation under control. Now, as Emperor Xianfeng had died, he had to discuss the matter with the empress dowagers. The counselors went to see them every day to report and discuss affairs of state. When Sushun mentioned the minting of new coins, West

Empress Dowager asked, "Is it so urgent? Can't it wait until we return to the capital?"

"Yes, it's urgent. If the inflation gets worse, the people will become dissatisfied with the government and riots may occur, even in the capital."

"Do you have enough copper?" she queried.

"I'm having copper transported from Yunnan Province to the capital. Once the new coins are in circulation, the situation will be better."

West Empress Dowager looked sidelong at East Empress Dowager, and asked for her opinion. All the while, East Empress Dowager was whispering to the young emperor, telling him to keep quiet. When asked, she just said, "It sounds good." She had no objection. West Empress Dowager doubted if East Empress Dowager had heard the discussion. Asking for her opinion was just a formality. So Sushun got the green light.

The clerical officials in the Summer Palace were very careful in choosing sides. Some would choose to follow Sushun, because he had power. Some compared Sushun to a mountain: hard, sturdy, immoveable. But Head Clerical Official Zao thought he was an ice mountain. Melt in no time. Quite a few of his colleagues agreed. Most of the clerical officials tried to stay in the wings, or better, in the audience, to watch the political opera in real life and to see how it would end.

* * *

When the sad news reached the capital that Emperor Xianfeng had died, Yixin wanted to go to the Summer Palace to mourn. Tradition. And suddenly came a secret missive, a message from the two empress dowagers, summoning Yixin to the Summer Palace. So he sent in a formal report, demanding to go to the palace to mourn for his late brother. The counselors could not say "no" to this. Yixin set off, as the late emperor's brother, not as a courtier.

Now, the Summer Palace was completely under Sushun's control. He even had spies among the eunuchs to eavesdrop on what the empress dowagers said about him. It cannot have been easy to send a secret letter to Yixin. It was said that one day Little An, West Empress Dowager's head eunuch, had a quarrel with East Empress Dowager's head maid. Little An cursed her while they were bickering. She began to cry, and went to complain to East Empress Dowager. Since Little An was West Empress Dowager's head eunuch, East Empress Dowager thought that it would be better to let her handle it, so she told her head maid to complain to West Empress Dowager. West Empress Dowager immediately sent for Little An, heard him out, and decided that Little An was at fault. Then she sent for the head eunuch of the Palace. He already knew about the spat, but feigned ignorance. Why step in the middle when two comets collide? He outranked both of the parties to the quarrel, but could hardly afford to offend either empress dowager.

When he had kowtowed to West Empress Dowager, she announced, "Little An annoys me. I don't wish to see him here anymore."

The head eunuch, still on his knees, said, "I'll send him back to the Forbidden City." West Empress Dowager nodded and added, "Give him twenty slaps before he leaves." Little An, prostrating himself, kowtowed and begged West Empress Dowager to pardon him. But West Empress Dowager was firm.

The head eunuch of the Palace took Little An to his place and told a eunuch to give him twenty slaps on the face. Then he sent Little An packing. A clerk and two soldiers escorted him. When they arrived in the capital, the clerk dropped off Little An at the Imperial Household Department. A petty official on duty there received them and gave the clerk a body receipt; he returned to the Summer Palace with the two soldiers. Then the petty official registered Little An's name.

When he was about to detain him in a cell for the night, Little An said, "Excuse me, Official. I have something very important to say."

The petty official said, "All right. Say it."

"Not to you."

The petty official was irritated and shouted, "Are you joking with me?"

"No. I'm not joking. Even if I tell you, you cannot do anything about it."

"Who do you want to speak to?"

"I must speak to His Excellency Baojun" (one of the courtiers in charge of the Imperial Household Department).

The petty official knew that Little An had been West Empress Dowager's head eunuch, and he didn't dare to offend him overmuch; so he sent somebody to let Baojun know. In two hours' time, Little An was taken to Baojun's residence. After Little An kowtowed to him, Baojun asked, "What do you wish to tell me?"

"Better read this letter, first, Your Excellency." He reached into his inner pocket. It was a short note from the two empress dowagers, ordering Yixin to the Summer Palace. Baojun realized the significance. He sent Little An back to the Forbidden City, and went to pick up Wenqiang; they went together to see Yixin.

If they wanted to deprive Sushun of his power, they would have to ally with the empress dowagers. As Yixin hadn't been appointed a counselor, he had to denounce the counselor system if he wanted to take over power from Sushun; it would not be enough to just drive Sushun out of the Secretarial Bureau. And if the counselor system were denounced, they would have to accept the empress dowager system — exactly what the empress dowagers had in mind. For backup, they had a letter delivered to Commander Shengbao, telling him to bring his troops to the capital.

* * *

There was a lot of work to do after an emperor's demise. First, everyone must wear white linen mourning clothes, which had to be made in great haste because these clothes could not be sewn before the emperor took his last breath — it would look like a curse, suggesting that he should die. Then the departed emperor must be dressed in thirteen layers of clothes, from the innermost thin summer clothes to the thickest winter clothes. It would be too much trouble to dress the stiff corpse with the thirteen layers of clothes, one after another, so a eunuch was used as a dummy. All the clothes were put on him, one by one, and then the whole stack was peeled off and put on the dead body of the emperor. Then there had to be two funerals. The first one was relatively simple. The late emperor was properly dressed, still lying on the deathbed. A table was set before the bed with all his favorite dishes. His son and all the courtiers knelt before the table and kowtowed nine times, howling in mourning. Then his head eunuch carried the cup of wine out of the building and poured it on the ground as a libation to the ghost of the deceased, underground. The ritual was thus finished.

After that, the son and all the courtiers went to the main room where the late emperor had held court. The son was placed on the throne, and all the courtiers knelt before him and kowtowed nine times. Thus, he was made the new emperor. The coronation would be held later, when they returned to the capital.

The next day, the young emperor and all the courtiers attended the final funeral. The late emperor had already been laid in the coffin, which had been removed to another building. Before the coffin, on a massive table, lay many dishes. Candles and incense were burning at one end of the table. A courtier from the Etiquette Ministry recited the "Eulogy To The Deceased." The young emperor and courtiers went down on their knees and wailed. Then wine on the table was poured on the ground again.

According to Chinese custom, a ceremony would be performed every seventh day from the day of the demise, and this would happen seven times (forty-nine days in all) and then again on the hundredth day. After that, the white mourning clothes could be taken off and normal dressing would resume.

On the second seventh-day, the ritual had just come to an end. Paper money was being burned. Just then, someone dressed in white rushed in and prostrated himself before the coffin, wailing grievously. It was the late emperor's brother, Yixin. The wailing of the other courtiers became louder, because it was considered that the louder the wailing, the more loyal they were to the emperor. (It is interesting to note that "loyal" offers no comparative term, such as "loyaler"; perhaps one can only be loyal, or disloyal. Yet that was the premise, here.)

The late emperor's tomb had been built outside the city of Peking. The coffin would be carried there for burial, after everyone returned to the capital.

CHAPTER 13

After the funeral, the empress dowagers wanted to see their brother-in-law Yixin. They were confident that they would find an ally in him. He could not be happy at being shut out from the center of power — the Secretarial Bureau. But they were afraid that Sushun might say that young widows should not see their young brother-in-law. Another social tradition in old China. Before they received Yixin, West Empress Dowager wanted to make sure that no one would eavesdrop, because Sushun had spies among the eunuchs. She sent some of the more suspicious eunuchs on a fool's errand to someplace far enough away that they couldn't get back in a couple of hours; then they sent the head eunuch of the palace to summon Yixin, telling him to use whatever ruse would do the trick.

The head eunuch waited outside the building until Yixin came out, accompanied by other courtiers including Sushun. He rushed up to make his formal announcement. The empress dowagers were summoning Yixin. A conspiracy? Yixin turned to Sushun and, to allay his suspicions, asked whether he could see the widows. Sushun asked the head eunuch: Why do the empress dowagers wish to see Yixin? He replied that they wished to know how things stood in the Forbidden City and how all those who had been left behind had fared. Entirely a family concern. Sushun did not show any opposition, so Yixin went with the head eunuch to see the empress dowagers.

"Somebody should go with Prince Yixin, so that we can at least know what they are talking about," Tu Han said, after Yixin and the head eunuch had left.

"You always lock the barn after the horse is gone. It's too late now," Zaihuan criticized him. They could hardly send someone chasing along behind.

After he kowtowed to the two widows, Yixin was seated. The empress dowagers made it look like a family reunion. It was supposed that East Empress Dowager should begin the conversation, but she was not a talkative woman and didn't even know how to get around to the important topic. So she began by asking when he had started out from the capital.

"Early on the 26th of the seventh moon."

"How long did it take you to reach here?"

"Five whole days."

"How's everything in the capital?"

"Everything's fine there. We are making all the preparations for the return of Empress Dowagers and Emperor."

"I hope we will return before the end of this year."

"That will be too late. The earlier, the better."

"Better after everything's properly prepared. Mustn't overlook anything," cut in West Empress Dowager.

"That's for sure. Can't afford a misstep. I'll take care of all the preparations myself when I am back there."

"Good. I think next month is the earliest we can leave here," said West Empress Dowager.

"That sounds good."

"What are people saying about the late Emperor's will, in the capital?" She wanted to lead the conversation to more significant things.

"Can Holy Mother Empress Dowager be more specific?" He didn't want to be easily led to where he already knew the conversation would go.

"About the counselor system?"

"We've had the counselor system before."

"Is it a life-long title?"

"Of course not. As soon as Emperor is grown up and takes control, there would be no need to have counselors anymore. Besides, the emperor has the right to take back the title. But generally the succeeding emperor won't do it, since the title was bestowed by the preceding emperor. Unless . . ."

"Unless what?" West Empress Dowager prodded.

"Unless the counselors do something seriously wrong. But now, the emperor can't denounce their titles, because his orders must go through their hands to be announced to the whole country. They won't let such an order out of the palace. What's the use, if no one knows there is such an order?" Ah. So, such an order would have to be issued through hands other than those of the counselors.

"What if we appoint you as a counselor?" asked West Empress Dowager.

"I beg the empress dowagers not to do that," Yixin said modestly.

"Why not?"

"No use. They are eight and I am one."

No use, indeed. A plan was fermenting in the busy mind of West Empress Dowager.

* * *

Although they hated each other politically, Sushun and Yixin were polite to each other socially. Sushun invited Yixin to his house for dinner after Yixin left the Summer Palace. Other counselors were there, too. A servant hurried in, bearing a small package. When Sushun opened it, everyone stared at the object in surprise. A brightly gleaming coin, the new proof.

"When will you put it into circulation?" Yixin asked Sushun.

"On the new emperor's coronation day." The coronation would be held when the empress dowagers and the emperor returned to the capital.

"Very good. It seems that you want to return to Peking as early as possible." That's what Yixin wanted.

"It depends on you," observed Sushun.

"Why me?" Yixin queried, baffled.

"You are in charge there. When you finish preparations to receive the empress dowagers and the emperor, we'll come," Sushun said with a smile. So, the man can smile, Yixin thought.

It was late when Yixin got back to his lodging. He sent a servant to fetch Head Clerical Official Zao, who came in civilian clothes and entered by a side door. They had a serious talk in an innermost room. Yixin inquired, "What do the counselors think of West Empress Dowager?"

"They think West Side is shrewd," answered Zao.

"Not only shrewd; she can also feign ignorance and say naïve things to set you a trap."

"That's a new one. Why does Prince say that?" said Zao.

"She wanted me in the Secretarial Bureau, working with the counselors."

"That's also a way out. If Prince heads the Secretarial Bureau, some counselors will take Prince's side. If anyone disobeys, Prince can squeeze him out of the Secretarial Bureau, though Prince can't take away his title of a counselor. If he's no longer in the Secretarial Bureau, what can he do?"

"That means I'd have a hand-to-hand combat with Sushun. I'd like to solve this problem when we are back in the capital." Now Head Clerical Official Zao knew that Prince Yixin intended to do away with the counselor system, not just to deprive the counselors of their power. That would bring in the empress dowager system.

Yihuan arrived to see his brother, Yixin, so Zao took his leave.

CHAPTER 14

Yixin and his supporters had been plotting against the counselors long before he came to the Summer Palace, but it was too early to let the empress dowagers know that. Women are generally known to have trouble keeping secrets. And this was a life and death secret.

Yixin did not visit them alone again during his stay in Rehe. The necessary message between them was exchanged through his younger brother, Yihuan, who had married West Empress Dowager's younger sister. It was natural for sisters to visit

After certain arrangements had been made, Yixin left the Summer Palace on September 16, in some haste lest he be detained. Would the counselors smell a rat? Besides, he had preparations to finish in the capital.

The date was fixed for the young emperor and the empress dowagers to return to the capital: October 26. They had been away nearly a year. Everyone was happy to go back home.

Just at the joyous moment came a letter from Commander Shengbao, paying respects to the empress dowagers and the emperor. Such a thing was unheard of. Queens and empress dowagers could not have any contact with the outside world, although anyone working in the government was welcome to pay homage to the emperor, by mail. That was normal. This letter had a special meaning to deliver; it supported the authority of the empress dowagers and denied that of the counselors. The tension between the empress dowagers and the counselors had surely leaked out. Now the counselors, especially Sushun, had an uneasy feeling.

They would have to do something to rebuff this, to refute it; if any other commanders or governors followed the example, it would be a real challenge to their authority. One of the counselors drafted a reply. They went to see the empress dowagers, taking the letter and the draft reply. First, they reported that the government armies had taken Anqing City, which had been occupied by the rebels. Then they discussed some other business. At last, Zaihuan mentioned the letter from Commander Shengbao and their reply, explaining that such a letter was against tradition. East Empress Dowager was surprised to hear that they would actually criticize somebody who merely wished to pay his respects to the empress dowagers, but West Empress Dowager said, "If it's against tradition, criticize him." She stamped her seal on the reply, and so did East Empress Dowager. Later, she explained to East Empress Dowager that she wanted to add a little more gunpowder to the keg on which the counselors were sitting. Furthermore, from the information Yixin sent via her sister, she knew Commander Shengbao would soon ask to come to the Summer Palace to show his last reverence to the late emperor, in person. She reckoned that if she gave in this time, she could persist next time, when they discussed his request.

* * *

Just as everyone was getting ready for the return journey, a report of suggestion, written by Critique Official Dong, arrived from the capital on September 12. This was a stone cast into an already undulating lake, and it caused not ripples but a big splash. The report said that since the emperor was so young, the two empress dowagers should sit behind a screen behind the throne, and hold court in behalf of the young emperor. Just what West Empress Dowager wanted. That was the empress dowager system, and it had been known in other dynasties before, but not in the Qing Dynasty. But West Empress Dowager felt that the time was not ripe to suggest such a thing. Don't serve the food before it is cooked. So she showed the report to East Empress Dowager, and they decided to keep it quiet for the time being.

The usual procedure was that all the reports must be registered by the Secretarial Bureau, then sent in through the Internal Registrar situated at the palace gate to the emperor (now to the two empress dowagers). After reading, the emperor would make marks on the reports that needed a reply or a decision.

The different marks showed different meanings like "known," "agreed," etc. Then all the reports would be returned to the Secretarial Bureau, who would draft replies or decisions in the emperor's name, according to the meanings of the marks on the reports. If they had different opinions, they could send in their own reports. Otherwise, they sent in the drafts for the emperor to approve or for the empress dowagers to mark with their seals. Back at the Secretarial Bureau, if there were corrections to be made, the drafts would be rewritten and then sent back to where the reports had come from. Occasionally the emperor, now the empress dowagers, would hold onto an inopportune report and never give it back to the Secretarial Bureau. It was sunk, or "flooded over," submerged under water. Saves a lot of trouble.

That day, all the reports except one were returned to the Secretarial Bureau. When the counselors found from the registration that one report was missing, they sent an imperial servant to the Internal Registrar to inquire about it. This was, strictly speaking, unnecessary because they must have known that it had been held back by the empress dowagers. The registrar sent someone to ask the empress dowagers about it, and having obtained the answer, he told the servant that West Empress Dowager had kept it. The servant brought back the message.

Zaihuan and Tu Han in particular took exception to this, and ordered the servant to go to the Internal Registrar to ask for the report back.

* * *

When the two empress dowagers saw that they could not keep the report any longer, they sat down together to discuss how to deal with the counselors. Under normal circumstances, no courtier would dare to do such a thing unless he wanted to be punished or even beheaded, depending on the emperor's mood at that time. But the counselors were now in charge of the emperor's body-guards, which made them bold enough to challenge the empress dowagers.

The two women were in a dilemma. They knew that the counselors commanded the armed men and might do something desperate, if they were forced too hard. But give an inch, lose a mile: the empress dowagers must not yield too easily.

East Empress Dowager maintained that they should avoid any confrontation with the counselors, but West Empress Dowager thought that they should treat the counselors as the dignity of empress dowagers required. Anyway, they decided to face the counselors the next day.

When they discussed important things with the counselors, the young emperor was always present to show that they spoke only in his behalf. So it was, that day.

"After due consideration," West Empress Dowager began, "we have decided that we agree to the report. So draft a reply."

"Empress Dowagers cannot do that," Zaihuan protested.

"Why not?"

Sushun thought they were treading dangerously; he said, "We will discuss it and send in a draft reply tomorrow." Thus saying, they retired from the presence of the two empress dowagers and the young emperor.

When the counselors were back in their room, they expressed their rage. This had to be the result of the meeting between the empress dowagers and Yixin. Duanhua, one of the chief counselors, said, "If we don't contradict it, such reports will come in over and over again."

"Right," Zaihuan remarked. "We must contradict it severely."

They drafted a reply in the name of the young emperor, saying that it was against the tradition of the Qing Dynasty to have the empress dowagers handle state affairs, and remarking that courtiers should never suggest such a thing. A political group can always find a reason why they should, or why the other group should not, do something.

The report of suggestion was lying before them now. The reason for the suggestion was that these were unusual times, which required an unusual approach.

CHAPTER 15

When the draft reply was sent in, West Empress Dowager read it first. East Empress Dowager had no ambition and no mind for these matters, anyway. Only for important things, West Empress Dowager went to seek her consultation.

Now, after she had read only the first few sentences, West Empress Dowager flared up. When she finished, she took the document to East Empress Dowager's chamber.

"They want to rebel."

"What do you mean?"

"They have written a reply that is totally different from what we told them to write yesterday." If anything a courtier did was against the wish of the emperor (or, now, against the wish of the empress dowagers), it was deemed a rebellion or betrayal. The result could be execution.

"Calm down," warned East Empress Dowager.

"I will. But we can't let them walk over us now, or they will be walking on our dead bodies before long."

"We'd better deal with them when we return to the capital. We'll have Yixin's support, then."

"And what should we do with this, now?" East Empress Dowager said nothing, so she continued. "At least we should ask them why they wrote the reply like this, and see what they say."

East Empress Dowager acquiesced.

On September 15, the counselors were summoned into their presence. The empress dowagers received them in the main room of their building. Everyone seemed a bit nervous. The young emperor hid in the arms of East Empress Dowager. A conflict of words could not be avoided since their views were so far apart and their personal interests were almost opposite.

"Who wrote this reply?" West Empress Dowager asked sternly.

"It's the result of our discussion," answered Zaihuan.

"Do you know that this reply should reflect Emperor's opinion?"

"Yes," Tu Han cut in, "but since Emperor is so young, the late emperor appointed us to handle things."

"But it's written in the emperor's name. How can Emperor oppose his own mothers?"

"We didn't write such things. We only contradict Critique Official Dong, who sent in this report," said Zaihuan.

"Why is what he said in his report wrong?"

"We've answered that question," Sushun said. "Empress Dowagers can read it for yourselves."

That was no way to address the empress dowagers. But he had said it. And he had said it so loudly that the young emperor was frightened and turned to hide his face in the silk of East Empress Dowager's gown.

"Can a courtier express his opinion to Emperor?" asked West Empress Dowager.

"No, he cannot, since the counselors will take care of things, one by one, in proper order," said Sushun stubbornly.

"Have you any respect for Emperor and Empress Dowagers?" West Empress Dowager was getting angrier by the minute.

"It's really not necessary for Empress Dowagers to read reports," he declared.

East Empress Dowager went pale. West Empress Dowager went red.

"Here is the emperor. Can he read the reports? If he can't, who can act for him, if not his mothers?" The voice of West Empress Dowager grew a bit higher, too.

"Why did the late emperor appoint us as counselors?" said Sushun.

But West Empress Dowager went on, "Now, in Emperor's name, I order you to rewrite the reply."

"According to our tradition, Empress Dowagers can only look after the young emperor; they cannot interfere in state affairs."

"Do you resist Emperor's order?" She slapped on the table.

"We are not resisting any orders from Emperor, but Empress Dowagers must abide by tradition," said Tu Han.

The voices were escalating. The young emperor was so terrified that he began to cry out and wet his pants, also wetting the clothes of East Empress Dowager. His crying interrupted the brawl. The counselors were embarrassed, and retreated silently to their resting room.

* * *

Sushun asked his brother Duanhua and their nephew Zaihuan, who was actually older than them, to dinner at his house. They talked while eating.

"If she wants to be in charge, good, let her take the reins. But if the horse has no legs, where can she go?" Duanhua blurted out, after downing a cup of wine.

That was their strategy. They were on strike. If no one worked for the emperor, hence for the empress dowagers, how could their orders get out of the palace and be carried out?

* * *

That afternoon, forgetting their afternoon nap, the two women discussed the situation.

"What shall we do now?" asked East Empress Dowager.

"I intended to keep it quiet for awhile, but they forced my hand. Now we have to leave it aside, until the broth cools."

But their rivals were not waiting. The next morning the empress dowagers waited for the reports to be delivered to them, but none came. It was not until late in the morning that the bad news came. The head eunuch of the palace dashed in to report to them that the counselors were on strike, and the whole palace was in panic. Everyone was afraid that something terrible would happen. The two empress dowagers looked at each other without a word. They instructed the head eunuch to go for further information.

They conversed once more. What could they do, if no one listened to them in the Summer Palace? Unless they returned to the capital, where they had Yixin for support. Suddenly into the mind of West Empress Dowager came an old saying: "Ten years is not too late for a gentleman to take his revenge." So, at last they gave in, and stamped their seals on the written reply to contradict the suggestion. When the counselors got it back, they enjoyed their victory over the empress dowagers. They had won the second round, regardless of the obvious fact that the empress dowagers were always above them in power and rank, like a sword hanging by a hair over their heads.

* * *

Commander Shengbao had passed a government test and was deemed a scholar. After two promotions as an official, he had been made a general, since rebellions were occurring in many provinces. He had been victorious in quite a few battles. As a result, he received many gifts of honor from the late emperor, including a peacock's tail feather and a yellow coat (no one could use this color except with the permission of the emperor). And finally, he had acquired the promotion to commander, with several generals under him. Although he had been defeated by the foreign troops while defending the capital, no one had challenged his authority and reputation because, at that time, defeat by the foreign armies was a matter of course. If a force armed with swords and spears, bows and arrows could defeat an army with guns and cannons, it would be a great surprise indeed. It was said that China had invented gunpowder, but only used it to make firecrackers.

When Commander Shengbao sent in a request, saying that he wished to come in person to pay his last respects to the late emperor, to show his loyalty and gratitude, Sushun wanted, at first, to refuse him; but at the insistence of the empress dowagers, he had to give in. Commander Shengbao brought his 500 bodyguards, for his own safety. Everyone in Rehe wanted to get on his good side. He was more than warmly welcomed. After he kowtowed and mourned before the coffin, he returned to his lodging place and received many visitors. But one important visitor he was expecting came at night. It was Head Clerical Official Zao. Commander Shengbao was arrogant, for he had so many merits. He treated his generals and officers as his slaves; many of them were, after all, illiterate. But he esteemed scholars and talented officials. He received Head Clerical Official Zao with due decorum, though his rank was much higher than that of the visitor. He told Zao that he had met Yixin on the way in, as Yixin was on his way back to the capital. Zao gathered that he knew most of what was going on already, and told him only new developments.

"Critique Official Dong is a blockhead," commented Commander Shengbao. "He deserves the reprimand from Sushun."

"I think such a suggestion should be made by someone with a much higher rank," said Zao.

Commander Shengbao agreed and added, "I've half a mind to do it myself, but this is not the right time."

"Better, after the empress dowagers and the emperor get safely back to the capital." Commander Shengbao nodded his head. So that was settled.

Before Commander Shengbao left Rehe, he gave 200 taels of silver to every official there. No one could reject it; that would be like smearing mud on his face. No one wanted to offend him. Besides, officials living on meager salary always need extra money. It was a gift, anyway, not a bribe. But what's the difference?

CHAPTER 16

Sushun always wanted to cut West Empress Dowager down to size, but he didn't succeed. Now he had another idea: he would go to see the two empress dowagers separately. He might get more done with East Empress Dowager alone. When his demand was made known to the empress dowagers, they had a conversation.

"I don't know why they want that," said East Empress Dowager.

"Because you are so good-hearted that they can trick you."

"That's what I'm afraid of. We'd better see them together."

"But if we receive them separately, you may hear things different than when we are together."

"What if they ask me to make decisions?"

"You can say you'll think about it."

"What if it's an emergency, and they need an immediate solution?"

West Empress Dowager knew that that was the problem, but after some consideration, she said, "For important matters, we have to use both seals on the papers. After you use your seal, they must still come to me. If it's inappropriate, I'll refuse. We'll play white face and red face" (in those days, no good cop/bad cop).

Sushun kowtowed to East Empress Dowager before he spoke. "I put my whole heart to work for the benefits of our empire, but still someone complains against me. How can I continue to work this way?" East Empress Dowager murmured something soothing.

"Since there are still wars in the southern provinces, we must save every tael of silver to support the wars," observed Sushun.

"You are right," responded East Empress Dowager.

"But not everyone thinks so," Sushun complained again.

"What's happened?" asked East Empress Dowager.

"Holy Mother Empress Dowager wants too many unnecessary things."

"Like what?"

"Like more bowls, plates and such things."

"Such things won't make us poorer."

"What if everyone else follows her example?"

"She is an empress dowager. Not everyone here is an empress dowager. And I know you work hard and are loyal to the emperor."

"But still, many are complaining behind my back."

"Don't listen to others. Just do your job. We trust you." East Empress Dowager comforted him.

"One more thing. There's gossip that Holy Mother Empress Dowager (West Empress Dowager) often receives visits from male relatives. It's against etiquette. Mother Queen Empress Dowager had better advise Holy Mother Empress Dowager not to do so." East Empress Dowager just nodded.

Sushun could think of nothing more to say, and had to retire. His goal was not achieved. For all his complaints, East Empress Dowager only gave him mild words — no gifts or honorary title. Nothing but an empty compliment.

The two empress dowagers met when Sushun left. East told West every-thing she could remember. Though indignant, West Empress Dowager said, "Sushun is right. We still have a war going on in the southern provinces. We must save every coin for it. From now on, I won't ask him for a thing." Mean-while, she said to herself, "If I do have power, some day, he will kneel before me and a eunuch will slap his face hard — and then execute him."

Then the chief counselors had a meeting. Duanhua said to Sushun, "East Side is pretty slow. She might not get what you said." Then he suggested to Zaihuan, "We must use the strategy: Retreat First For the Purpose of Advance." They decided to try it. So the next day, when they went to see the empress dowagers, they put up an oral resignation from some of the insignificant posi-tions. Generally, when a courtier sent in a resignation, the emperor would refuse the resignation and say some words of encouragement, even give a gift or an honorary title, which was just what they wanted. But this time, the empress dowagers accepted their resignations and gave all these positions to other court-iers. Their subterfuge failed. And they could not withdraw the resignations.

* * *

On the day they were to leave the Summer Palace, they were divided into two groups. The group that set out first mainly comprised the empress dowa-gers, the young emperor and seven counselors, and all the other courtiers. The second group consisted of Sushun and Yihuan, escorting the late emperor's coffin. This group could not move quickly. And they were not in a hurry, as a matter of fact. But the empress dowagers wanted to reach the capital as soon as possible. They urged the others to move along. They wished that they could have grown wings and flown to Peking, out of danger from the counselors. They were not even in a mood to appreciate the beautiful scenery along the road, the colored leaves, the blue sky dotted sparsely with fluffy clouds and sometimes a vulture swooping down upon its prey in the distance.

At length, they drew to a halt at a place near to the capital. All the courtiers who had remained in Peking with Yixin came out to welcome them. At the sight of Yixin and the courtiers, the empress dowagers were overwhelmed with a sense of relief. Ronglu was among them. Cixi's devoted cousin, he was now a high-ranking officer in command of an army guarding the capital.

There was a temporary residence for the empress dowagers and the emperor. They lodged there for the night. After a rest, after washing the dust off their faces and hands, and after tea, the empress dowagers received Yixin.

East Empress Dowager asked, "Is everything all right in the capital?"

"Everything's all right and everything is ready," was the answer. (That covers a lot of ground.) Both empress dowagers understood. East asked, "How about the Forbidden City?"

"They are ready to welcome Empress Dowagers and Emperor back."

They arrived in the capital on November 1. Once inside the Forbidden City, the two empress dowagers felt truly safe. Even assassins could not easily get in. After a rest, the empress dowagers sent for Yixin again, who came immediately and reported all the arrangements he had made. Everything was ready for action.

Yixin had met with three prime ministers who disliked Sushun and had great influence among the courtiers. They readily gave Yixin their support. Prime ministers were quite often scholars, and quite often had old students among the courtiers, like an old tree with many branches. A minister had a chance to be the head examiner; and the candidates who passed the government examination were traditionally considered to be the students of the examiners. And prime ministers were promoted from ministers.

The next day, when all the courtiers were in the resting room, the empress dowagers summoned Yixin and those prime ministers and Wenqiang, who was Yixin's trusty follower. The counselors were not included.

Zaihuan shouted, "Empress Dowagers can't summon courtiers. Against tradition!" But they ignored him.

The empress dowagers told those prime ministers how the counselors had disobeyed them, even bullied them. Once, the counselors had argued so fiercely that they frightened the young emperor, so that he had begun to cry and even wet his pants, coincidentally soiling the clothes of East Empress Dowager. The prime ministers were outraged, and wanted justice to be done. Prime Minister Zhou said, "Why didn't Empress Dowagers punish them?"

"They are counselors appointed by the late emperor. Can counselors be punished?" asked West Empress Dowager.

"Why not?" said Prime Minister Zhou. "Empress Dowagers can issue an order to deprive them of the title of counsellorship first, and then punish them."

At the suggestion, East Empress Dowager turned her back to them and, like a magician, produced from her inner pocket a small scroll, the order prewritten on October 21 when they were still in the Summer Palace. East

Empress Dowager had hidden it on her person all this time. She handed it to Yixin, telling him to read it to the prime ministers. Yixin unrolled the scroll and read it to them.

It accused the counselors, especially the three chief counselors, of the following crimes: When they were assisting the late emperor, they had handled state matters improperly, causing the foreigners to invade so that the late emperor had to leave the capital; while at the Summer Palace, they had dissuaded the late emperor from returning to the capital when peace was restored, so that his health had deteriorated and he had died there; they had opposed the empress dowagers in handling state affairs.

Each of these crimes warranted a death sentence, but the order only stripped the counselors of their titles. That was not enough, now, for they would counterattack later on. A second order was issued for the arrest of the three chief counselors and the removal of the other five counselors from office.

Yixin took the written orders and went back to the resting room with the prime ministers and Wenqiang. When he read the orders, Zaihuan yelled, "We've just arrived. Where did these orders come from?" Only counselors could issue orders (in the emperor's name, of course).

Actually, anyone can issue orders, if he or she has enough support. Armed support.

Yixin ordered the palace guards to tie up Zaihuan and Duanhua and put them into the imperial prison, where only high-ranking courtiers were "entitled" to be imprisoned. The other five counselors were sent home to await further orders. It was November 2, 1861.

Sushun was still free, since he had not arrived yet. He was on the way. He had better be in irons and fetters before the news reached him. If he got wind that his partners were in jail, he would either rebel or slip away, trouble in either case.

Yihuan, Yixin's brother, was with Sushun. They would stay for the night in a small town. Yixin dispatched a messenger with a written order to take Sushun into custody. The order was delivered to Yihuan, who was to carry it out. A plan was formed for the arrest. Yihuan sent for Sushun's head bodyguard. When he came, Yihuan asked him whether he was loyal to the emperor or to Sushun. Tough question. Better answer carefully. Something serious must have happened between Sushun and the emperor, that is, between Sushun and the emperor's two mothers. Of course, the head bodyguard could not say that he was loyal to Sushun; he swore his loyalty to the emperor.

Yihuan ordered him to lead the way to Sushun's temporary residence. A group of soldiers followed them. When Sushun's other guards saw this, they didn't know what to do. They looked at the head guard, but he kept his eyes fixed on the ground. So they just let Yihuan and the group of soldiers pass before them. The residence was already surrounded by other soldiers. Most of Sushun's guards were with the late emperor's coffin. Why — would someone want to steal the coffin, or the corpse? No; but many valuable things were in the coffin, to be buried with the deceased. If anything happened to the coffin, even if nothing was stolen, anyone who shared the responsibility would be severely punished. Sushun had sent most of his guards to assure its absolute safety.

The soldiers disarmed Sushun's guards. When the soldiers broke into Sushun's room, he was sleeping with his two concubines. Sushun was furious at being woken up — then the soldiers seized him. Two soldiers held him in a kneeling position while Yihuan read him the order written in the young emperor's name. It was midnight, November 4.

PART TWO
A BALANCING ACT

CHAPTER 17

With all the counselors either arrested or removed from office, a new power center had to be established. Yixin gathered his loyal supporters. This time they decided that there should be six secretaries in the Bureau. Besides Yixin himself, Wenqiang, Baojun and the former head clerical official Zao were all made secretaries. Yixin gave the positions to his supporters in recognition for services rendered. Yixin's father-in-law would be a secretary, too. He was too old to perform any actual duties, but he was put there as an advisor. Another secretary was chosen from courtiers of the Han Clan, to balance the racial proportion in the Bureau. The list was approved by the empress dowagers. Yixin was made the head secretary. There was an unspoken bargain — West Empress Dowager made Yixin head secretary and Yixin supported the empress dowager system. Power re-allotted.

When Yihuan brought Sushun to the capital, he reported to Yixin on his arrest. Had Sushun said anything along the way? Yihuan told his brother that Sushun had said that West Empress Dowager was a poisonous snake and would bite anyone, anytime she thought it was necessary. Yixin ignored the warning.

Sushun was put into the same prison with the other two counselors. Sushun had advised them to kill the empress dowagers on the way to the capital, but they didn't follow his advice, being scornful of women. Now the three of them accused one another of being slow in decision, negligent in stratagem and unnecessarily merciful to enemies; but all to no avail. Sushun wanted to slip a letter out to his faithful supporters, so that they could think of some way to rescue him; but no jailor would dare to help in such an endeavor. That dog wouldn't hunt. Then he planned that, if they tried him in court, he would plead vehemently and ask for hard evidence, to delay the verdict as long as possible, so that he might find a way to escape. But that dog wouldn't hunt, either. They were not about to try him in court.

The Secretarial Bureau had a meeting to discuss the offences that the three chief counselors had committed. There was no debate, no opposition. No one defended Sushun. They concluded unanimously that there were eight offences.

(1) When the late Emperor was lying on his deathbed and wanted them to draft a will, the chief counselors put in some words that were not what the late Emperor meant. They refused to follow the instructions of the empress dowagers, and did everything according to their own inclinations.

(2) They insisted that they alone were the counselors and would not listen to the empress dowagers, and stated that the empress dowagers should not read reports.

(3) They said that the empress dowagers should not see the princes, who were the late emperor's relatives. They sought to isolate the empress dowagers.

(4) Sushun even sat on the throne, and used the late emperor's belongings.

(5) Sushun refused to give the empress dowagers things they asked for.

(6) Sushun strove to estrange one empress dowager from the other.

(7) Even when Sushun was in custody, he spoke ill of the empress dowagers.

(8) While Sushun was escorting the late emperor's coffin to the capital, he lived with his concubines. (Inconsistent with a state of mourning. Against tradition.)

When these accusations had been handed in to the Secretarial Bureau, Yixin reported the result of the meeting to the empress dowagers. They had just signed an order to execute the chief counselors, Sushun, Duanhua and Zaihuan, immediately, with no right to appeal.

Sushun was executed promptly and publicly. A courtier was sent to supervise it. Sushun would be carried in a wooden cage (tradition), on a cart drawn by a donkey. The courtier knew that if Sushun was aware that the game was up, he would resist like a wild tiger, he would struggle to his last breath. He would surely be subdued at last, but no one wanted that kind of trouble, so when he saw Sushun in the prison cell, he lied to him:

"They are having a meeting and want me to bring you there for interrogation."

"They treat me so unfairly. I helped the late Emperor to handle all the affairs
of state, in such a difficult time. I must let them know."

Sushun walked out of the cell, complaining, and followed the courtier to
the prison gate. But when he was shoved into the cage on a cart and sent off in a
different direction, he knew he was trapped. He didn't say anything more, only
closed his eyes. He intended to tell the onlookers what he knew about West
Empress Dowager and Yixin before he was beheaded.

Jailors know that there are three kinds of prisoners with a death sentence.
If a prisoner heard the death sentence and was scared silly, it was the first kind
and easy to deal with. The second kind was the one who would shriek and holler
and stamp his feet; but with his energy thus exhausted, nothing would happen
at the execution site. The last kind was the most difficult to handle. Realizing he
was about to be put to death, the prisoner was very calm and said nothing; then
something would surely happen before the execution.

The news of Sushun's impending execution spread fast. People thronged to
the execution grounds, at a spacious market place. All the vendors were cleared
out and an execution space was set up. Behind the space was a table where the
courtier would sit to oversee the event. The place was crowded with onlookers.
More people lined up on both sides along the route where the prisoner's cart was
expected to pass. It was not until noon that the dismal parade appeared. By now,
all sorts of debris covered the cage, the cart, and the prisoner, from rotten vegetables to broken eggs, from traces of phlegm to rocks and clods of mud. No
wonder. Today, everyone who hated him, even those who merely disliked him,
came to see him in his disgrace. It was customary to behead the prisoner when
the sun was at its zenith. When the sun was shining overhead, the ghost of the
prisoner could do no harm to the executioner when it escaped from the dead
body.

Prison has always been the worst place in the world, no matter where and
when. Once he's in prison, whether guilty or not, the prisoner's family must
bribe the jailors or the prisoner will be ill-treated. Same with the executioner. He
can make the prisoner die fast, or die slowly.

Not long after the prisoner's cart arrived, an official came on horseback to
announce the emperor's order of execution. Sushun refused to kneel and began
shouting insulting things about West Empress Dowager and Yixin. A jailor
slapped him hard on his face. Another kicked him behind his knees so that he

went down, but before he could fall on his stomach, the jailor who had kicked him pulled his pigtail to stop his fall, thus making him stay on his knees. Then the executioner came forward. He didn't bring down the sharp wide-bladed sword the way people imagine. He aimed the point of his sword behind the prisoner's neck and pushed very swiftly between two cervical vertebrae, thus severing the head. At the same time, he kicked the body down to elude the blood spurting out.

Another courtier was dispatched to the prison to announce to Duanhua and Zaihuan that their time had come. But before he made the announcement, he had a sumptuous meal prepared for them. The last meal. He sat with them and drank with them, like an old friend. At least they knew each other, since they had worked together for the same emperor. After the dinner was over, he gave them his grim news. They were to end their own lives, with a little help from the jailors if necessary. They could choose between poisoning or hanging themselves. They were each locked separately in a room. In each room on a table there was a rope, and a cup of wine with poison in it. But when neither of them proved willing to make the move, and the jailors had to step in. The men were tied down on a long bench, and a thin piece of rice paper was placed over their noses and mouths. Then the jailors sprinkled water on the paper, which stuck on the face to block the air. They were smothered. This was on November 8.

Another order was issued, announcing that Sushun's estate including his personal property would be confiscated. Government clerks, headed by Secretary Wenqiang, went to his residences to register all the items and moved them into the national treasury.

Sushun had two sons. The elder one had been adopted by his brother Duanhua, who had been in the imperial prison and had no son of his own. If he died and no one inherited his princely title, the emperor would take back the title. Since Duanhua had followed the late emperor to the Summer Palace in Rehe, the son had been living with his brother in Sushun's residence. Secretary Wenqiang knew the situation and sent the two sons to live at Duanhua's place, since Sushun's residence would be confiscated and given to another courtier (someone who had made great contributions to the empire). The sons were allowed to take whatever they wanted, plus their personal belongings. While the sons were making their selection, the servants and maids furtively filched a few valuables for themselves. Even the sons' tutor joined in the stealthy plundering. The servants and maids were dismissed, with a bit of money and their own belongings. The family members were moved to smaller houses and were allowed enough means to live on. This was very lenient treatment. As a more severe punishment, his family might have become slaves, or be sent to hard labor, or be executed altogether.

A cache of letters were found in Sushun's study. When he was at the height of his power, many officials and officers had written to him, vying for favor. Some of his acolytes had even implied in their letters that Sushun should usurp the throne. Secretary Wenqiang knew the value of these letters. If they became public, the government would be in a real bind; he had to handle the matter with extraordinary care. He bundled the letters into a package, and took it to see Yixin. Yixin called together the members of the Bureau and they discussed how to dispose of them. It would be impossible to punish everyone who had had correspondence with Sushun. Too many courtiers were involved. It would cause mayhem. The best course was to burn all the letters and act as if they never existed. The empress dowagers gave their assent. The letters were burned, before an audience of courtiers.

Then came another order. For the other five counselors. The late emperor's brother-in-law was pardoned, because everyone knew he was innocent. Others were removed from office and would never be employed again by the govern-ment. One of them was banished to a distant province, because he had worked the longest as a secretary of state but could not stand up to Sushun.

West Empress Dowager resented Tu Han, also a counselor, who had often contradicted her while they were at the Summer Palace. But she had to go easy on him, because his father had been the late emperor's head tutor and East Empress Dowager forgave him on account of that. West Empress Dowager couldn't insist on a severe punishment; the late emperor had been her husband, too. The wheel of destiny turns around the human relationship.

When a formal statement announced the new secretaries to the public, both the courtiers and the people at large welcomed it. Many had found it unfair when the late emperor failed to appoint his own brother as one of the counselors; his recent appointment as the head secretary was seen as a good way to make amends. Yihuan, his brother, was now in charge of the garrison troops of the Forbidden City. The job of his dreams. His childhood wish came true. He had always wanted to be a general or a commander.

CHAPTER 18

There was a tradition that everything the late emperor had used must be either given to the courtiers as mementos, or burned. Almost everything was given to the courtiers, four items each, even clothes and shoes. A list was made up of who was eligible. Special individuals, like Yixin, got more than four items. But all these things were not to be used; they should be displayed as an honor from the emperor.

Then a red-letter day was chosen to carry the coffin to the tomb. It was said that every emperor's tomb, no matter of which dynasty, was equipped with arrows, swords and other defensive devices to prevent any unauthorized entry to steal the valuables buried there. And the location of the entrance to the tomb should be kept secret: the tomb builders, who knew the secret, were buried alive in the tomb.

From the day the late emperor died until the hundredth day, all the courtiers wore the same linen mourning clothes. By the end of that period, the white had gone dark gray and shabby. Shaving was not permitted, so that the beard and the hair on the front of the scalp, usually shaven clean, had grown long. The courtiers looked like beggars; the first thing every courtier did on the hundred-first day was to shave and change clothes.

Now the young emperor was back in the Forbidden City. Time to bring in more tutors. Three more scholars were appointed. The empress dowagers put Prince Wei in charge of the emperor's education; he would manage everything concerning the education except the teaching itself. The most difficult task was how to discipline the young emperor, who was still a child. No one really could reproach the emperor, except for the empress dowagers. But Prince Wei could not report every trivial offense, or the empress dowagers would think that he was a useless old fop. By tradition, the emperor could have another boy of his age as a studymate, to have lessons together, even to play together during recesses. Prince Wei sent his own son, Yiqiang. It was an honor to be able to study with the emperor, but the studymate was really a scapegoat. Whenever the emperor made a mistake, the studymate would be scolded in lieu of the emperor. When the emperor saw that his playmate and studymate taking the blame for him, he would (presumably) behave better or study harder. But the studymate had an advantage later, when they both became adults. The emperor would surely make amends for all the undue censures he had taken for him.

* * *

West Empress Dowager was very eager to implement the empress dowager system, but it would be unseemly to prod Yixin. Instead, she seized every opportunity to bestow favors on him, first of all by doubling his salary. Yixin took the hint and called a meeting with all the courtiers who were familiar with the empress dowager system in the previous dynasties. With reference to all the examples in history, they drafted a set of rules and handed them in. West Empress Dowager was not satisfied with some of the items and sent the list back for a re-draft. The ball was passed back and forth several times, until at last West Empress Dowager was content.

The essential rules were that the empress dowagers could receive the government officials and officers to discuss the state affairs in lieu of the emperor (by tradition, empress dowagers could only see male family members, not male courtiers) and the empress dowagers would decide on the appointment and removal, promotion and demotion of all the government officials and officers in behalf of the young emperor; and the empress dowagers could issue orders in his name.

West Empress Dowager had some experience in handling reports, but that was not enough if she wanted to rule the country independently. She had some scholars compile a book, taking all the good examples from Chinese history for her reference. West Empress Dowager knew that there had been one real empress in the long history of China. She wanted to learn from her experience as a ruler. When the book was finished, she ordered the scholars to come to her by turns to explain to her all the texts, one by one. They were not, formally, her tutors, but they gave her invaluable lessons.

The coronation took place on November 11, and a ceremony endowing the empress dowagers with the responsibility for state affairs took place on December 2. Every day after that, the young emperor sat on the throne and held court, with a desk before him. A screen, a frame covered with yellow gauze, stood behind the throne. The "mothers" sat behind the screen, vaguely visible like flowers seen through a mist. Two rows of courtiers would stand in front of the emperor's desk, after the ritual of kowtows. Yixin, the uncle, stood to the left of the desk.

* * *

Ambitious people often want to make things better when they have the power to effect a change. So did West Empress Dowager. She had learned that most of the previous dynasties had crumbled due to corruption among the officials. How could she prevent that happening again? She encouraged the critique officials to reveal every instance of corruption; many such reports came to her notice. And many of them criticized Commander Shengbao, who was fighting now in Anhui Province.

Commander Shengbao was a man of self-importance and bad temper. The only one he had esteemed and obeyed was the late Emperor Xianfeng, who had elevated him to his present position. Now, Emperor Xianfeng was dead. No one alive was worthy of his homage and absolute obedience. To him, the young emperor was nothing but a child; and the empress dowagers were useless women. He looked upon Yixin as someone who needed his support. Without Shengbao, how could these people have gotten the upper hand over Sushun and the other counselors? He liked to quote from *The Art of War*, written by Sun Tse, an ancient strategist and commander: "When a commander is away fighting, he can ignore the king's orders." After all, the king was out of touch with the reality of the battlefield, and his orders could not be well suited for the evolving situation.

Commander Shengbao despised his generals, some of whom were illiterate. He would rebuke them constantly. If any general offended him, he would have him beaten, in public. And he spent money lavishly — so he had to accept bribes. He always had women with him, wherever he went with his troops. This was flatly against military law, but he didn't care about laws. Laws were not made for individuals like him. Whenever he saw an attractive woman along the way, he just ordered his bodyguards to take her along — despite the family's protestations.

The empress dowagers and Yixin were always lenient with him because of his support. But every camel's back has a limit, and finally the last straw came. There lived a landlord by the name of Miao Peiling who recruited and trained an army of his own, in 1856, to defend his homeland against the Nian Army. In 1857, when Commander Shengbao was sent to fight the Nian Army in Anhui Province, Miao had already won a reputation for bravery in combat. Commander Shengbao liked such persons, and sent a man to persuade Miao to join the government army. He enticed Miao with the title of a general. Miao accepted, and brought his army to where Commander Shengbao was encamped.

In 1860, when the foreign troops approached Peking, Commander Shengbao was summoned to defend the capital. He wanted Miao to go with him, but Miao had his own plans and refused to go north. Miao misjudged the situation; he thought thatthe Qing Government would soon be overthrown. He wished to be a warlord, with a stretch of land of his own to rule independently. In April of 1861, Miao began to fight openly against the government. In August of the same year, he took a city from the government army. He sent someone to contact the Peaceful Army and invited the Shrewdness King to come north to form an alliance. In February 1862, Shrewdness King sent a detachment north. Leader Zhang of the Nian Army joined them and the three of them attacked a town under government control.The Qing Government ordered Commander Shengbao to the rescue, because Miao had been under him before his betrayal. Commander Shengbao wrote a letter to Miao, promising the restoration of his former title and full rights if he would turn back to the side of the government. Meanwhile, Younger Zeng had defeated Shrewdness King and occupied Anqing City. Miao thought that the Peaceful Army would soon be annihilated andthe Qing Government was a safe partner now. So he came to join Commander Shengbao again. Commander Shengbao kept his promise and handed in a report to put that into effect. West Empress Dowager was less impressed; she refused to give his former title back to him, because of his betrayal.

Shrewdness King escaped and needed to traverse the area controlled by Miao. Miao lured Shrewdness King to his encampment and took him captive. Miao handed him over to Commander Shengbao, who reported to West Empress Dowager and asked permission to escort the captive to the capital himself. West Empress Dowager declined, and ordered him to execute Shrewdness King immediately. And so he did. Then Commander Shengbao thought that Miao should be rewarded for the capture of one of the two most powerful kings of the Peaceful Army at the time. The most suitable reward, in his opinion, would be to give his title back. He wrote a report to that effect. Then a reply came, saying that Miao was pardoned for his betrayal; but the capture of Shrewdness King was not enough. If he could wipe out Leader Zhang of the Nian Army, he would get back his title. This put Commander Shengbao on the spot. He had made a promise, and now he could not keep it. He persisted in sending reports, but all in vain.

Elder Zeng governed four provinces, including Anhui. He didn't like to have Commander Shengbao staying in his area. And Shengbao, though a commander, had no province of his own to govern. Why hang around fending off thieves on behalf of someone else? He wrote to ask West Empress Dowager to make him the governor of Anhui Province. West Empress Dowager began to dislike him for his effrontery and his domineering attitude. Hard to trust him, too, since he had taken up with the fickle Miao. She gave the post to one of Elder Zeng's commanders and ordered Commander Shengbao to move his army to Shanxi Province to fight the Hui Clan rebels. At first, Commander Shengbao declined, with a lame excuse, and recommended another commander to go instead; but at West Empress Dowager's insistence, he had to leave for Shanxi Province in August, 1862. In September, he was repulsed by the rebels. He summoned Miao to Shanxi Province to help him, without even writing a report to request permission. West Empress Dowager and Yixin were shocked at this and ordered other government troops to encircle Miao's army. If Miao should betray them again and ally with the Hui Clan rebels, the situation there would be critical.

West Empress Dowager and Yixin decided it was time to clip Shengbao's wings. He might rebel, too. Time to get him back to the capital, but without his troops. Shengbao was offered two juicy positions: Military Minister, or head of the Imperial Household Department (where there were so many opportunities to line one's pockets). Shengbao rebuffed both offers. He mistook this for a ruse to lure him into the capital and kill him. Instead, he tied his own noose. No one could save him.

On January 22, 1863, an order was secretly dispatched to have Shengbao taken into custody and escorted to the capital. Difficult task. If he screwed up, Shengbao would go on the attack. A general in his area was tapped for the job. The general moved his troops as if he were going to assault the Hui Clan rebels. A sudden shift and he closed in on Shengbao, surrounding his residence at night. Shengbao was asleep with one of his women. As the order in the emperor's name was read to him, removing him from his post and placing him under arrest, he knew he was trapped. He was accused of the following crimes:

- Taking women with him on campaign, against military law.
- Embezzling money intended for military purposes.
- Keeping the wife of Shrewdness King as his concubine, when she should have been delivered to the government as a family member of the rebel leader.
- Taking bribes from Shrewdness King's two brothers and hiding them in his army, when they should have been delivered to the government for execution.

When Shengbao was arrested, most of his women ran away. The wife of Shrewdness King remained, because she had nowhere to go. Shengbao was not in irons and fetters; he was carried in a palanquin, just as if he were still the commander. An officer and 200 soldiers escorted him. The group proceeded very slowly. One night they lodged in a deserted house, in a small village. Suddenly there came a regiment of infantry. They took all the luggage belonging to Shengbao, and Shrewdness King's wife. Some infantrymen were recognized: another general who hated Shengbao had sent them. Shengbao was in a fury. He refused to go further and wanted his things back. He wrote a letter to the new commander (the general who had arrested him), and the commander ordered the general to return Shengbao's belongings. Shengbao got back his gear, but not the wife. The general sent these words to Shengbao: "Since she was the wife of a rebel leader, I must deliver her to the government." Actually, he kept her for himself, because indeed she was so beautiful that no man would resist her.

The group reached the capital on March 23, without any further disturbance. The officer escorted Shengbao directly to the imperial prison. Shengbao was put in a room, not in a cell. A former private advisor of his, Cai, by name, came to see him and comforted him. Cai promised to do his best to help him, as he was now a critique official. (He was very talented. At bribery.) But before he could do anything, a report came from one General Li. General Li had originally been with the Nian Army and later had joined the Peaceful Army under Shrewdness King. He had occupied an important town, linking the Peaceful Army north of the town to its other half, south of the town. Messages passing between the two parts had to pass through his area. For one reason or another, Shrewdness King had not trusted him. Lack of trust is always dangerous in politics. General Li had feared for his life. Commander Shengbao had learned of his situation and persuaded him to turn himself over to the government. Li was given the title of a general as a reward. Since he was now working for the government, he had cut off the connection between the two parts of the Peaceful Army. Big help to the war effort. And he had always been grateful to Commander Shengbao — especially now, as the Peaceful Army was in a decline. At this juncture, Li suggested in his report that he was willing to give up his general's title for the pardon of Shengbao. Unheard of. Yixin was afraid that if the government gave him a flat refusal, he might go back to the Peaceful Army or the Nian Army. He was still controlling a geographically strategic area. After a meeting among the secretaries, they determined to put his request in suspension for the time being and wrote a letter to Elder Zeng. The letter advised him to make necessary preparations, should General Li betray the government.

(Much later, according to stories from those days, General Li had a dispute with General Chen. As General Chen was Prince Yihuan's favorite general, he always got the upper hand; General Li resented the unfairness. He had a secret plan, but it leaked out. The governor of Anhui Province found out about it. He invited General Li to his residence for dinner, detained him, and killed him in the back garden. Then he sent money to his family to assuage them. General Li's troops dispersed. General Li's family was satisfied, because if General Li had openly rebelled the whole family would have been executed.)

Critique Official Cai was as sly as a fox. If he couldn't be sure of the result, he wouldn't take action. He was in no position to know West Empress Dowager's attitude towards Shengbao. But he had promised, and so he must do something if he wanted to build up his good reputation. He went to see another critique official, whose brother had also been a former private advisor of Shengbao. He convinced that official to write a report to plead Shengbao's case. At first, Yixin had wished to spare Shengbao's life, so he had let the matter drop, as if he had forgotten about it. When the two reports came in, he could no longer sit by. He had to assign Prime Minister Zhou and Secretary Li to judge the case. They interrogated Shengbao and he claimed that he had done nothing wrong. He said, "If I did so many things wrong, why not arrest me earlier?" Pretty lame. But they took time to cross-examine him, item by item, until General Li was talked into submission and withdrew his request. Then the critique official who had pleaded for Shengbao was removed from office and his report was refuted.

If Shengbao had begged for his life, he might have been pardoned, since his offense was different from Sushun's. However, he insulted the judges. When Prime Minister Zhou asked him if he had taken women against their will, he shouted that he had raped many women, including every woman in Prime Minister Zhou's household — and Shengbao had, in fact, passed Zhou's hometown on his march to the war zone. He had not actually committed any such offense along the way, and only said this to vent his own rage, but such an act was so repugnant that even Yixin was disgusted. Shengbao's opinion, Prime Minister Zhou should be grateful to him. How could he sit in judgment? Sushun, when he was in power, had often bullied Zhou, who had then been a minister. Zhou hadn't even dared to complain. And Sushun had been brought down only with Shengbao's support. If not for him, how could Zhou have become a prime minister? Shengbao's conduct throughout the whole process showed that he had no regret for all his errors. If they allowed him to live, he would always be a thorn in their side. West Empress Dowager persisted in demanding the death penalty, so he was sentenced to death, by hanging himself. They didn't dare to execute him in public, like Sushun, for fear that he would cry out too many embarrassing palace secrets before his head fell off.

Why did West Empress Dowager want Shengbao dead? She couldn't tolerate defiance. And since she had had a disagreement with Yixin, she wished to remove him from office at the proper time and have a freer hand in state affairs. What if Yixin and Shengbao united against her, as she and Yixin had done against Sushun? Better get rid of a potential ally for Yixin. Then, too, she was afraid that Shengbao might reveal some secrets about her conflict with Sushun, or some other information that would tarnish her prestige.

CHAPTER 19

Since Concubine Dowager Li had a daughter, West Empress Dowager would have liked to have a daughter of her own; but she could never give birth to a daughter now that her emperor husband had died. Prince Yixin had a daughter, very clever and demure, one year older than the daughter of Concubine Dowager Li and two years older than the young emperor, her son. It seemed that she was endowed with a talent for repartee. If she said something, no one could contradict her. She always had a good reason, a logical reason, for whatever she said. West Empress Dowager had seen her more than once when she had come into the Forbidden City with her mother on special occasions.

West Empress Dowager wanted to adopt her as her daughter. This had to be considered a friendly gesture, an honor, but Yixin didn't like it because he would lose the only daughter he had. He might not have another. Besides, when his daughter was made a princess, who must kowtow to whom when they met? An insoluble problem of ritual. But Yixin could not refuse West Empress Dowager's kind wish.

His daughter went to live in the Forbidden City. Everyone there called her Big Princess, because she was the oldest of the three children. The young emperor loved to tease the daughter of Concubine Dowager Li, but he never teased Big Princess. He respected her and always listened to her.

Once, after they had watched a few operas, West Empress Dowager asked Big Princess if she liked them. She replied, "I don't know how they acted, good or bad, but I don't like these operas."

West Empress Dowager was surprised to hear it. She said, "I saw you sitting very attentively. If you didn't like them, I would have thought you would be fidgety."

But what she said next was quite surprising for a young girl. "How could I be fidgety, when I was with Empress Dowagers watching operas?"

West Empress Dowager nearly blushed. She hadn't even appreciated how properly the girl behaved. Who could be angry with such a nice, clever young girl?

When Big Princess reached the age of thirteen, West Empress Dowager wanted to find a husband for her. Of course, many courtiers wanted to marry their sons to Big Princess, not only because Big Princess was wise and demure, but also because marriage ties to West Empress Dowager would greatly help the father in his career. Someone went to see Yihuan, Big Princess's uncle, and expressed his desire to propose his son as the imperial son-in-law. He hoped that Yihuan could help him, since he worked for Yihuan and was always loyal to him. Yihuan asked his wife, West Empress Dowager's sister, to visit her in the Forbidden City and serve as matchmaker. West Empress Dowager was discreet in choosing a husband for her daughter. She said to her sister, "I must look at the boy, first, before I can make up my mind."

They arranged that the sister and Yihuan would hold a banquet at their residence for the empress dowagers to come to watch some new operas, and at the same time to meet the boy. On that day, court was held only briefly. The empress dowagers and the emperor went to Yihuan's residence. Other princes and their families, imperial cousins and their families and others belonging to the imperial household, were invited, too. When the empress dowagers and the emperor arrived, everyone knelt before the gate of the residence to welcome them. It was arranged that, before the performance began, West Empress Dowager would receive the boy privately in another room. The boy was handsome. At first sight, West Empress Dowager liked him; but when she asked what his name was, the boy stammered, unable to get the words out. Not because he was nervous, but because he was born like that. West Empress Dowager couldn't ask him any more questions, and dismissed him in disappointment. But the good performances cheered her up.

Eventually, West Empress Dowager married Big Princess to the son of Emperor Xianfeng's brother-in-law, the one who had been a counselor and had been pardoned. The son was studious, quiet as a mouse — but not so healthy. The son was sixteen years old, then, while Big Princess was only thirteen. A few years after they were married, the son began to be seriously ill. Tuberculosis again.

One day, a celebration was going on for the birthday of West Empress Dowager. All the imperial household and imperial relatives were present for the occasion. The husband of Princess Rong An, the daughter of Concubine Dowager Li, was there, too. But the emperor didn't see the husband of Princess Rongshou (Big Princess's formal title). He asked his head eunuch about it. The head eunuch whispered, "He's dying."

"But I see Big Princess is watching operas with Holy Mother Empress Dowager. Shouldn't she be at home, looking after her husband?"

"Big Princess doesn't want Holy Mother Empress Dowager to know it. It is Holy Mother Empress Dowager who married her to that husband. Besides, today is the red-letter day, Holy Mother Empress Dowager's birthday. Big Princess doesn't want the sad information to dampen the happy celebration. If Big Princess is absent, Holy Mother Empress Dowager will surely ask why, and the disturbing truth will come out."

So after the performance, the emperor took Big Princess to another room and inquired after her husband, and his health. Tears seeped down her cheeks, but she could not sob out loud, because it would offend West Empress Dowager. The emperor could offer only words to comfort her. Before long, the husband died and Big Princess became a widow; but she often went to the Forbidden City to see West Empress Dowager.

Every order issued in the young emperor's name, every appointment of officials and officers as well as their removals from posts, had to be approved by the two empress dowagers. They had absolute power. Yixin was only an executive, fulfilling their decisions. But West Empress Dowager was not fully satisfied. First, she had only half the power. Second, Yixin could not be totally controlled. He often disagreed with her. Part of their growing distance had to do with Little An. West Empress Dowager's head eunuch often spoke ill of Yixin, for Yixin disliked him. But since Little An had delivered that secret letter that had caused Sushun's downfall, he had West Empress Dowager's full trust. He had reminded West Empress Dowager of Sushun's spies among the eunuchs. These spies had been arrested and thrown into jail

As West Empress Dowager's head eunuch and her favorite eunuch, Little An did many things against the law. He took bribes and stuck his nose in other people's business. Even the young emperor detested him, because he was disrespectful. In fact, the emperor often secretly vowed to kill Little An some day. Of course, Little An could never guess that. He only knew how to gain the trust of West Empress Dowager. He did everything she wanted; but in the process, he had made a lot of enemies. He often went to the palace supplies office, which Yixin governed, with a long list. He would requisition all sorts of things, plates and bowls, etc., in the name of West Empress Dowager. Actually, he would demand things that were not actually needed, just to have the people there acknowledge his authority. But one day when he went there again Yixin was present, and he refused most of the items requested. At dinner that evening, Little An ordered the cooks to put the food in coarse china bowls like those used by ordinary people. When West Empress Dowager asked about it, he reported that Yixin had refused to give him fine china bowls. Thereafter, West Empress Dowager was sure that Yixin despised her, and her resentment grew.

* * *

West Empress Dowager often sent Little An to see her mother, bringing gifts like ginseng and edibles. Little An enjoyed the task, because he could get tips. Her mother now lived with one of her sons, just ordinary in every way. West Empress Dowager conferred on each brother an honorary title, but no official positions. The brother living with her mother wanted a good official position, and often begged Little An to convey his wish to his sister; but Little An didn't dare to mention it to West Empress Dowager. Little An knew that West Empress Dowager would not hear of such a thing, because her brother was a fool. What would she do, when he made mistakes? If she did not punish him, all the courtiers would complain or even criticize her. But she could not punish a brother.

But as the brother kept importuning him, he plucked up his courage one day and told West Empress Dowager that her brother desired to be appointed to a good official position. West Empress Dowager warned him not to interfere in political affairs. The ancestors of Qing Dynasty had instructed that a eunuch who interfered with anything political should be put to death.

Little An was frustrated, and decided to teach the brother a lesson. The next time he went there, the brother importuned him once more. He told him that he had mentioned the request to his sister and that she had promised to give him a very good official position; he should wait patiently for the appointment to be announced. The brother was very happy and excited. He thanked Little An abundantly. But the appointment never came. He sent his mother to visit his sister in the Forbidden City. When the mother saw West Empress Dowager, she mentioned it. With great deliberation, West Empress Dowager told her mother that her brother was not an able man and was unsuitable to any of the official positions. She told her mother to advise her brother to enjoy his life as it was.

CHAPTER 20

Every army needs provisions and arms. Since the Chinese army was still in the iron age, there was no apparent need to invest in an "arms race," but they did need food, so provisions had to be found. A new provisions governor was appointed when the old one died. West Empress Dowager thought of Wu Tang, who had given her family 300 taels of silver in their time of need (albeit by mistake). She had promised her mother that, if she could, she would repay him for the favor. And now she could. But what if Yixin opposed her? She decided not to push the idea without first eliciting broad support.

The next day, during a routine meeting with the secretaries, she suddenly asked, "How is Wu Tang?" She meant, is he capable, upright, good or bad? Wu's favor to her family was known to almost all the courtiers in the central government.

Yixin knew what West Empress Dowager wanted, but Wu Tang was, at that time, a good and capable official, so Yixin replied, "He's good and capable."

"So," said West Empress Dowager, "Why not let him take over the post of Provisions Governor?"

"Good," agreed East Empress Dowager, who also knew his history. And the secretaries had no objection. Wu was appointed Provisions Governor. This job was really a challenge. West Empress Dowager only wanted to return the favor and give him a promotion.

* * *

Anqing City was strategically located, like a gate to Nanking City. Anyone who controlled the Anqing City area could control the Nanking City area. The leaders of the Peaceful Army felt that their duty was to defend what was left, especially Anqing City and Nanking City. Wrong strategy, but that's history. Since Anqing City was still occupied by the Peaceful Army, the government army couldn't surround Nanking City, because the Peaceful Army in Anqing City would come to the rescue, assaulting them from behind. Elder Zeng laid out a strategy to take Anqing City first. He gave the difficult task to another brother of his, the younger Zeng, who was mentioned before. The Peaceful Army put up a stubborn and brutal resistance against the fierce attack of the Xiang Army headed by Younger Zeng. Shrewdness King sent strong reinforcements to relieve them, but was beaten back. On September 5, 1861, the Xiang Army occupied Anqing City and marched along the Yangtze River, by land and by water, to assault Nanking City, the capital of the Peaceful Heavenly Kingdom.

West Empress Dowager appointed Elder Zeng as the Two River General Governor (a general governor governed more than one province; a governor ruled only one province), and gave him total charge of the war against the Peaceful Army. Younger Zeng launched wave after wave to assail Nanking City, which was in a critical situation anyway. Since Shrewdness King had died, Heavenly King had called Loyalty King back to the capital to defend it; but Loyalty King had his own tactics. He led his army of some 10,000 strong to advance towards Shaoxing City and soon took it and then occupied another city, Ningbo. Thus Hangzhou City, the capital of Zhejiang Province, was exposed to the Peaceful Army, which surrounded it and cut off the food supply. Nearly 30,000 people starved to death. Government reinforcements came to the rescue from another province but were blocked somewhere between Jiangxi Province and Zhejiang Province, and at last were defeated by the Peaceful Army. Hangzhou City fell into the hands of Loyalty King. Many mandarins and officers either fought to the death or committed suicide, because even if they managed to flee from the war zone, they would be arrested as cowards and probably killed anyway: martial law. Lose your life, and your reputation as well. When they fought to the death or committed suicide, they salvaged their brave reputations, at least, and their families could hope for a comfortable pension from the government.

When the Peaceful Army surrounded Hangzhou City, the governor of Zhejiang Province had asked Elder Zeng to send troops to his rescue. Zeng had not complied because the governor hadn't supplied his Xiang Army with rations according to the arrangement by the Secretarial Bureau. So when Hangzhou City was conquered by Loyalty King, the governor committed suicide.

Loyalty King's goal in attacking these cities was to draw away the government troops that were assailing Nanking City, for that was the greatest threat to the Peaceful Heavenly Kingdom. But in January 1862, West Empress Dowager appointed Zuo Zongtang governor of Zhejiang Province and in February Zuo led his troops into the province to fight the Peaceful Army. Loyalty King's strategy failed.

While Governor Zuo captured town after town, city after city that had been occupied by the Peaceful Army, Loyalty King led his army towards Shanghai. West Empress Dowager wanted Younger Zeng to go to defend Shanghai, but Younger Zeng was set on taking Nanking City. He thought that it was more important to take the capital of the Peaceful Heavenly Kingdom than to defend Shanghai. In February, West Empress Dowager had to order Li Hong-zhuang to reinforce Shanghai. Zuo and Li were both scholars and had worked under Elder Zeng, and Li was Zeng's pupil. But neither one completely obeyed Elder Zeng after they were made governors. In March, Governor Li organized his own army with the help of Elder Zeng; it was equipped with new weapons and was called the Huai Army.

The wealthy people of Shanghai were afraid of the Peaceful Army and wanted Governor Li to come as soon as possible. They even leased foreign steam-ships to fetch the Huai Army. Governor Li arrived in Shanghai in April and duly vanquished the Peaceful Army. In June, Governor Zuo wiped out more of the Peaceful Army in Zhejiang Province; he was appointed General Governor of Zhejiang and Fujian Provinces.

Heavenly King called Loyalty King back to defend the capital. In September 1862, Loyalty King gathered his 20,000 troops and marched west to attack Younger Zeng; but he could not prevail. He entered Nanking City with his troops. Meanwhile, the Huai Army continued to assault the Peaceful Army that was still fighting in that area. When Loyalty King was back in the capital, he suggested to Heavenly King that they should get out of Nanking City while the getting was good, and fight their way through to someplace else where they would have room to maneuver. Heavenly King refused. Too bad. Surrounded in the city, he would be like a fish in a bowl, waiting for the net to drop. If he could fight his way out of the encirclement, he would be like a fish in the ocean. Wrong strategy always means failure.

When the Peaceful Army attacked Shanghai, many foreigners were living there. After the treaty was signed in Peking, after the Second Opium War, some of the foreigners had organized armies to fight against the Peaceful Heavenly Kingdom for the Qing Government. They helped the Huai Army. In November 1862, Governor Li took Suzhou City. In December, and West Empress Dowager appointed him governor of Jiangsu Province; but later Suzhou City was reoccu-pied by Admiration King of the Peaceful Army.

In 1863, Wing King moved into Sichuan Province, but was defeated and killed there by the government army. In December 1863, Admiration King, of the Peaceful Army in Suzhou City, was betrayed and killed. In March 1864, Governor Zuo took Jiaxing City and Hangzhou City, the last two cities under the control of the Peaceful Army in that province. In June 1, 1864, Heavenly King died, apparently of illness. (Some history books say that he swallowed poison.) On July 19, 1864, the Xiang Army used explosives to burst open a part of the city wall, and they rushed in. The Peaceful Army would not surrender; they defended the city alley by alley, until nearly every one of them was dead. That night, disguised as soldiers of the government army, Loyalty King took the son of Heavenly King and escaped with the fleeing crowds through the city gate opposite to where the government army had entered; but they were separated in the chaos. Loyalty King hid in a temple outside the city, but the government troops were searching everywhere. They found him. He was escorted to where Elder Zeng was encamped, and he was executed on the spot. It was August 7, 1864. The son of Heavenly King fled with some of his attendants to Fujian Province. There are two different rumors about what became of him. One said that he was captured later, and killed; a variation has it that some other boy was executed, but the real son was hidden somewhere else, and was never found. A happier rumor suggests that some attendants took him on board a steamship and resettled in San Francisco, and later came back to join the revolutionary movement.

* * *

The Peaceful Army was annihilated during 1864, but the Nian Army kept fighting against the government. The difficulty with the Nian Army was that they didn't have a settlement to be surrounded. West Empress Dowager ordered Elder Zeng to take charge. Elder Zeng stationed all the troops under his command in a huge, loose circle around the area that the Nian Army moved in; then he would shrink the circle, like a tightening noose. Or, rather, he would close in and bring the Nian Army into sharper focus, and then pounce. The stratagem sounded good, but it took time to bring it to realization. After quite some time had passed with no report of success, critique officials started handing in reports saying that Elder Zeng was trifling with his duties and must be removed. Their deduction was based on the reasoning that the stronger Peaceful Army had been wiped out, and yet the Nian Army was still there. A moving target is harder to hit, but they didn't think about that. West Empress Dowager ordered

Governor Li, Elder Zeng's protégé, to take over, and Elder Zeng resumed his former position as the Two River General Governor.

At that time, the Nian Army had split into two parts. The part went west was called the West Nian Army and, not surprisingly, the part that remained where they were was called the East Nian Army. Governor Li was to fight the East Nian Army and West Empress Dowager ordered Governor Zuo to move his troops west to combat the West Nian Army. Then she gave Zuo's post to Provisions Governor Wu Tang, who at last had a province to govern.

Governor Li had to follow his tutor's tactics; there was not much else to be done, given the situation. Only now the Nian Army had split, and its strength was diminished. An advantage for Governor Li. The East Nian Army was forced to retreat into a small area between two rivers, where the government army launched a surprise attack, at night. The East Nian Army was annihilated. Now, the West Nian Army moved north, towards the capital. And it got very close. West Empress Dowager was in a panic. She ordered her trusted cousin Ronglu to bring his troops to block their advance, which he did; then the West Nian Army made its way south. Part of the West Nian Army went further south and was subdued in Yangzhou City area and its leader was executed on January 5, 1868. The other part went to Shandong Province and was vanquished there in August of that year. That was the end of the Nian Army.

* * *

In the north, beyond the Great Wall, was the original habitat of the Manchu Clan and there lay all the tombs of the emperors of the Qing Dynasty. A vast stretch of plain served as pasture for horses, and all the horses for the government cavalry came from there. But robbers in the region also rode on horseback. They came and went in a flash. The Horseback Robbers became a real headache to the local government; and every time the government was tipped off to the robbers' location, they would pull their disappearing act. The cavalry would arrive, but the horseback robbers had vanished. Now 500 of them were closing in on the imperial sepulchers. Serious trouble. If any imperial mausoleum was dug open and the treasure was stolen, the chief officials of the local government would all be put to death. An urgent report was therefore sent in. West Empress Dowager had a serious talk with the secretaries. No army could be spared from the south, where battles were still being waged; they would have to dispatch a newly-trained division, equipped with rifles. Prince Yihuan was in charge of this special division. Ronglu was his aide, and was given the title of Wing General. Secretary Wenqiang proposed that he himself should head a detachment selected from that division. The ladies consented. Secretary Wenqiang told Ronglu to choose the soldiers from the division to form a detachment.

Ronglu was born of the Manchu Clan. His grandfather and father had both died in Guangxi Province, fighting the Peaceful Army when it had just begun its mutiny. As a reward to the family, in appreciation of the feats they had performed, Ronglu had been given a post as an official in the Construction Ministry. When Sushun was the minister, Ronglu had nearly been put in jail on a false accusation of embezzlement. But when Wenqiang was made minister, he had greatly appreciated Ronglu's adept handling of the ministerial business, and so when Prince Yihuan wanted to reorganize the special division and strengthen its discipline, Secretary Wenqiang recommended Ronglu to help him. Ronglu knew who was who and what was what in the division.

That particular division was notorious for its poor discipline and inability to fight. West Empress Dowager was anxious. She sent Little An to have a look. Little An went there anonymously. He saw quite a few uniformed men walking around carrying birdcages, and others eating food bought from vendors. The scene looked like a market place or a public park. West Empress Dowager shared her concerns with Secretary Wenqiang, but Wenqiang soothed her. He said that it was because those men were living in the big city, with too much luxury to distract them from their duties. Put them in a difficult spot, and they would come around. Maybe it was true. Secretary Wenqiang led his detachment off to the mausoleums, and the horseback robbers galloped away before they arrived. Wenqiang helped the local government to reorganize the local defensive forces, and then he allowed Ronglu to take charge of the detachment to chase the robbers. He himself came back to the capital and reported to the empress dowagers that the imperial graves were safe.

CHAPTER 21

The ancestors of the Qing Dynasty had set up a few rules to govern the roles of the imperial eunuchs: not to interfere in matters beyond the scope of their duties, for example; not to leave the capital, on whatever pretext, etc. Breaking any of the rules meant death, so no eunuch in the Qing Dynasty dared to fool around — except the two head eunuchs who served during the reign of West Empress Dowager. The first was Little An. The second was Li Lianying.

Little An (1844-1869) had no respect for the young emperor or for East Empress Dowager who both, in turn, disliked him intensely. But who would quarrel with West Empress Dowager on account of Little An? Little An grew ever more arrogant and bold.

Once, when the late emperor was still alive, his son was answering a question put by his mother, Concubine Yan. Little An interrupted — that's an offense already, though a minor one, and it added steam to the son's already brewing hatred. Little An often interrupted when the son was talking to his mother. Someone who hated Little An taught the son how to punish him. This time, he yelled, "Shut up!" Everyone in the room, the maids, the eunuchs, even his mother was surprised. Quite unexpected from a six year old.

Little An flushed. He forced a smile and said, "Why is Big Brother angry with me?"

The son pretended to be a grown-up and said, "How dare you to speak to me like that?" Then he summoned the head eunuch of the palace. It meant that he wanted to punish Little An for his impertinence. Little An knew that he had overstepped. He was used to thinking of the son as an ordinary boy, and he had merely tried to throw in some witty words to please the mother. But this time he was caught. Even Concubine Yan could not protect him when the head eunuch came. So he went down on his knees.

"Slap your own face." The boy was red with anger. Concubine Yan could not say anything in Little An's behalf, since he had made the wrong move in front of so many people. It was an obvious offense. He had no choice but to slap his own face.

"Slap hard. One hundred!" the son ordered.

He had to slap himself, hard. Another eunuch counted to one hundred. He had to thank Big Brother for ordering him to slap himself on the face. Tradition. At night, when he went back to his own bedroom, he looked at his swollen face. He would avenge himself by saying false things about the little emperor to his mother. He often did that, especially after Concubine Yan became West Empress Dowager, to make her angry with someone.

Since East Empress Dowager was not ambitious and left West Empress Dowager a free hand in managing state affairs, Little An was encouraged to transgress the law, and under the protection of West Empress Dowager he took bribes like he was picking apples from a tree. One evening after West Empress

Dowager went to bed, he stole out of the Forbidden City and dropped in at the Imperial Household Department. There were already some eunuchs there, hanging out with the clerks. That was their gathering place. They drank and gambled there. Their favorite game was dice. When Little An made his appearance, everyone got on their feet to greet him. Someone asked him to sit at the table and play for a while. Generally, when Little An played, the gamblers would let him win. Bribery in disguise. But today, Clerk Telu, a close friend of Little An, pulled him aside and whispered in his ear. They sat at another table, loaded with food and wine. They drank and ate, and talked business. In this case the business was: how to help a certain person to solve his problems, and earn some pocket money in the process. They even bargained over how much the person should give them, like haggling at the market.

"Somebody wants to have a painting by West Empress Dowager," said Clerk Telu. "He will pay fifty taels of silver."

"Is that all? You call that business?"

"That's the bonus," Clerk Telu winked at Little An. "And here's the big deal."

Official Zhao had had an assignment to collect taxes and send the revenue to the South River Camp for military support. But the South River Camp had been vanquished and the commander had died. He should have sent the money to Elder Zeng, who had been made a general governor then.

Thus Official Zhao had an embezzlement case pending against him and was wanted by the local government. He had been hiding in Peking ever since. Now, after so many years, although his case was still open, no one would really be looking for him. However, he could not always stay in hiding. He wanted to bribe someone powerful enough to close his case, and then get him a position such as mayor in a rich town. But first he wanted "to wash himself clean of the dirt." His exact words.

"He's a clever guy, hiding in the capital," commented Little An, "Who will notice him in this big city?"

"He is willing to pay 20,000 taels of silver when it's done." Clerk Telu smiled like a real salesman.

That was not a small sum. Little An's heart beat a bit faster. Since he was always at West Empress Dowager's side when she was reading reports, Little An was familiar with how these things were handled. He knew that the case must be closed first, and after that, the assignment could be addressed. To achieve this, someone relevant to the case should send in a report. Then he could do something to get the case closed. But as far as Little An could remember, all the higher officials related to the case were already dead. He asked Clerk Telu whether the fellow had joined the army. No. Too bad — if he had been in the army, he could have claimed to have shared in some commendable action which could be used to offset his offenses.

Now, 20,000 taels of silver was worth straining his brains a bit. Suddenly, he bethought himself of Wu Tang, the Provisions Governor who had no province to govern and whose responsibilities were to gather provisions for the govern- ment army. Provisions Governor Wu was West Empress Dowager's favorite governor. If he could write a report and throw in a few good words for the fellow in question, everything would be fine. He mentioned Provisions Governor Wu to Clerk Telu, who shook his head. It was Provisions Governor Wu who had it in for him in the first place. Now, that's a real problem. But he saw in his mind's eye the money dangling before his face.

Then Clerk Telu made an arrangement for Little An to meet Official Zhao, at his house. When Little An arrived, Zhao was not there yet. Clerk Telu said, "I've told him to come a bit late. So we can talk."

"What about?" asked Little An.

"I told him to bring a down payment of 1,000 taels." He smiled to Little An.

"Sounds great."

"But when he comes, Second Esquire An had better be prepared to share a few little secrets from the palace, so that he will have confidence that I've found the right person to solve his problems." (Esquire? In China, all sorts of terms are used to express one's esteem when addressing people of different social status. English appears not to allow for quite the same degree of concern for respect, and there is no word in English corresponding to the Chinese word "Ye." We will borrow the word "Esquire," for now. The ordinal number denotes that Little An was the second son in his family.)

"No problem."

Zhao arrived, and Clerk Telu made the introductions. "This is Second Esquire An, West Empress Dowager's superintendent" (one could hardly call him a eunuch, to his face). Zhao took half a step back with his left foot, and bent his right knee half way down (left knee, too), with his right arm straight down- ward, the finger tips almost touching the floor: the salute of a subordinate to his superiors, and cried, "Superintendent An!" Little An just nodded his acknowl- edgement, as if he really were his immediate subordinate. Then Clerk Telu turned to Little An, saying, "This is Fourth Esquire Zhao." (Because he was an official, Clerk Telu must call him Esquire, too.) He interrupted hastily, "Just call me Fourth Zhao." (A show of modesty. Only his elders, or his superiors, or his closest friends could call him Fourth Zhao.) Then they sat down to dinner, and talked.

"You are lucky that I could get Superintendent An here. Superintendent An is very busy, seldom free . . . What can Superintendent An tell us about West Empress Dowager, anything to open our eyes, or shall I say, to open our ears?" Clerk Telu wanted to be witty, to show his intimacy with Little An.

Little An told them how West Empress Dowager had sent him on a life-and-death errand to carry a secret letter to the capital, and how they (Little An meant that he had had a part in it.) had brought down the counselors from power. Even Clerk Telu didn't know all that, close as he was to the Forbidden City. Both the listeners showed their esteem — more than Little An deserved. After a few cups of wine (no glasses, yet, in China — a porcelain cup was used), Little An began to brag how powerful he was as West Empress Dowager's favorite eunuch. At this, Zhao showed more confidence than he really felt. After dinner, Clerk Telu had Zhao tell Little An directly about his problems and requests. Nothing new, but that was the procedure. Since he was an official, Zhao knew a lot about such things and they couldn't pull the wool over his eyes. They should at least hint to him through which channel they would address his problems. Clerk Telu wanted to mention somebody working in the Secretarial Bureau, but Little An objected. He feared that if word got out, Yixin would nail him. He decided to mention Provisions Governor Wu Tang, because if word spread, Wu Tang would not dare to say anything since he owed everything he had to West Empress Dowager, and he was her head eunuch.

But the name of Provisions Governor Wu made Zhao nervous. "Oh, no no no no no! His Excellency Wu is the person who wants me. If His Excellency Wu knows where I am, His Excellency Wu will have me arrested."

"Don't worry," Little An soothed him. "I will manage it. You just wait and see." By now, all of officialdom knew that Provisions Governor Wu was West Empress Dowager's favorite (some would add the word "lapdog" here), because of the good turn his servant had done for him, by mistake, by helping her family many years before. Zhao thought that Provisions Governor Wu could not reject any request from West Empress Dowager. But he didn't know that Little An would never dare to mention such a thing to her in the first place. He planned to achieve it all by himself, in her name. Zhao had, indeed, brought a silver note of 1,000 taels, and gave it to Little An as earnest money. The project began.

Little An was not content with 20,000 taels. He said to Clerk Telu, "Can you tell Zhao that if he pays 30,000 taels, I'll get him a very good position?" Clerk Telu said, "Sure. I'll let him know." The next day when they met, Clerk Telu reported, "Zhao said okay. But he doesn't have that much money in hand right now. He must borrow it, and will pay when he gets the appointment notice and documents." Little An knew that Zhao didn't trust him. He wanted to wait and see. He was lost in his own contemplation and almost missed Clerk Telu's next comment: ". . . that the 1,000 taels is a festival gift, not a down payment. If we can't succeed, we don't need to return it."

Now Little An put on his thinking cap. He had better come up with a plan to get the deal done. It was not every day that he could earn 30,000 taels. His monthly salary was only 20 taels; and a eunuch or a maid could be fined for breaking something or for any other infraction. The fine would be deducted from the salary. But they had free board and food.

The shine had come off the reputation of Provisions Governor Wu; West Empress Dowager often received reports criticizing him, but she "flooded" them to protect him. Little An knew all this. He went to the Internal Registrar to copy the record of these reports that had gone missing. Little An thought that if Provisions Governor Wu became aware how West Empress Dowager had protected him, he would find himself constrained to do anything that she wished, or that Little An wished in her name. But how could he get the message over to Provisions Governor Wu? Before long, an opportunity presented itself to him.

The calendar showed that the Chinese New Year was approaching, the grandest festival of the year. The festival gifts were on the way. All the mandarins in the provinces would send gifts to the empress dowagers and the emperor, to all the princes, to the ministers, or to those whose help might potentially be needed in the future. Special gifts were sent to those with special relationships.

One day, West Empress Dowager dispatched Little An to her mother's house to deliver some festival gifts. There, Little An met a messenger from Provisions Governor Wu, who sent to the mother of West Empress Dowager 100,000 taels in notes every year out of gratitude to West Empress Dowager. The messenger knew Little An by reputation and was exceedingly polite to him. Little An had not expected this coincidental meeting or he could have taken this opportunity to carry out his plan. Too bad. He wasn't prepared.

Little An was a real schemer. He should have gone into the army; he would have become a great military strategist. Too late now, all the generals would resign out of shame if they were asked to fight under someone who had lost his manhood. Still, in his present circumstances, he had plenty of opportunity to exercise his strategic thinking, and now he was struck with a good notion.

When he returned to the Forbidden City, he informed West Empress Dowager of the encounter with the messenger from Provisions Governor Wu, adding that the messenger had wanted to get in touch with him.

"What for?"

"It's not I, Empress Dowager's slave, that he seeks. He wants me to deliver a message to Empress Dowager from His Excellency Wu." A consummate liar.

"And why would that be?"

"His Excellency Wu desires to know what special things Empress Dowager would like from his area."

"How kind. Always thinking of me."

"Empress Dowager had better ask for something, anything, so that His Excellency Wu won't feel that his offer of gratitude is ignored."

"That's right. Let him get some embroidered silk fabric with new patterns in Suzhou City." Suzhou City is famous for its Su Embroidery; its patterns of Chinese gardens with grottos and pavilions are known throughout the world.

Now Little An had a cover, and could write a good composition. He could openly go to see the messenger without anyone surmising what was going on between them. For one of the ancestral rules for eunuchs was to ban them from contacting any officials without an assigned task from any of the imperial family members. It was hoped that this would help prevent the eunuchs from engaging in illegal activity. The lesson had been learned from the previous Ming Dynasty.

Little An had Clerk Telu notify the messenger to meet him at his house. As the messenger didn't know where Little An's house was, Clerk Telu took him there the next day and left him with Little An, so that he would appear not to know what transpired. Little An was polite to the messenger. At that time, the attitude of one person towards another depended on who wanted to ask a favor of whom. The one asking a favor was always polite, or even pleasing, and *vice versa*. Little An was a difficult person, but the promise of 30,000 taels did away with his arrogance.

After exchanging a few pleasantries, Little An took out a piece of paper listing the things West Empress Dowager wanted. Then he lowered his voice and added, "Empress Dowager has another wish. Someone must know Empress Dowager's brother." He told the messenger the whole story and then mentioned the name of the person and his request, adding, "If His Excellency Wu can send in a report to close his case, Empress Dowager's brother will see it as a favor done to himself." He implied that it would certainly please West Empress Dowager, too. When the messenger was taking his leave, Little An suddenly produced from his inner pocket a big envelope and handed it to him, saying, "It's important to give this letter directly to His Excellency Wu." The messenger nodded and stuffed it into his own inner pocket, together with the list. Little An saw him to the door. In the envelope were copies of all the critique reports against Provisions Governor Wu and a memo about Official Zhao's case.

Since that day, Little An had been expecting a response. As a matter of fact, he had been expecting 30,000 taels. After a month and a day, the messenger came again. He delivered to Little An's home some culinary delicacies as a small gift from Provisions Governor Wu. The gift was meant as a message to indicate that the response from Provisions Governor Wu had come. Then the messenger went to the home of Clerical Official Fang, of the Secretarial Bureau, who was a good friend of Provisions Governor Wu. As Clerical Official Fang was at work, the messenger left a small gift together with a large envelope for him. When Fang came home, in the evening, he found the two things. He read the letter, then the memo. The letter said that it was Provisions Governor Wu who had built up the case against Official Zhao, who was quite corrupt, and he could hardly write a report now to say that Official Zhao was innocent. He hinted in the letter that he understood this was the wish of West Empress Dowager, but he could not contradict himself. He did not know what to do, and needed his help. At the end of the letter, he asked Fang to keep the matter confidential.

Clerical Official Fang sent for the messenger. He wanted to know the details. The messenger told Fang that Little An had come to him and put in this request. Now, Fang understood that it was all Little An's monkey business. It wasn't the first time that Little An had done such things in the name of West Empress Dowager. So he wrote a reply to Provisions Governor Wu, and told him to forget the whole thing.

As the messenger never came to Little An with the long-expected news, Little An had to seek him out. The messenger said, as instructed, "His Excellency Wu has asked someone to handle the matter for him." Hmm. That did not sound good. Things were not moving according to plan.

Later, when Clerk Telu learned that Clerical Official Fang had received a letter from Provisions Governor Wu, he met Little An in the evening and said, "I think we are in trouble. If they want me to tell them where to find Official Zhao, what should I say?"

"Don't worry. I'll take care of it." But Little An was alarmed, himself. What if West Empress Dowager got wind of this? Would she forgive him this time? He'd better go pay a visit to Clerical Official Fang. Generally, Little An had no respect for clerical officials in the Secretarial Bureau, because they were not of a high rank. But today, he addressed him as Esquire Fang. Fang didn't think highly of Little An, either, but he didn't want to offend him. So he told Little An that Provisions Governor Wu couldn't contradict himself by writing such a report, unless West Empress Dowager ordered him to do so. (Implied: not through you, Little An.) Then he added, "But His Excellency Wu will let him go without offi-cially closing the case. We don't want to know where he is or what he's doing." So saying, Fang gave the memo back to Little An. ("Forget it. Nothing happened.") Little An was off the hook. What a relief.

The next evening when Little An met Clerk Telu, he said, "It's not entirely a failure. At least we got half the job done."

"How so?"

Little An told him the result of his meeting with Clerical Official Fang, adding, "He wanted us to wash him clean. Now we've got him out of the dirt. That's half the job." Clerk Telu understood that Little An wanted half the money. He promised to ask for it. Two days later, someone came from the Imperial Household Department and wanted to see Little An. He thought that it must be Clerk Telu, with the money. But it was another clerk, saying that Prince Yixin wanted to see him. Little An's heart jumped. What's this? His mind spinning, he followed the clerk to the Imperial Household Department; Yixin was in charge. Little An kowtowed before Yixin. Generally, Yixin would bid a person to stand up after kowtowing, but not this time; so Little An remained prostrate. Yixin began to censure him for all the unlawful things he had done. He reprimanded him for almost half an hour and then bade him to leave, with one last warning that if he did any such thing again, he would be punished severely. Little An nodded, mutely, and left.

Now, almost everyone knew that Little An had been scolded by Prince Yixin. He felt humiliated and swore to take his revenge. Bad news awaited him when he met Clerk Telu in the evening. Official Zhao was afraid that things might change, since Prince Yixin knew about it, so he refused even to pay half of the money until his problem was really solved. Little An hated Yixin all the more.

Even West Empress Dowager knew that he had been scolded by Yixin, but she had no idea what for; so Little An took his chance to slander Yixin. He told West Empress Dowager that Yixin had not really castigated him. He was only a eunuch, not worth the time for a prince to reprimand. Yixin was really blaming West Empress Dowager — for squandering money. This thoroughly piqued West Empress Dowager. Now a real opera would begin. Little An would be the happy audience.

CHAPTER 22

Finally, the rupture between West Empress Dowager and Yixin broke out into the open. This was caused by Critique Official Cai, who sent in a report of accusation saying that Yixin was haughty, took bribes, aspired after absolute power and showed unequal treatment to the courtiers. At the end of his report he suggested removing Yixin and appointing Yihuan (Yixin's brother, West Empress Dowager's brother-in-law) as the head of Secretarial Bureau.

Critique Official Cai was sly as a fox and greedy as a wolf. He wanted a promotion. He wanted to do something to please West Empress Dowager, and her annoyance with Yixin presented an opportunity. But he didn't want to do anything rash. Better check the facts, through Little An; but Little An did not want to be seen with him. Maybe discretion is the better part of ambition. Still, by roundabout means, Little An gave Cai a hint and a nod, and offered to protect Cai if Yixin sought to retaliate (a disingenuous offer, since critique officials had the right to criticize anyone; while eunuchs had to watch their own backs).

Now, Critique Official Cai took pains, more than ever, to choose his words while drafting the report. Each word should have the right weight so that when it hit, it would hit hard. Hard enough to knock down a powerful man. He read it through several times and made a couple of changes. Then he copied it in the formal calligraphic style, and handed it in.

West Empress Dowager never expected to read such a report, but when she came upon it, she felt that it scratched just where she itched. She knew Yixin had many supporters, like a venerable oak with deep roots in the ground. She needed an ally. She went to see East Empress Dowager and showed her the critique report, adding, "If we don't pull him back now, he'll go over the cliff." From the report, East Empress Dowager naturally thought that Yixin had really committed all the offenses he was accused of and so she agreed with West Empress Dowager.

"We'll remove him from all his offices, to teach him a lesson," suggested West Empress Dowager.

"Must we go that far?"

"Well, will he listen to you, if you ask him nicely to stop doing such things?" pressed West Empress Dowager.

"Hmm." East Empress Dowager had seen Yixin contradict West Empress Dowager several times; she had to agree. Still, East Empress Dowager thought they would reinstate him, if he learned his lesson; but West Empress Dowager wanted to remove Yixin for good.

On March 30, 1865, West Empress Dowager told Yixin that a certain critique official had sent in a report accusing him of certain things. Yixin was so surprised that he asked who had accused him. West Empress Dowager told him. Cai had been a private counselor to Commander Shengbao, and after Shengbao's arrest, had come to the capital and bribed his way into the Critique Department.

"Cai is not a good official. He still has a case pending against him in Sichuan Province for fraud. He should be under arrest, himself," said Yixin. Actually, according to tradition, he had to say, "I know I'm wrong. I deserve to be executed, or punished." And he had to kneel and kowtow, to beg pardon.

West Empress Dowager was infuriated. Insolence! Contempt! She convened Prime Minister Zhou and other high courtiers. She thought that Prime Minister Zhou would side with her, as he had during her struggle for power with Sushun. But when she tasked them with discussing how to penalize Yixin, the courtiers were stunned. Rebellions were still flaring up all over the country. Absolute unity was needed in the ruling group. No one said anything.

West Empress Dowager fumed, and commanded Prime Minister Zhou to give his opinion. He could only promise to discuss it with the other courtiers. Finally, they were permitted to withdraw to their resting room. She knew, now, that Prime Minister Zhou was with Yixin, not with her. So she added another Prime Minister, Wo Ren, to the list of those handling Yixin's case.

Prime Minister Wo Ren was known to be conservative. He despised the new and the modern. He despised the foreigners. He was not particularly impressed with Yixin's handling of the negotiations with the foreigners during the war and afterward. In short, he shared West Empress Dowager's desire to take an ax to Yixin.

On April 1, when West Empress Dowager received prime ministers Zhou and Wo Ren and the others, she declared her decision to remove Yixin from all his offices. She had already threatened Yixin with that once before when he had argued with her. (Yixin had replied that she could do that, if she liked, only observing that he was a prince by birth and she could never deprive him of this title.)

West Empress Dowager resented Yixin's continuous disrespect. Now was the opportunity to show her authority as an empress dowager. She wanted him to obey her. She wanted everyone to obey her.

The prime ministers then called for Critique Official Cai to provide evidence to back up his accusation. He said he had no hard evidence; he had made the statement based on hearsay. When Prime Minister Wo Ren asked from whom he had heard such rumors, Cai had to come up with some names. He mentioned two officials working in the Judicial Ministry. They were summoned before the prime ministers and other courtiers. Under questioning, they said that they had not told Critique Official Cai anything, and did not even know him.

While all this was going on, some of the princes sent in a petition suggesting to restore Yixin to his former offices. The head of the Secretarial Bureau ought to back his accusations with evidence, and such an important decision should not be based on personal sentiment. Besides, the foreign countries might not be willing to talk to any other person, since they knew Yixin so well; this could become an international incident. West Empress Dowager had not expected so many courtiers and even princes to plead on Yixin's behalf. Apparently, the time was not right for her to reach for absolute authority. Time to back pedal, a little. Instead of insisting, she had the princes and courtiers discuss the matter. Meeting with other secretaries, she placated them and said that if all the courtiers wanted Yixin to continue as head of the Secretarial Bureau, they could hand in a petition. The secretaries were pleased and went about preparing just such a petition. But before the cabinet met to discuss the case, on April 4, West Empress Dowager summoned the two prime ministers and a few other cabinet members and told them that Yixin was no longer suitable to be the head of the Secretarial Bureau.

At the joint meeting Wenqiang, now in charge of the Secretarial Bureau, quoted what West Empress Dowager had said to them; the members of the cabinet were quite surprised. Could West Empress Dowager have said one thing to the secretaries and another thing to the members of the cabinet? Had they only known the reason, they would not have been surprised after all. After West Empress Dowager met with the secretaries, Little An reported to her that Yixin was organizing his supporters for an all-out fight. This, of course, was not true; but she believed him and went into a rage. Now, the group of secretaries and the group of cabinet members called each other liars. Wenqiang said that if West Empress Dowager meant what she had said yesterday, she could not have said what the cabinet members supposed she had said this morning. A cabinet member retorted that West Empress Dowager had indeed said it, and they had "supposed" nothing.

In the Qing Dynasty, every time the courtiers came to see the emperor (now, the empress dowagers), the Courtier Before the Throne would lead them to the throne. At the time of these events, the eighth prince was serving as the Courtier Before the Throne — the eighth brother of the late emperor — so both groups agreed to ask the eighth prince what West Empress Dowager had actually said. In he came, and gave his word of honor in asserting that what West Empress Dowager was reported to have said yesterday was true, and what she was reported to have said this morning was true, too. West Empress Dowager had actually said different things on different days. Now, no one could be sure what West Empress Dowager really wanted. They had to adjourn the meeting.

On April 5, West Empress Dowager issued orders to reassign some of Yixin's posts. On April 8, Yihuan came back from his task of overseeing the construction of the late emperor's tomb. He had a talk with Secretary Zao, former Clerical Official Zao, and he asked him to draft a report for him to the empress dowagers. His report said that Yixin had done his duties extremely well and that his only flaw was his attitude towards the empress dowagers; and that if the empress dowagers could forgive him, it would be a blessing to the country. West Empress Dowager also gave this report to the joint meeting for discussion.

At the joint meeting on April 9, Prime Minister Wo Ren, the chairman, announced, "It will take too much time for everyone to express his opinion, so I have drafted a report. I will read it to you, and if no one disagrees, we can hand in to the empress dowagers." The natural lethargy of bureaucrats can usually be relied upon, but Prime Minister Zhou saw through the ruse. This matter was too important to consign to inertia, allowing Wo Ren put words in all their mouths. So Zhou said, "We are not in a hurry. Besides, we must discuss Prince Yihuan's new report." Many of the courtiers opposed removing Yixin from his post as head of the Secretarial Bureau; and another prince produced a draft of his own, which coincided with the majority opinion. Even Prime Minister Wo Ren had to accept it.

When the report was handed in, West Empress Dowager realized that, if she went ahead, all the courtiers might submit their resignations. She tried another tactic. On April 11, she gave Yixin back his post as head of Foreign Relations, in deference to the notion that the foreign governments would make trouble if Yixin were removed as chief diplomat. Now, for the second round. The investigations into the accusations against Yixin went on until the end of April, and produced no evidence whatsoever. How could Yixin be punished? As a concession, Yixin resigned as the head of Imperial Household Department. Now, West Empress Dowager could appoint someone who would obey her and give her everything she wanted. At the same time, the other secretaries persuaded Yixin to file a self-criticism report. Fear of foreign aggression, recognition that she had little support for this move among the courtiers, and the submission shown by Yixin all contributed to softening West Empress Dowager. She yielded, this time.

On May 8, the empress dowagers received Yixin, who wept for having been falsely accused — but the empress dowagers took them as tears of repentance. Even West Side was touched, and gave an order to restore him as head of the Secretarial Bureau. A political storm subsided, to everyone's relief.

* * *

Water was flowing under the bridge all this time. The emperor was not a little boy anymore. He was fifteen, now. The empress dowagers began to think about selecting a queen and some imperial concubines for him. Even wedding preparations were slowly getting under way. What a grand ceremony that would be. The empress dowagers and the emperor must wear new gowns with dragons embroidered on them. Generally, this special imperial apparel was sewn and embroidered in Suzhou, and then transported to the capital. The southern provinces were renowned for their wealth and scenery, as well as their textiles; people in the north envied the south.

Little An thought to himself that, if he could be sent there on an imperial errand, he would enjoy the sightseeing and, coincidentally, receive many valuable gifts from the governors and local officials. Who wouldn't wish to curry favor with him, the favorite head eunuch of the most powerful person in the empire? There were rules to forbid eunuchs leaving the capital; but who would say "no" if West Empress Dowager agreed to it?

Whenever the imperial family had things custom made, the expenses reported were always much higher than the real costs. This was an open secret.

"Empress Dowager," Little An said, one day, "The emperor's wedding will be so expensive. We must make sure we are not excessively over-charged."

"How can we do that, not knowing the real costs?"

"I've thought of a way. If Empress Dowager sends me to supervise the work being done, I'll know what the expenses are and how much they can report. With the money saved, we can buy more things for the wedding."

West Empress Dowager thought that suggestion had some merit, so he made his preparations. He would take two huge ships and sail south on the Grand Canal, which had been dug hundreds of years ago in the Sui Dynasty. It ran from north to south, through many provinces. One of them was Shandong Province. The governor of Shandong was a courtier known for his courage and probity — a courtier who loathed Little An for all his misdeeds.

Little An thought that it would be best if he could get the emperor's consent to his journey; but he could not ask him directly. He asked the emperor's head eunuch to speak to the emperor in his behalf. Now, the emperor's head eunuch hated Little An, too, for his insolence to the emperor. He did however, mention Little An's request to the emperor; and the emperor in turn asked his head eunuch what to do. He was still young, and this was clearly a tricky business, beyond his depth. The head eunuch offered to say something suitable to Little An, and suggested that the emperor should pretend to know nothing about it.

Little An saw him next day and asked what was the emperor's attitude; the head eunuch said, "The emperor didn't say anything. I think he won't have any objection to it, since Holy Mother Empress Dowager thinks it's all right."

Little An was so excited that he began to brag about his trip. Soon, almost everyone knew about it; but no one said anything to him. When Yixin heard, he was happy; most of the courtiers were also delighted. Those who had had favors from Little An didn't dare to speak to him about it. This was a very serious matter, and it involved West Empress Dowager. They all knew that they must tread very cautiously. One step, one word amiss, and they would be condemned. Through his head eunuch the emperor learned everything about Little An. He sent a secret message to the governor of Shandong Province, instructing him to arrest and execute Little An, if he traveled through his domain.

Chapter 23

Since the government army's defeat at the hand of the foreign troops in 1860, West Empress Dowager and Yixin had realized that they must learn from the foreigners and adopt their advanced science and technology. They began to buy guns and cannons from the Western merchants. They also bought steam-ships and warships. But in the long run, this was not a feasible way to strengthen the country. They began to have factories built to make these things in China. They sent young people overseas to study engineering and develop technical skills. Elder Zeng and Governor Li respectively set up the Machine Bureau and the Manufacturing Bureau in Shanghai. Yixin established the Foreign Languages School in Peking, so that the government could have interpreters for diplomatic affairs and translators to render science books into Chinese. Science courses were also taught there. Provincial governments were tasked with recommending students, and young officials working in the central government could also take part in the entrance exam. All the teachers were foreigners. Was this an early "Great Leap Forward"?

These were grand plans, and Empress Dowager Cixi is remembered, among other reasons, for the enormous efforts undertaken during her reign to drag China into the modern world. But such things are easier said than done. Many conservatives in the court were against it. Prime Minister Wo Ren was the most obdurate. They were revolted by untraditional, foreign trends. China had always been the center of the world. How could they condescend to learn from other countries? Prime Minister Wo Ren said, "We can surely find men with such talents within the vast territory of China." But few students were registering for the entrance exam for the Foreign Language School, and West Empress Dowager discussed the problem with the secretaries. They concluded that they would have to make Wo Ren renounce his reactionary ideas and desist in his opposi-tion before they could succeed. Accordingly, West Empress Dowager ordered Prime Minister Wo Ren to go ahead and find such men for the government. Wo Ren thought that it was a practical joke; he didn't take it seriously. He offhand-edly replied that he had no such persons in mind and could not recommend any.

The first net they had cast came up without catching him, so West Empress Dowager appointed him an advisor to the Foreign Affairs Yamen. To the Prime Minister, who had always resisted all things foreign, it would look like he was slapping his own face if he went even to sit in that Yamen. How could he go there, where the courtiers and officials had direct contact with foreigners? He handed in a report saying that he was too old to work in the Foreign Affairs Yamen. Yixin assured him that he would not have to go there every day, and would not be assigned any routine chores; his sole duty there was to give advice, when needed, since he was a senior official, so experienced. Implied: he only had to accept the post. Nothing more. And nothing less. But accepting the post was precisely what he could not do without losing face entirely. What a bind! When Yixin pressed him again, he could not say "no." Neither could he say "yes." He could hardly breathe. No way out, now, but to send in a report of resignation or retirement, and he was not prepared to do that either. So he had to abandon his obstructionism. Thereafter, West Empress Dowager and Yixin eased up on him, and gradually the voice of other opposing courtiers became muted. West Empress Dowager and the secretaries carried on with their project.

* * *

In the northwest of China, there are many minority peoples. At that time, the Hui Clan had taken up arms against Qing Government almost simultaneously with the Nian Army. Fortunately, they had not gotten very far. Battling both the Peaceful Army and the Nian Army, the government army had had just enough forces to impede the advance of the Hui Clan rebels towards Peking. Now, with the Peaceful Army and the Nian Army defeated, West Empress Dowager wanted to put down the Hui Clan rebellion for once and for all. She appointed Governor Zuo General Governor of Shanxi Province and Gansu Province. He often compared himself to Zhuge Liang, the greatest commander and strategist in the Three Kingdoms period in Chinese history. Before Governor Zuo went to the northwest, the empress dowagers summoned him to the capital to see for themselves what kind of person he was. They also wanted to talk with him about his war plan in the northwest.

Governor Zuo arrived in the capital and lodged in Yanliang Temple. Every temple at that time had guest rooms. Yanliang Temple had originally been the residence of a prince and later was converted into a temple. Since it was close to the Forbidden City, high-ranking officers from local governments would lodge there when they were summoned to the capital. After Governor Zuo had settled in, he went to visit Yixin, who held a grand dinner for him. Among the other guests were the secretaries, who were also eager to talk over the war plans. Governor Zuo launched into a lengthy presentation: his analysis of the situation, his strategy, and the tactics he had in mind — "the stick plus the carrot." He intended to give the Hui food to eat and land to plow, and induce them to settle down. After a time, anyone who was still rebelling would be slaughtered.

His analysis listed all the disadvantages of the region: the land was barren and the people were poor; there were no rivers to transport provisions; the rival Han and Hui Clans were mingled together in a potentially explosive situation;

112

there were few cows to help plow the fields, and seeds and agricultural equipment were in short supply; and as a result, far less tax could be collected there
than in the other provinces. Then he added, "Furthermore, the price of rice there
is several times higher than elsewhere in our country. Suppose a soldier eats two
catties of rice a day (the catty is a Chinese unit of measure, a little over a pound).
That costs three taels a month. That's what they spend on a soldier in the
southern provinces. But here, on three taels a month, a soldier can only eat rice,
no meat or vegetables." Time to revisit the budget.

Yixin and the other secretaries all agreed. Then Yixin asked, "How much do
you estimate, to do all this and maintain your troops?"

"Something on the order of 3,500,000 taels per year."

"How long do you think it will take?"

"About five years." Governor Zuo stroked his beard.

The cost was really skyrocketing. Yixin just said, "We'll report to the
empress dowagers and see what they say."

On the day of the Mid-Autumn Festival, Governor Zuo went to see the
empress dowagers, with a little trepidation. He recited to himself the rituals of
conduct that must govern his presentation. The Etiquette Ministry had taught
him what to do. Everyone had to learn the rituals before being brought into the
presence of the empress dowagers. Stepping over the high threshold (for keeping
out evil spirits) and entering the reception hall, he took a couple of paces
forward and knelt on a cushion that had been placed there especially for him.
(Only elder courtiers enjoyed such a privilege.) Then he took off his hat, placed it
on the brick floor beside him, and carefully kowtowed. He stayed on his knees,
on the cushion, while he answered questions from the empress dowagers.

West Empress Dowager addressed him first. "You have had a difficult time,
these years."

"Just doing my duty," Governor Zuo replied modestly.

"How was your trip here?" West Empress Dowager was concerned with
the general situation outside the capital.

"Pretty quiet everywhere, after the war. If the people can live in peace and
have enough to eat, there won't be any rebellion." A straight-talking man.

"That's what we are expecting. It depends on the governors." West
Empress Dowager hinted that Zuo was one of those responsible.

"How long do you think you will need to finish your task in the northwest?" said East Empress Dowager.

"It should take around five years to have things well established, barring any possible backfire." Zuo said, still kneeling. Maybe it sounded a little boastful, but the empress dowagers were happy to hear it. The interview ended and Governor Zuo withdrew; but he forgot to pick up his hat on the floor.

When he got back to his lodging, a eunuch brought him some moon cakes sent by the empress dowagers as the festival gift. Then another eunuch came, carrying his hat. One of his private advisors realized that they could not just say "Thank you." They were expected to "buy" it back from him. One more funny little form of graft. But once a custom was established, everybody had to follow it. If they refused to pay for the hat, the eunuchs would start a rumor, making Governor Zuo look ridiculous. After some bargaining, 3,000 taels were paid in silver notes. The eunuchs would divide it among them.

Following Governor Zuo's departure, Governor Li arrived in the capital. In Peking, Governor Li was even more famous than Governor Zuo. The empress dowagers had summoned Governor Li to discuss the reorganization of his Huai Army. It was peacetime now. No need for so many standing armies. Governor Li was advised to keep only the young and strong, and send the rest home. Then they wanted Governor Li to persuade Elder Zeng to accept the position of Governor of Zhidi Province (now Hebei Province). Since Peking was located in that province, its governor was deemed the leader of all the governors, including the general governors. But Elder Zeng had declined, saying that he was too old and in poor health. Elder Zeng was the most famous governor; and he had a very good reputation. The empress dowagers didn't want him to retire early.

West Empress Dowager had phe empress dowagerslayed a little trick on him when he was put in charge of all the troops arrayed against the Peaceful Army. At that time, many courtiers had been afraid that Elder Zeng might turn on the government and overthrow Qing Dynasty, then declare himself emperor of a new dynasty. The empress dowagers had feared it, too. So they had appointed Zuo as Governor of Zhejiang Province and Li as Governor of Jiangsu Province, to weaken Elder Zeng's power. Although Elder Zeng did not manifest any desire to be emperor himself, some of his followers had indeed tried to persuade him to try I; but Zuo and Li, though they had worked under Elder Zeng, would never have supported an imperial bid from him. They owed too much to the late emperor and to the empress dowagers.

In 1858, Li had studied under Elder Zeng and served as a sort of assistant. Then they had a falling out, and Li left. They made up, later, and when Elder Zeng was appointed Two River General Governor, he gave Li a position; then Li

114

became governor, himself. Li was a man who always put his own interests first, as he understood them. Since West Empress Dowager gave him such a governor's post, he wouldn't support Elder Zeng against her. Li liked the bird in hand; no need to go after two in the bush.

Governor Zuo was born in Hunan Province. He had passed two government tests and lived as a tutor in his village and trained the local people to defend the village against the Peaceful Army. Then he went to work under the Governor of Hunan Province, directing military affairs. When Elder Zeng organized his army, Zuo sent him men, provisions, and money, and in the following years they boosted each other's careers. But Zuo always had a different opinion from Elder Zeng about war strategies, and he resisted Elder Zeng's domination. Their relationship became tense. West Empress Dowager promoted Zuo until he was equal in rank with Elder Zeng; now, Zuo could hardly support Elder Zeng in unseating the emperor, putting himself above Zuo once again.

Urged by the empress dowagers and the secretaries, Elder Zeng accepted the post of governor of Zhidi Province. He arrived in the capital and took up his temporary residence in the temple. When people in Peking found out that he was due to reach the capital on a certain day, many of them lined up along the route along which he was supposed to pass. People wanted to see what he looked like. They already knew that Governor Zuo was a bit fat, like a rich merchant, whereas Governor Li was tall, like a strong fighter. When Elder Zeng made his appearance, many were disappointed. He was lean, and average of height. If it were not for his official clothes, he would certainly be mistaken for a provincial squire. Someone in the crowd was skilled in the ancient craft of face-reading, and announced that it was surprising to find that Elder Zeng could be a governor. According to face-reading theory, Elder Zeng had been destined to be executed! He must have committed many good deeds, thus changing his fate — though not his face.

During the interview, the empress dowagers inquired and Elder Zeng answered, after his fashion. He was exceedingly cautious. A situation like this could backfire so unexpectedly. He was unbearably tense.

"Was everything satisfactory in the south, before you left?" asked West Empress Dowager.

"Yes. Everything is in order."

"How is the disarmament process going?"

"20,000 were sent home and 30,000 remain to be reorganized."

"They didn't make things difficult for you?"

"No. They are happy to go home."

"How's your health?" cut in East Empress Dowager.

"Better. I think the worst is over." Elder Zeng started to breathe again.

"You still take medicine every day?" asked East Empress Dowager, softly.

"Yes." His heartbeat started to settle down.

"When you arrive in Baoding City (capital of Zhidi Province), the first thing to do is to train the local army," said West Empress Dowager.

"I will. And I will strengthen the defense along the coast."

"If you need anything, or have any problem, just send in a report."

The interview ended. Elder Zeng kowtowed, stood up, and backed out of the room. He left the capital the next day and went to take up his post as the governor of Zhidi Province.

CHAPTER 24

On August 13, 1869, two colossal ships sailed down the Grand Canal, with music floating out of the cabin and pennants fluttering in the breeze. On one of the banners was a picture of a three-legged bird, the legendary bird, the bird kept by the goddess queen. She would send it abroad to gather things for her. Little An put up the banner to imply that he was sent by West Empress Dowager to gather whatever he could get (for her, of course, not for himself). He forgot that West Empress Dowager was always careful to show that she was not taking anything that was not her due. Another indiscretion on Little An's part. An error. A fatal error.

Little An had bought a girl from a poor family to be his wife. Strange thing for a eunuch to do? This absurdity had a history of its own, originating in the earlier dynasties. Eunuchs, upon attaining a certain status, would certainly start to hanker for a normal life. Not surprisingly, being normal, to them, meant having a family. Sometimes, a eunuch might even adopt a son to inherit his name and property. But no girl would marry a man who was not a man; so a eunuch could only buy a girl from a poor family. How could she object? At least she wouldn't be starved. But still, some girls would rather be nuns than be married to eunuchs. It was said that a eunuch would do a girl harm, struggling to sate his frustrated appetites. Poor girl.

In any case, here was Little An, and here was his wife with him. There were attendants on board and hired musicians to help him enjoy his journey. He had brought some boxes of gems (some of them stolen from the palace); he planned to sell them in the southern provinces and buy silk there, which he could sell when he was back in the capital. Little An was a real schemer. All along the way, he collected "tips" and even forced some of the more timid officials to give him silver notes. Racketeering his way into Shandong Province, he noted that there was no welcome party in sight. The Governor there was known for his integrity. He abhorred misconduct. In fact, he abhorred Little An, and he had sworn to kill him, if ever he had the chance. Now the chance presented itself.

When the Governor was informed that Little An had entered his province, he ordered the mayor of the town where Little An stopped for the night to go and arrest him. The mayor held back, for fear of offending West Empress Dowager. At that time, a mayor had quite a few advisors to help him manage all kinds of matters, from legal to his personal affairs. One of these advisors counseled him to keep to the cellar, as this promised to be quite a tornado. The mayor offered some pretext for not going; the governor was not surprised. He dispatched an officer to do the job. Little An was not about to slip out of his domain like a fish slipping out of a net. The next governor might let him go; who would dare to arrest him?

The officer sped along the route Little An had taken; at last, he overtook him. He introduced himself to Little An and extended an invitation on behalf of the governor to visit his yamen (the local government administration building, and the governor's seat).

"What does he want with me?"

"Oh, I wouldn't know," replied the officer. "I am not privy to such high level matters."

Maybe the governor wanted to treat him to a banquet, offer him some mementos, a little something to remember him by. So off he went with the officer, to see the Governor. Memorable it was: he was immediately locked up. The Governor ordered Little An brought into his presence, and started an interrogation. "Do you know that sneaking out of the capital is against the rules of our ancestors? How dare you?"

"I am sent on an imperial mission by West Empress Dowager. I am not sneaking out of the capital!" Little An declared, in an angry voice.

"Then where are your official documents?"

"I don't have any documents. But if you don't believe it, you can write to West Empress Dowager to verify what I say. West Empress Dowager can confirm it."

"Everyone who travels on an official errand has official documents. If you can't produce any documents, you surely have sneaked out." Then the Governor ordered his guards to throw Little An into prison, cutting short his pleas. With the fish safely caught, he wrote a report to the Secretarial Bureau and dispatched it to the capital by the quickest available means. The report stated that a eunuch had been apprehended, having sneaked out of the capital, contravening the rules set up by the venerable ancestors, and should be executed. But he didn't wait for a written reply. He had Little An summarily executed on September 14, lest West Empress Dowager order him to release the captive (who would no doubt then take his revenge). Now, if West Empress Dowager wanted to punish him — that, he would accept. At least he knew that he had dealt with Little An. (Another version of this episode suggests that he did wait for instructions from the Forbidden City, and received the approval to go ahead with the execution.) When the jailor went to Little An's cell, he said that the Governor wanted to see him. Little An fell for it again: maybe West Empress Dowager had heard of his plight and ordered him released. But he was not brought to the Governor; he was shoved into a cage and thrown on a cart. No more dissembling, on either side. The situation was clear enough, now. The executioner walked along side as the cart lurched toward the town center. There were few people to observe the scene, as it was done in the black of night. The Governor took every precaution to avoid unnecessary complications.

It was said that he had Little An's body exposed for three days, with the body stripped of pants. This was to disprove a rumor that was going around that Little An had only pretended to be a eunuch but in fact was a lover to West Empress Dowager. That would be why West Empress Dowager had indulged him so much. A rumor can never be killed by a show of power, only by revealing the facts. This particular revelation killed the rumor quite handily. And West Empress Dowager was thankful, when she learned of it later.

At this point in time, West Empress Dowager was not well. Therefore, the report about Little An went to East Empress Dowager, who decided, in consultation with the emperor and with the support of the secretaries and many other courtiers, to execute Little An. When the order drafted by the Secretarial Bureau was sent to West Empress Dowager for her to mark with her seal, she was irate; but she could do nothing to stop it. She could not change the rules set by the venerable ancestors and furthermore, all the courtiers insisted that the rule be observed, so that other eunuchs would not be encouraged to try their own luck. Then the emperor, who had been tipped off by a certain clever official, told her about the three-legged bird. Now, if she refused to execute Little An, people would think that she really had sent him to collect gifts and bribes for her, which would mar her reputation. She had to approve the order, to show that she had had nothing to do with Little An's sneaking out of the capital.

Every end is a beginning. For whom would Little An's end provide a new start? Li Lianying just happened to be waiting in the wings. Li had been in the Forbidden City for several years already but he hadn't had a chance even to appear in the presence of West Empress Dowager. Little An allowed no one to threaten his position.

Generally, the ritual that made one a eunuch was performed in the early years. The older the candidate, the riskier the operation. Li was already around thirty years old when he decided to play that card. He was an avid gambler, if not always a lucky one. Because of his constant losses, he had racked up enormous gambling debts. He left his hometown to escape from his debtors, and he lost himself in the capital. He looked up an old eunuch he had once known, in the Forbidden City. Since he didn't have a job, he often went to visit the old eunuch; and he learned that all the eunuchs who had ever served to comb the hair of West Empress Dowager had been either reproached or even punished, except for Little An. No one had done the job to her satisfaction yet. Li thought that, if he had to learn a new trade, he might as well try this one. If he could become her favorite eunuch, it would be worth the sacrifice. A long shot; but what other option did he have? Now, where could he learn the fine points of ladies' hair-dressing? Off he went to the most prestigious brothels, not for the usual reason but to learn how they did their hair. These women knew the most elaborate coiffures. He disguised himself as a vendor of cosmetics and flowers, and assiduously studied, for months, until he had mastered every aspect of hair design.

Then he went back to see the old eunuch and expressed his intention to join the ranks. Astonished, the old eunuch advised Li to do no such thing. Too risky.

"Only one out of every ten survives, at your age."

"So, I'll be the one that lives."

Li felt that his luck was improving. His determination won over the old eunuch and he took Li under his wing. Who could do the job? This would require a specialist, a most experienced practitioner. He knew such an expert, and he took Li to see him. This line of work had been handed down in the family, and if anyone could do it, he could. Li was made to lie down on a wooden bed and his limbs were tied to the bedposts. A flourish of the knife, a searing pain, a wave of colors before his eyes — Li fainted. The old man applied medicine to stop the bleeding. "If there is no infection before it heals, he is safe," he said. After a period of recovery, Li walked back into the Forbidden City, as a eunuch. There, he was drilled in all the court etiquette, and finally, he was qualified to be recommended to West Empress Dowager as a hair stylist. But that could only happen after Little An was gone. Should he be concerned that his predecessor had been killed? Little An had been a fool, in Li's opinion; he would be more careful.

Now, through the old eunuch, he made it known to West Empress Dowager that he was a hair stylist. West Empress Dowager summoned him and warned him that if he couldn't do her hair to her satisfaction, he would be punished for boasting. In fact, she was greatly satisfied. He became her favorite eunuch, and later her head eunuch.

CHAPTER 25

Elder Zeng arrived in Zhidi Province as Governor. The new Two River General Governor was Ma, who was from a family of the Hui Clan, although his ancestors had immigrated to Shandong Province on the east coast of China and he had been born there. Ma was a capable man. He had fought with the Nian Army and was always victorious in battle. He was promoted quickly. When he was appointed the Two River General Governor, he organized a new army to be trained in the use of rifles. Every morning he would go to see his army drilling. He liked to watch the soldiers at target practice. After that, he went back to his yamen for breakfast. His yamen was very close to the drilling ground, so he would walk there and back. No need to ride on horseback or be carried in a palanquin. Only a few bodyguards escorted him.

In the olden days in China, especially in the period of the later dynasties, poor people who were wronged or falsely accused had nowhere to turn. They could lodge no official complaint or suit. The lowest local government would reject their cases, so they would commit desperate acts, seeking to have wrongs righted. Sometimes, someone would throw himself on the ground to block the path of an official from a higher local government. For example, if his case was turned away by a mayor, he would throw himself down on his knees in the governor's path and cry, "I've been wronged!" or "Help me to right the wrong!" A sympathetic official, conditions permitting, might take the person to his yamen and listen to his case. Another official would merely flick his hand, and his body-guards would drive the petitioner away.

One morning when Governor Ma was on his way back to his yamen, a man appeared out of nowhere and threw himself on his knees, crying, "Your Excellency, right this wrong for me!" But the next moment, the man grabbed Governor Ma's right wrist with his left hand and plunged a sharp dagger into Governor Ma's chest. Governor Ma cried, "It's you!" before he fell. The bodyguards caught the man and held him. Governor Ma was carried into his bedroom and laid on his bed. Doctors came running. As the bad news spread, the local general, whose duty it was to defend the city, came running. The judicial official and other officials came running. There was nothing anyone could do. Governor Ma died the next day.

They questioned the killer, Zhang by name. Prisoner Zhang gave a full confession, which was written down: Zhang was conscripted into the Nian Army and always wanted to go over to the government side, but had no opportunity. Ma was, at that time, the Mayor of Hefei City in Anhui Province. Zhang captured Ma during a battle but refrained from killing him on the condition that Ma would help Zhang and other two men, Zao and Shi, to join the government army. Ma promised to persuade the governor to make an arrangement, so the four of them swore to be brothers. This was serious business. The betrayal of a sworn brother was more serious than the betrayal of a friend. As every family has its pecking order, they decided to go by seniority. Ma was the oldest and so was Eldest Brother, Zao was second, Shi the third and Zhang the youngest brother. They let Ma go back to Hefei City. Ma did arrange for his three sworn brothers to join the government army, and he organized the turncoat troops and made himself the leader, with the sworn brothers as his officers. Aided by them, he won quite a few battles and this helped facilitate his rising through the ranks. When the Nian Army was subdued, Ma had already been promoted to Financial Official of Anhui Province, right under the governor and right above the judicial official. His three sworn brothers worked under him, in his yamen. But it was said that at this point Ma began to show a disdain for them because he had always been a government official and the other three had originally been outlaws. Miles apart.

Once things settled down, Second Brother Zao wanted to fetch his wife from his home village. Zhang advised him to delay a little longer, in case the situation changed. Zhang was a sensitive man and smelled that something was not quite right, but Zao couldn't wait and fetched his wife anyway. When she arrived, she thought it would be politic to pay a visit to Ma's wife. Unfortunately, Ma was home when Zao's wife came to call. He was stunned to behold such a charming woman. He could not get her out of his mind. He had no intention of letting this treasure pass him by. And the treasure proved willing enough to make itself available. Ma and Zao's wife soon gratified each other's desire. Both of them considered Zao an obstacle, now, a thorn in their flesh. Ma took to sending Zao away on errands to remote locations, as far away and as often as possible. These errands generally brought Zao some extra money and he was happy to be given the opportunity.

The affair gradually became public knowledge. Paper can't hold back fire for long, as a Chinese saying goes. Everyone in the yamen knew, but no on dared to mention it to Zao. Except Zhang, who finally could tolerate it no more. One day Zao came back from another trip and Zhang burned his ears with the story. Zao didn't believe him. Then, by degrees, Zao realized it was true. Insulted, outraged, he wanted to kill his wife. (He didn't dare to kill Ma.) But Zhang said to him, "You have no proof, so if you kill your wife it is murder, and you will be executed. It's not worth your life. But if you don't want your wife anymore, you can give her to Ma. Thus we can still be brothers. A man may find a wife anywhere." Zao thought it over, and agreed that that would be better; so he found a chance to propose this to Ma. But much to his surprise, Ma flared up, saying that Zao was insulting his superiors. When Zao told Zhang what had happened, Zhang was deeply alarmed. That could only mean that Zao was in danger. Zhang advised him to make himself scarce, for his own safety, but Zao would not listen to him. And a few days later, Zao was dispatched on another errand. This time he was to bring back some weaponry for the provincial government. Zhang suspected foul play, so he and Shi escorted Zao to the town he was to visit. Nothing happened all the way there. Zao laughed at his two sworn brothers; so they clapped him on the back and went home.

When Zao reached the place, he was kept waiting for a long time. Then an officer came up and arrested him. He was accused of spying for the rebels lurking undercover amidst the government officials; and now he was accused of seeking to deliver weapons to the remaining rebels. He was executed at once, without the least sham of a trial. The old Chinese martial law.

When Zhang and Shi learned the astounding news, they realized that they were in danger now, too. They split up and went into hiding. Shi was found later in Shanxi Province, but Ma let him go because he looked harmless, at the time. Zhang, however, had disappeared. He had secreted himself in a remote village in the mountains, vowing to avenge his second sworn brother. Such a betrayal must be set right. He practiced the martial arts so that when he next met Ma, he would succeed in his first strike. After many years of practice, he felt he was ready. He acquired a dagger and a deadly poison. And then, like a bear coming out of hibernation, he set forth. He didn't know where Ma was by then, but Ma made that part easy: he was the Two River General Governor, and everyone knew him. Zhang arrived in the city and stationed himself near the yamen, disguised as a beggar, and observed Ma's comings and goings. Easy.

Hearing this confession, the officials were alarmed. If this got out, Ma's brilliant reputation would be tarnished forever. They would do one last favor to their late governor. They invented another scenario:

Zhang was in the Peaceful Army. When the Peaceful Army failed, Zhang escaped to Ningbo City on the coast of the Taiwan Channel in Zhejiang Province. He lived there under an assumed name and opened a pawnshop. He also conducted a bit of business on the side with the pirates on the South China Sea. At that time, Ma was the governor of Zhejiang Province. Ma ambushed and killed more than fifty pirates, many of whom were Zhang's friends. This interrupted Zhang's business with the pirates, and he began to develop a sense of animosity against Governor Ma. Then Governor Ma decided that the pawn business exploited the poor and should be banned. He put up a notice to that effect, which put Zhang out of business. Zhang had no way to make a living, and so hated Ma all the more. Meanwhile, Zhang's wife had eloped with another man and took the family's valuables with her. Zhang went to Governor Ma's yamen, requesting that his wife be apprehended, but Ma considered the case too trivial and he refused to accept it. Now Zhang was really bitter. He had no family and no means to live on. If he was going to die, he would die together with Governor Ma. He made the preparations. He stationed himself near the governor's yamen, disguised as a beggar, and awaited the proper moment. One morning when Governor Ma was on his way back from the drilling ground, he dashed up and assassinated him.

This scenario made Ma look like a good governor, even a martyr, who had died in the line of duty, although it sounded a little contrived as far as the motive for murder. The genuine version was more dramatic, with romance, with passion; it was believed by the general public, and was written into operas and plays that were great successes in Shanghai.

The general and the judicial official knew that their invented scenario would have to be signed by the prisoner himself or it could not be reported to the central government; but Zhang refused to sign it. Some officials even began to suspect that there might be someone else behind the assassination. Maybe the Xiang Army formed by Elder Zeng had refused to work under Governor Ma, who was not a Xiang Army official. It was well known that Governor Ma had always been quick to reprimand the Xiang Army. But if that were the truth, it would be a serious problem indeed.

The story, in all its different versions, spread to the capital in tandem with the official reports. The empress dowagers and the secretaries were confused. If the assassination had really been backed by someone in the Xiang Army, it was too terrible to be passed over without responding. Measures should be taken immediately. The Xiang army had been organized by Elder Zeng, so West Empress Dowager ordered Elder Zeng to go back to Nanking City to resume the post of the Two River General Governor. She also sent the Minister of Judicial Affairs to investigate, and she moved Governor Li from another province to be the Governor of Zhidi Province, replacing Elder Zeng.

The Minister of Judicial Affairs was a venerable old man, 68 already. He should have retired by then. He brought along two of his subordinates, and the three of them discussed how to investigate the case. If the assassination had been backed by someone in the Xiang Army and if their investigation got too close to the truth, it might force the Xiang Army to revolt, putting Elder Zeng in a dilemma. Better not lead the investigation in that direction. The Minister was a man of integrity and wanted to proceed according to law, but he also knew that a mutiny would disturb the peace that had so dearly been achieved, and West Empress Dowager would hardly appreciate that.

But two officials in the local government insisted on digging until they got to the bottom of the case. So, on the advice of his two adjutants, the minister invited those two local officials to take part in the investigation and the interrogation. Once, when they were questioning prisoner Zhang, who persisted in his own story, the two local officials asked permission to torture the truth out of him. But if they only beat the prisoner, he could surely endure it and would say nothing new; if they tortured him very severely, he might die. And that would be the worst of all possible outcomes. Whichever official had ordered the torture would be punished, maybe killed. Who would take the responsibility? Not the Minister; he didn't even support the idea. So the two local officials could not insist. The Minister was afraid that if the prisoner, under torture, broke down and started naming names, he might give names of people who were really not the ones behind the assassination. What if he fingered someone else, for revenge?

What if he mentioned the name of Elder Zeng, even though that could not be right? This was a delicate case. In the end, they had to use the invented scenario as the formal document of the interrogation, even without the prisoner's signature. Then they sent the report, signed by both Elder Zeng and the Minister, to West Empress Dowager, with a note attached to explain the dilemma. West Empress Dowager accepted the report and explanation, and ordered the prisoner executed. However, Zhang lived on in dramatic history as a hero, and the late Governor Ma as a sinister and ungrateful rogue. Who wrote history, this time, the people or the government?

The Minister, having swallowed his compunctions in order to meet the higher interest of preserving the peace, felt that he had not performed his duties in complete accordance with the law and his conscience. He submitted his own resignation and a petition of retirement for the two officials, who would return to the capital. The resigned minister went directly back to his hometown.

CHAPTER 26

During the war against the Peaceful Army, the Qing Government had established a military division on the Yangtze River, and placed it under the command of Elder Zeng. A general had direct control of the division, which consisted of several battalions with an officer at the head of each. This division's discipline was the worst in the country, unimaginably bad. The soldiers even took to dressing in ordinary clothes and robbing the merchant ships on the river. When Elder Zeng was alive, West Empress Dowager and Yixin had tolerated the division's misconduct. Now Elder Zeng was gone and many critique reports came in complaining about the situation. Finally, West Empress Dowager decided she would have to take action. She appointed Deputy Minister Peng of the Military Ministry as an imperial representative to investigate the case. An imperial representative acted on behalf of the emperor and, under emergency conditions, could execute corrupt officials before reporting to the emperor.

Imperial Representative Peng set out for the Yangtze River, disguised as a country squire. As he was a frugal man and never wore silk or brocade or satin, his disguise was convincing. Starting on the upper reaches of the Yangtze, he traveled downstream. Everywhere along the way, wherever the division's ships were at anchor, he heard and sometimes saw with his own eyes how the soldiers bullied people and took things from them — even their daughters and sisters.

Peng donned his official regalia and went to inspect a battalion. He asked the officer how he was preparing his men. The officer answered, with all due reference, "In reply to Your Excellency the Imperial Representative, your humble servant is training them in archery." Archery? To combat warships equipped with cannons? He dismissed the officer on the spot.

One day, he entered Zhejiang Province and anchored near Jiaxing Town, which was at the Grand Canal. He went ashore in plain clothes, with his page, and sauntered along the country road, enjoying the scenery along the waterway. Weeping willow trees adorned either bank and sails were profiled in the distance, against the clear sky. A boy rode by on the back of a water buffalo, piping a tune on his fife. Imperial Representative Peng entered the town by the north gate. He felt hungry, and stepped into a waterfront eatery. He found an empty table near the window and sat down. Two division soldiers came in and sat at the next table. While he ate, Peng watched the two soldiers. When they finished a dish, they would cast the bowl out the window into the water below. The restaurant counted the dishes served and charged the customer by the count; the two soldiers had no bowls or plates on their table — nothing to pay. Peng paid for his own lunch, and left the restaurant. Strolling in the street, he saw a large building and went in. It was an entertainment house: a storyteller would sit at the back, on a dais, and regale the audience with a story. The rest of the space was occupied by tables and benches for the listeners. The entertainment house would sell tea and snacks to them. Generally, the storyteller would recount a novel, in serials, something like "The Three Kingdoms." He would change his voice to suit the characters of the novel; he could even imitate a female voice. Usually, at the most dramatic or intriguing point in the story, he would say, "Time's up, today. If my respected listeners wish to know how the story goes on, please come early tomorrow."

When Peng walked in, the house was practically full. Only one table was vacant, and it was right in the middle, just in front of the dais. Peng walked over and sat down. Everyone stared at him, eyes wide in consternation. A waiter hurried over and urged him to move, begged him to move, but how could he move? This was the only available table. Just then a battalion officer came in, followed by two soldiers. The faces around Peng turned pale and the waiter started to quake. The soldiers shouted insults and forced Peng to give up his spot; he stood up and walked out.

Imperial Representative Peng returned to his ship and called in the mayor of the town. He asked him about the battalion officer, adding, "Why don't you punish him?"

"Your Excellency the Imperial Representative, people don't dare to accuse him. Your humble servant has no witness to produce evidence against him. Once a man came to my yamen but the next day was found killed at his home."

Peng knew that if he sent the Mayor to arrest the officer, the soldiers might riot. Instead, they laid out a plan together. The battalion officer received an invitation from the Mayor, for a dinner. The officer could not think why the Mayor would choose to hold a dinner just now, but neither could he refuse the offer of free food. When he went into the yamen, he did not see signs of any festivities. He almost backed out, when he was seized by a band of policemen. He was bought before Peng, who had borrowed the mayor's yamen, and he was interrogated. The battalion officer recognized Peng and he knew the game was up. Punishment must be close at hand. He never thought the punishment would be this swift, nor this absolute. He kowtowed, begging for his life. Peng had his crimes read out, in detail, then had him executed — to the great delight of the townspeople.

After a thorough investigation he returned to the capital and submitted a report to West Empress Dowager, suggesting the removal of the division general and many of his battalion officers. West Empress Dowager approved his report and appointed a new general and many new officers.

* * *

A son was born to Prince Yihuan and his wife, the sister of West Empress Dowager. The son later became Emperor Guangxu, who succeeded the present young emperor. West Empress Dowager was happy to have a nephew and gave him and his parents many gifts. When the boy was one month old, a feast was held in his honor. All the princes, imperial relatives and courtiers were invited. Prince Yihuan's residence was crowded with guests. But birds of a feather flock together; people mingled in different groups, according to rank. The princes and imperial relations were clustered together in one room, the ministers in another, and the critique officials in still another. There they could carp and gossip to their hearts' content, deriding other courtiers and officials. Critique officials were sharp witted and sharp tongued.

Ronglu, now Deputy Minister of the Construction Ministry, was in charge of the arrangements for the feast. It was he who had decided which rank sat in which room. He also hired two opera troupes to perform and a troupe of acrobats to amuse the younger guests. The young emperor's tutor, Li, liked to mix with the critique officials, although he was also a member of the Secretarial Bureau and could go to the room with the ministers. Many of the critique officials were renowned scholars. Tutor Li was also a scholar and he preferred to talk about books and poetry rather than vulgar topics like food and women.

When Tutor Li entered the room, they were talking about the outcome of this year's final government exam. Many critique officials shook their heads and sighed. Some candidates had been passed, even with wrong words on their test papers. Correct writing was the basic requirement. When Tutor Li was told of it, he was shocked. How could it happen? Incredibly, most of the examiners appointed this year were not scholars. They were not qualified to evaluate the test papers. And, although Tutor Li had been made the head of the department of critique officials, he was not bold enough to criticize anything involving West Empress Dowager. His ambition now was to make the young emperor a scholar. Only a scholar could rule a country well.

But he was disappointed in the young emperor, because he did not like to study. The more his mother pressed him, the more he resisted. Once, when the emperor was unable to recite a text, Tutor Li struggled again with his frustration. He could not castigate this pupil, this regal boy who was immune to criticism. Only when West Empress Dowager reprimanded the tutor for neglecting his duties did the emperor's tears begin to show. Only this could make him feel ashamed of himself and begin to study harder.

Yixin's son Zaizhen, the studymate, didn't like reading, either. But the emperor gradually came to enjoy his company, because he knew all sorts of things from outside the Forbidden City and told the emperor about them during recess.

CHAPTER 27

Now, the emperor was grown up. He was seventeen in the year 1872. Time for the empress dowagers to turn over the leadership. They were no longer needed to act in his behalf. The third emperor of the Qing Dynasty had even handled state affairs at the age of fourteen. West Empress Dowager was not about to give up power that easily, however, and she managed to keep stalling. Now she decided that they should select a queen and hold the ceremony instating him as the ruler after his marriage. In March, the selection of candidates began.

The girls were all selected from the families of the courtiers of the Manchu Clan and the Mongolian Clan. Tradition prohibited the emperor from selecting a Han girl even to be his concubine. Most people in China are ethnic Hans; the Manchu and the Mongolian are minorities, but the Manchu Clan was the ruling clan at that time and the Mongolian Clan was their ally. Many girls were selected and sent to the two empress dowagers for a further round of selection. On the fateful day all the finalists waited outside the Forbidden City, attired in beautiful gowns. Most of the girls wished to be chosen, but there were a few who did not like the idea of living like a bird in a cage. Some were in love with boys from their hometowns and had been looking forward to a happy and relatively free life. They had heard that life in the Forbidden City was full of perils. A wrong word could cost them their lives, and the empress dowagers had a fearful reputation.

The "mothers" winnowed them down until only ten were left, and then four. Finally, the emperor himself was permitted to give an opinion and decide which of the four girls would be queen. Another would be the imperial concubine, and the remaining two would just be concubines.

Of the four candidates, West Empress Dowager preferred the girl from the Fucai family. She was only fourteen, but quite particularly lovely. East Empress Dowager preferred the girl from the Alute family. She was nineteen, two years older than the emperor, but she was smart and demure, though not as strikingly beautiful. General opinion held that an emperor should choose his queen for her character and propriety, because many beautiful queens had brought destruction to China.

On this, one of the most important days in his life, the emperor stood before the four girls. He had understood the hint from West Empress Dowager. But East Empress Dowager thought the girl was too young to handle the intricacies of life in the Forbidden City, the queen's responsibilities, while a more mature queen would be better equipped to look after the emperor and help him in many regards. The emperor himself was inclined to that opinion, and so he handed the jade *ruyi*, an ornament and symbol created for that express purpose, to the Alute girl. West Empress Dowager, unaccustomed as she was to being crossed, held

East Empress Dowager responsible for this shocking disobedience. It was March 11.

The four girls were sent back home to wait for the wedding day. Life had changed for them, and much more would change as preparations went forward for the nuptials, especially in the future queen's family. Since her selection, she had to be treated as the queen, no longer as their daughter. Any family members received by her must kneel and kowtow. At meals, the mother had to serve the dishes, waiting at the table like an imperial maid. The future queen must sit and eat alone. She probably ate quickly, so that her mother would not be required to stand there too long. And she could no longer meet whomever she wanted, especially her brothers or male cousins. Meanwhile, the family received a great deal of wedding gifts and congratulations from everyone at court.

On March 24, the empress dowagers announced that the wedding would be held on October 16.

On August 23 and September 19, the emperor sent wedding gifts to the queen's family, as prescribed by the ancestors: 200 taels of gold, 10,000 taels of silver, tea containers of gold and silver, silver cups, 1,000 scrolls of brocade, and twenty horses. Maybe that does not sound like much, considering they came from the imperial family. But these were no ordinary tea containers, cups and horses: the coins were struck from a special mold, with a dragon on one side and a phoenix on the other. The horses were all white and came equipped with leather saddles, bright brass stirrups and reins. And the horses had been trained to walk to the rhythm of music.

Now, the queen's family had to prepare the dowry. According to the tradition of the Manchu Clan, the dowry must be carried into the Forbidden City beforehand. It was divided into 360 packages, each with two poles attached and borne on the shoulders by two men (or four men, for the heavier ones). The packages were open on top to display the contents inside. While the dowry was being carried towards the Forbidden City, crowds after crowds of people rushed forward to get an eyeful. They almost blocked the streets. Soldiers were sent to maintain order. Generally, they would whip the people into submission, but during these nuptial days they were required to find gentler ways to keep the streets clear. As the procession passed, people gaped at the jewels, the clothing, and the curios.

On the wedding day the Empthe emperoreror sent a luxuriously adorned palanquin to the queen's home. An imperial representative went along, carrying the queen's seal, which was made of gold. All the household came out and got to their knees to receive the queen's seal. During this time, the queen was being attired. Four ladies-in-waiting attended to her. One combed her hair into a wedding style. Another helped her into the bridal clothes, while another changed the queen's shoes. The last exercised her cosmetic skills on the queen's face. Then the queen emerged from her room, ladies in tow, and went down on her knees to accept the seal. Everyone kowtowed to the queen, and the air was suffused with congratulations and jubilation. The queen then stepped into the palanquin, a kind of miniature Chinese pavilion built of wood, with a pointed decorated roof, and a small curtained window at each side and a curtained doorway at the front. The bearers lifted the palanquin by two poles that ran along the sides, hoisted it onto their shoulders, and carried her off to the Forbidden City. In front of the palanquin thousands of people formed a procession on horseback, including guards, musicians, eunuchs bearing all manner of supplies, and the ladies-in-waiting. The procession, led by the imperial representative, stretched for miles. The road was lined with people. As night fell, members of the procession lit 300 pairs of palace lanterns that cast a glorious light on the parade.

The emperor was waiting impatiently in the Forbidden City, checking the time and fidgeting restlessly. The other three girls were carried into the Forbidden City (with considerably less pomp). When the emperor was informed that his concubines had arrived, one after another, he just nodded. At last, the bells and drums over the front gate of the Forbidden City sounded, announcing the arrival of the queen. The emperor departed his bachelor's rooms for the wedding room in another building. Now began a series of complicated ceremonies.

The queen's palanquin stopped and she was helped out, with an apple in each hand. The apple, in China, represented safety — the two words were pronounced the same in Chinese. One lady-in-waiting came to take the apples from her hands, and another lady handed the queen a gilded jar, its mouth sealed with red gauze. In the jar were small pieces of gold and silver, rubies and other gems, and grains of rice and wheat. This was called the Treasure Jar; it symbolized all forms of blessings and prosperity. Next, the queen had to step over a saddle with the two apples under it. Just at that moment, the emperor appeared. When the queen got to the other side of the saddle, she found herself standing face to face with him. Loud music accompanied the ceremony. They kowtowed to each other, on a red rug. Then they kowtowed to Heaven and Earth, and to the God of Longevity. After that, the queen had to go to kowtow to the Kitchen God.

Nominally, the queen was to manage the cooking at the palace, though she certainly never did any cooking herself. Now the emperor retired to another room to have a rest, and the queen went into the wedding room to be attired for the remainder of the night. Her hairdo was arranged in another style, more casual and fit for lying on the pillow, and she was dressed in softer, looser garments. Then the emperor came in, and the attendants withdrew, leaving the new couple to get acquainted.

The emperor's concubines were presented to the empress dowagers first. West Empress Dowager was especially kind to the Imperial Concubine. When the queen went to see the empress dowagers next day, West Empress Dowager didn't even speak to her, only nodded to acknowledge her kowtow. This was a bad sign, and everyone in the Forbidden City understood it immediately. But the wedding was complete, after three years of preparation and an expenditure of 20 million taels of silver.

* * *

After the wedding, on February 23, 1873, the emperor took up the reins of power, namely, he read the reports, made the decisions and appointed the officials and officers. West Empress Dowager advised him to continue consulting her on important matters, since, as she said, it would take time for him to develop the necessary experience and judgment. West Empress Dowager was not pleased to have been thus retired. She had nothing to do. And the emperor had chosen his queen against her will. Now, she learned that the emperor slept with the queen almost every night, and seldom went to the chamber of the imperial concubine whom she so much preferred.

Whenever the emperor came to pay homage to her, she would repeat that the he should spend more time with the imperial concubine. She would reproach the queen for indecent behavior. She even reprimanded the queen, to her face, saying that she must not be jealous of others. The queen thereafter advised the emperor to visit the imperial concubine more often. But the emperor was livid; could his mother not keep out of any of his business, not even his marital life? So he stopped going to see the imperial concubine altogether. But, unwilling to endure West Empress Dowager's scolding, he no longer went to the queen's chamber, either. He simply began to sleep in his study, saying that he wanted more time for reading.

Once, he complained to East Empress Dowager that his mother so often found fault with him. East Empress Dowager observed that his mother had too much time on her hands, and suggested that he find something to occupy her time; perhaps she would be happier, and criticize him less.

Then some officials in the imperial construction group suggested rebuilding the Round-Bright Garden which the foreigners had burned. That might be a useful way to occupy his mother for a time, although it was a far cry from the life-and-death matters she was accustomed to. West Empress Dowager expressed some interest. But Yixin and the other courtiers opposed the idea, because the imperial treasury had been drawn down with all the wars. The country urgently needed to build a navy to protect against any further invasion from foreign countries, and resources were scarce. Still, the emperor was desperate to give his mother something to do, and West Empress Dowager certainly felt entitled to a reward after relinquishing her grip on power. The construction officials went to the site to estimate the cost, and suggested raising the money through donations; the emperor duly ordered the courtiers to donate money for it.

As long as the emperor didn't demand money from the treasury, Yixin said nothing more. In fact, he donated 20,000 taels of silver. But many courtiers refused. The emperor couldn't punish them for that. In the end, he only gathered a few hundred thousand taels, far short of the budgeted amount.

Critique Official Sun filed a report to oppose the construction plan. The emperor flew into a rage; he wanted to find a way to punish him, before the other courtiers scuttled his plan altogether. He asked the secretaries about Critique Official Sun. The secretaries surmised that he would be looking for faults, something he could pin on him; but Yixin replied that when the late Emperor had escaped to the Summer Palace in Rehe, this critique official had tried to commit suicide by jumping into a well. A faithful servant to the late emperor: how could the present emperor punish someone who had been so loyal to his honorable father? Then another critique official, You, handed in a similar report. The emperor was angry, but in fact this served his interest after all — nothing special about this official; he could punish him and set an example to the others. Critique Official You was dismissed. Yixin advised the emperor that it was not appropriate to remove a critique official over such a matter during difficult times. When he persisted, Yixin reported to West Empress Dowager, who sent for the emperor and counseled him not to remove critique officials over trivial matters.

Next, he ordered all the governors to make a donation; but they complained that they had no funds to spare since there was so much urgent work to be done, now that the fighting had stopped. Even Governor Wu of Sichuan Province excused himself, saying that when he could collect enough money he would send it to the capital. The construction officials questioned that, because Sichuan Province was known to be rich; but the emperor's plans were frustrated for now.

At about that time, a merchant by the name of Li presented himself to the official in charge of construction and let it be known that he was prepared to donate timber for the Round-Bright Garden. The emperor was delighted. He ordered the official to arrange for the timber to be transported to the capital, and promised that when the construction was finished he would give the merchant a high official position. The emperor took to sneaking out of the Forbidden City on the pretext that he wished to inspect the ruins of the garden, to see how to rebuild it.

But in further conversations, Merchant Li admitted to the official that the wood was in the forest of the remote mountains in Guizhou Province, far, far away in the southwest. The enormous trees had to be chopped down, hauled to the nearest stream, floated down to the closest town and shipped from there to the capital. This would be an enormous undertaking in itself, requiring many men, much time, and plenty of money. The official was stunned. This was not at all what had been represented. He could not report this awkward situation to the emperor. Then Merchant Li said that he could help to buy lumber from foreign merchants. Better come up with something. The official knew that if he didn't produce wood for the emperor, he would lose the position at least and his liberty very likely. Besides, if he had Merchant Li buy the wood, the government would pay for it. The money would not come out of his own pocket, and furthermore, he would get a commission. He agreed to the merchant's proposal, and gave him 500 taels of silver as traveling expense.

Merchant Li was clever, wasn't he? He was even cleverer than that. He was a great imposter. It was true that he had had dealings with foreigners; but he often cheated them and then disappeared. Eventually the foreigners in question moved on, and when they left China he went on to swindle the next ones. Once, a foreigner had wanted to purchase a piece of land; Merchant Li sold him a stretch of property but it turned out to be swamp. The price had been low, after all, so the foreigner thought he would have to make the best of a bad situation. Then he found out that the land belonged to the local government, not to Li, in any case. But Li was gone. The foreigner was ruined. He searched for Merchant

Li, but was never able to track him down. The foreigner died, and with his dying breath uttered the wish that his ghost could find Merchant Li.

Now, Merchant Li went to Hong Kong, lodged in a suite in a grand hotel and put up a notice "Lumber needed for the imperial garden." When the word got around, he was swarmed with wood salesmen. A French merchant offered the best price. Li ordered 35,000 square feet of wood for 10,000 taels of silver. Reckoning that he had promised to donate 10,000 taels, he reported the cost as having been 30,000. That would leave 10,000: a good profit for him. The contract said that when the wood arrived in Tianjin City, the government would send an official to receive the shipment and make the payment. But when the French merchant reached the harbor, no one was there to receive him.

Merchant Li had reported the price to the official in charge; when he, in turn, informed the construction officials, they acknowledged that the price was high — even by their standards — and they decided not to accept the shipment. The French merchant complained to the French envoy; the envoy contacted the Foreign Affairs Yamen. The swindle was exposed for all to see.

The official in charge had to report to the emperor, who was irate. He told the empress dowagers. Merchant Li was put to death and the official was removed from office. The French merchant had died anyway, so the deal was off. Now, the construction plan was abandoned for good.

* * *

When the emperor came into power, he remembered his studymate and playmate Zaizhen, and made him his Courtier Before the Throne so that they would still see each other all the time. When they had nothing better to do, Zaizhen would tell the emperor funny stories. Or stories he thought were funny.

"One day," he told the emperor, "the wife of the French envoy came to see my mother — ." The emperor interrupted and asked, "Does a foreigner really have red eyebrows and green eyes?" (A eunuch had told him that.)

Zaizheng replied, "They have green eyes, yes. But they don't have red eyebrows."

"How do they behave?" asked the emperor.

"Their rule is, ladies first. When a newcomer arrives, the men must stand up, but the women remain seated. And men always kiss women's hands," Zaizhen gravely answered.

"I was told that the women and the men socialize together. Is that so?"

"Oh, yes. They greet each other by gripping each other's hands. They embrace each other and even kiss each other on the mouth."

"Have you been kissed by a foreign woman?" The emperor was curious. He was still a teenager.

"No. I haven't had such pleasure. They don't kiss us, because they know we don't like to be kissed."

"Have you touched a foreign woman's hands?"

"Yes! On the day when the French envoy's wife came to see my mother, I went into our guest room, too. I was about to withdraw, but the French woman asked me to stay. By the way, she can speak some Chinese, though she speaks poorly. She shook hands with me, but I had gooseflesh all over."

"Why? Are there thorns on her hand?"

"No. It wasn't painful; but the hair on her arm is very long."

"That must look like a monkey's!" the emperor joked.

"Yes! But she is prettier than a monkey." They both laughed.

CHAPTER 28

At seventeen, the emperor was fully a man, and ready to have a wife. But he could not approach his queen, whom he loved, for fear of antagonizing his mother — who would take it out on the queen. He disliked the imperial concubine because his mother had forced her on him. And he could not go to the other two concubines without going to the imperial concubine.

Driven by passion and frustration, and gradually learning more of the life of ordinary people, he began to find everything outside the Forbidden City interesting, intriguing, compelling. He wanted to witness it, to have a taste of it. He began to sneak out, in disguise, and wandered in the streets. He visited restaurants renowned for certain dishes, and sampled the delicacies civilians enjoyed; he visited the bazaars, and savored the energy and life. Once, he came upon a courtier who was singing a few airs from some well-known operas. Many courtiers or even princes delighted in singing, and some even acted out the scenes among relatives and friends. Just for fun. The emperor liked operas, too. A few days later, he promoted the courtier so that he could see more of him. The courtier secretly introduced him to a host of other vulgarities, which only whetted his appetites further. Life in the Forbidden City was unbearably circumscribed. The most exciting entertainment was the opera, but one can hardly watch operas every day. The emperor was finally reduced to patronizing the common whorehouses. He couldn't show his face at one of the better brothels, where he might be recognized by a member of the court; so he found himself like a golden pheasant mingling with scavenger birds in the dismalest corners of the city. All these activities of the emperor were known to Ronglu, who was then in charge of the enforcement of law and order in the capital. He had undercover security men all over Peking, gathering all kinds of information for him. But Ronglu didn't tell anyone about the emperor's behavior; he only ordered his men to protect him, discreetly.

The emperor's furtive trips became so frequent that he neglected his studies. He often refused to go to class, for no apparent reason, simply notifying the tutors, "Not today." Customarily, it was up to the tutors to decide whether there would be classes or not; but with this emperor, it was different. What could they say?

When the secretaries found out about it, they had to discuss it. This was no mere security risk; this was serious. Yixin was the sixth uncle of the emperor; Yihuan was the seventh uncle. They were joined by several elderly courtiers who had watched the young emperor grow up. They submitted a report to admonish the emperor, adding, at the end, that they hoped that the emperor would grant them a reception, as they had additional important matters to report in person. The emperor had already heard enough, however; he didn't even read their report. The secretaries and courtiers waited for the emperor to see them, but days went by without any hope of reception. Finally, they simply presented themselves. Since Yixin was the head of the Secretarial Bureau, he began. "Has Emperor read our report?"

"No, I haven't yet." The emperor, a bit nervous, pretended to speak nonchalantly. He picked up the report, which was still lying sealed in its envelope, and slit it open. As he glanced down the page, the color drained from his face. Serious allegations, even if they were veiled. He put down the report and said, "Alright, I understand, now. I will study harder. Is that all right?" He sounded irritated. But these seasoned courtiers pressed on.

"There's more to it than that," said Yixin. He took out another copy and read it aloud. Before he could finish it, the emperor shouted indignantly, "What if I let you be emperor?" Every one of the courtiers was stunned. Secretary Wenqiang, who was not well these days, sighed and collapsed on the floor. The emperor was in a panic and regretted his outburst. The eunuchs waiting outside the building rushed in to help Wenqiang to his feet. Such a thing had never happened since the beginning of the Qing Dynasty.

Yihuan, the seventh uncle, said, "If the emperor will be more careful in his conduct, it will be a blessing to our Qing Dynasty."

"I know that everything is my fault. What's wrong with my behavior?"

"The first responsibility for a young emperor is to study hard. The second responsibility is for a young emperor not do things that an emperor should not do," added Yihuan.

"What have I done to deserve such censure?"

"Emperor should not slip out of the Forbidden City."

"You have been listening to rumors. How could I have managed to do such a thing?"

"Emperor knows whether it is rumor or not rumor." Far be it from him to declare that the emperor was lying.

"Do you have any proof? If you don't, you are spreading rumors."

Under the circumstances, Yihuan had no choice but to tell the emperor what he had learned. The emperor must be made to take this matter seriously and reconsider his conduct. A recitation of excursions ensued, where the emperor had gone, what games he had engaged in. On such and such a day, the emperor had gone to buy books. On such and such a day, the emperor had dined at such and such a restaurant, where he had ordered such and such dishes and paid such and such a sum. At least he forbore to name the brothels at which the emperor had ended his evenings. The emperor was speechless. No defense.

Then the Secretarial Bureau sought to punish the officials in charge of the imperial construction work. They had caused distractions, disruptions, expense and embarrassment by instigating the emperor to renovate the Round-Bright Garden. But the emperor did not agree. It had suited him, at the time, to try that project. When Yixin insisted, the emperor flew into a rage and issued an order to remove Yixin from all his offices — a tactic he had learned from his mother. Other secretaries came hurrying, trying to reason with the emperor. He wrote another order, removing every secretary from the Secretarial Bureau. He summoned the ministers and other courtiers and asked them to discuss what punishment the emperor should inflict upon the secretaries.

Ronglu was not the only one with eyes and ears. West Empress Dowager had her own people working here and there. Eunuchs from the emperor's quarters ran to her with news of his latest exploits. She hastened to see East Empress Dowager. They sent for the emperor. The man with two mothers presented himself to the formidable ladies. East Empress Dowager said to him, "How can you dismiss all the secretaries? Do you want the empire to crumble in your hands?" The emperor could say nothing. Then West Empress Dowager told the emperor to rescind his orders, and in the end he had to do so, though reluctantly. The tempest blew over.

On November 28, 1874, the emperor was suddenly taken ill. An imperial doctor was summoned. A cold. Not to worry. Everybody catches cold, from time to time. He prescribed various medicines; but they had no effect. The doctor seemed perplexed; not much to do but wait for further signs and symptoms to appear. In the meanwhile, he could only prescribe some general tonics. Red spots broke out on the emperor's skin a few days later. Smallpox? The doctor was relieved; the treatment was clear, now that he knew what it was.

The empress dowagers asked, "Are you sure you can cure him?"

"Oh, yes. If it *is* smallpox."

What if it was not? West Empress Dowager was annoyed, but she could not rebuke the doctor. Not that she was afraid he would poison the emperor — but it's better not to rattle a doctor's nerves, and make him prescribe the wrong medicine. By tradition, one was always careful not to upset a court doctor by rebuking him. On the contrary! West Empress Dowager offered to promote the doctor if he succeeded in healing her son.

There was another tradition that, when anyone in the palace suffered from smallpox, the Goddess of Smallpox would be set up in an unoccupied room and joss sticks and candles would be burned before the icon. It worked. After a few days, the emperor's rash gradually disappeared. There was an air of relief throughout the palace. The empress dowagers were at rest. However, to their dismay, other signs quickly appeared. Now the doctor was in a plight. Unambiguous symptoms; unspeakable diagnosis. Could he tell the mothers that their son had the fatal disease of syphilis? It did not make sense, in any case. It was impossible. The emperor could not have been exposed to the disease. Of course, the treatment was ineffective. The emperor was weaker every day. The doctor had to watch what he said; no point blackening the emperor's name — which was more important than his life. Besides, revealing the truth would not help anyone. There was nothing anyone could do. It was a terminal disease at that time.

As the emperor's health declined, Yixin was anxious to get a reliable prognosis. He sent for the doctor. At first, the doctor held back. After considerable tergiversation, he was backed into a corner. Yixin threatened him, saying that if the doctor didn't let him know what was happening, he would be held liable when the emperor died. He was compelled to tell the truth. Yixin was stunned. Never thought of that. Incredible. And, he agreed, better make sure the empress dowagers did not find out.

* * *

During the emperor's sickness, the empress dowagers had resumed their role in handling state affairs in his behalf. That suited West Empress Dowager just brilliantly. She was disappointed in her son, anyway; in her opinion, he had never listened to her since taking over, and he lacked talent. Now, everybody was in a stir, theorizing as to who should succeed to the throne when the emperor was summoned to Heaven by his ancestors.

According to both logic and common sense, the successor should be chosen from the next generation: an adopted son of the present Emperor. But West Empress Dowager thought differently. If the successor came from the next generation, the present queen would become the empress dowager. West Empress Dowager would be nothing but the grandmother. She would lose power forever. Unthinkable. She sent Ronglu, now a high-ranking courtier, to convene all the highest members of the court to discuss the issue. A subtle question. Who would dare to express an opinion? They demurred, saying the empress dowagers were best suited to make such an important decision.

West Empress Dowager's sister had married Yixin's brother Yihuan; they had a son who was only four years old. Perfect — West Empress Dowager could stay in power, now, on the same pretext as before.

"His mother is my sister," she would say; "his father is my brother-in-law. I am his aunt twice over. He is really my own flesh and blood."

East Empress Dowager had no better candidate to present. Certainly. She would still enjoy her special status, too — as long as she showed no ambition. The courtiers could say nothing, as the selection of the future emperor was a family matter, although it certainly concerned the entire empire. West Empress Dowager made the decision, and that was that. Then she promoted Ronglu to be one of the heads of the Imperial Household Department. Ronglu could see more of West Empress Dowager now.

The emperor died on January 12, 1875, and the successor to the throne was named Emperor Guangxu (1871-1908). He was brought in as the adopted son of Emperor Xianfeng, the husband of West Empress Dowager, not of her son Emperor Tongzhi, so recently departed: Emperor Guangxu was the cousin of

Emperor Tongzhi, belonging to the same generation. Now West Empress Dowager was his adoptive mother.

Yihuan's younger brother, the ninth one, Prince Fu, was sent to fetch Yihuan's son, the future emperor. The child's mother, West Empress Dowager's sister, was overwhelmed. What an honor, what a surprise, to see her son become emperor. What a blow, to lose her son forever. And how would the child get on, wrested from all he knew?

"Will the wet nurse go to the Forbidden City, too?" asked the mother.

"No. They have hired another nurse already," answered Prince Fu.

"But please let West Empress Dowager know that my son can't leave this wet nurse," she pleaded, almost in tears.

"My sister-in-law, you must say Emperor now, not Son, anymore."

It was night. The child was asleep. When they woke him up, he began to cry. Off they went to the Forbidden City, the mother carrying the boy in her arms, in a heated palanquin. When they reached the palace and were presented to the empress dowagers, the child was asleep. But when the new wet nurse took him, he began to cry again. He cried and cried, and could not be consoled. And in the end, indeed, the empress dowagers had to send for the original wet nurse.

Just a month after the new emperor's coronation, the queen of the recently deceased Emperor Tongzhi died. Suicide? That was the official story. But general opinion was that West Empress Dowager had compelled her to end her life, either by swallowing a lump of gold or by starving herself. The imperial palace is full of secrets that no historian can solve.

At this time, Princess Rong An, the daughter of Concubine Dowager Li, was pregnant. When she heard that her stepbrother Emperor Tongzhi had died, she was distraught. She wept so hard that her baby aborted. She herself was taken with smallpox, and died not long after. It was said that Emperor Tongzhi needed a companion in Heaven, and he took his stepsister with him.

CHAPTER 29

A critique official turned in a report. He said, "There is a pawnshop owner named Li [that's a very common surname in China] who has been falsely claiming that he is a relative of Minister Ho, of the Construction Ministry. On that basis he has been getting away with all sorts of illegal things — fraud and extortion. He is also a go-between in other unlawful transactions. He mingles with the courtiers and his residence is as magnificent and luxurious as those of the ministers. How can a pawnshop owner come by such luxuries? This critique official begs to have this pawnshop owner deported to his hometown so that the capital can be purified of such an unhealthy influence." Then he added, in another paragraph, "As for courtiers, especially ministers, they should not mix with such base people, feasting together and giving each other presents. This critique official begs to have an order issued to prohibit such behavior among the courtiers."

West Empress Dowager was surprised. Minister Ho was a scholar. Could he really be fraternizing with such people? But maybe the report was not reliable; a critique official was allowed to write a report based on rumor. She deputized her head Eunuch Li to gather the facts. Head Eunuch Li, or Li the Tanner, as people called him behind his back, was cleverer than Little An. He did whatever he liked, but without leaving any evidence behind. He spent half a day having inquiries made, and then he came back to report to West Empress Dowager.

Merchant Li, the pawnshop owner, came from Shanxi Province. He had had a building constructed, taking up a great expanse of space in a market place, and he opened a large pawnshop dealing in curios and also selling books. But the poor were not buying books, and the poor did not have curios to pawn. His customers were all well-heeled officials and courtiers. He therefore bought an official title so that he could wear official clothes on certain occasions. He even knew a prince who collected antiques. With so many high-level contacts, he began to feel that he could step outside the circumference of the law. These dealings became open secrets, and eventually attracted the notice of the critique officials.

And this was just at the time that West Empress Dowager had decided to utilize the critique force to discipline officialdom and re-establish her own authority. She gave the report to the Secretarial Bureau for discussion and investigation. The Secretarial Bureau ordered the Judicial Ministry to arrest the pawnshop owner. Investigation revealed that, while building his shop, he had encroached on government land and had taken over a whole lot that belonged to a charitable organization. The Judicial Ministry set him a penalty of a beating of sixty lashes and one year's imprisonment; after that, he would be deported to his hometown under parole of his local government.

But the critique officials were really aiming at Minister Ho. They wanted to hit the tiger, not the fly. Another critique official filed a report asking what was actually the relationship between Minister Ho and the pawnshop owner. After perusing this document, West Empress Dowager demanded an explanation. Minister Ho replied, in his report, that he did not have any relationship with the pawnshop owner except for chance meetings on those occasions when he went to buy some books. Now, if that was the truth, he was not guilty of anything. But was it? As a matter of fact, Minister Ho had taken the wife of the pawnshop owner as his "dry daughter" — something like a God-daughter, but without any religious significance. When the wife died, Minister Ho had made one of his own maids his dry daughter, and married her to the pawnshop owner. So the men did have a relationship, as dry father-in-law and dry son-in-law. Furthermore, to show his gratitude for marrying his dry daughter to him, the pawnshop owner bought a young girl and presented her to Minister Ho as a concubine. Minister Ho's wife had long since passed away, so Minister Ho made the girl his wife. Now the pawnshop owner had a young dry mother-in-law. If the girl were still a concubine, he would not be expected to show any respect to her when they met, but as the wife of Minister Ho, he should go down on his knees before her and kowtow to her on certain occasions.

The critique officials accused Minister Ho of lying about his relationship with the pawnshop owner. Minister Ho was demoted to deputy general critique official, since there was no other vacancy at an appropriate level. Now, all the critique officials were opposed to that, and it was not a very wise move on the part of the Secretarial Bureau. Had they made the appointment without serious consideration? One critique official asked if this appointment was intended to indicate that a critique official should lie and cheat. Not quite the result intended. So the Secretarial Bureau had to let him retire, with the promise that his son would get a promotion.

* * *

After five years, General Governor Zuo had at last put an end to the Hui Clan rebellion, as promised. Just as he was about to return victoriously to the capital, an international incident erupted in Xinjiang Province. West Empress Dowager ordered him to stay there for a while longer: if war should break out in Xinjiang, between Russia and China, he would be needed.

Russia had occupied Yili Town, in Xinjiang Province, quite some time ago. They had declared that they were only keeping it for Qing Government until Qing Government was capable of ruling the town peacefully and efficiently — many Russian merchants and working people lived in Yili Town and the Russian government felt a very touching responsibility to look after their welfare. At least Russia still acknowledged that Yili belonged to China, which had been busy dealing with rebellions. Now, the rebellions had been extinguished. Qing Government put the issue of Yili Town back on the agenda. They delivered a diplomatic note to Russia, stating that it was time to hand it over. Both governments agreed to have a talk, in St. Petersburg. (It would be hard to get farther from Peking and still be in Russia, but St. Petersburg was Russia's capital. Fair enough.)

The Qing Government sent courtier Chonghou as imperial representative. He was a veteran of the Foreign Affairs Yamen and knew how to deal with foreigners. Courtiers usually tried to guess what West Empress Dowager really wished, so that they could perform to her satisfaction. But this time Imperial Representative Chonghou got it wrong. He believed that West Empress Dowager wished to avoid war at any cost. He gave in to Russian demands more than necessary; and worst of all, he did not send a copy of the draft documents back to the Forbidden City for approval. He understood that he had been given full authority to negotiate and sign the treaty. He really did not get it right, at all. In fact, having concluded an agreement, he began the long trip back to the Chinese court without awaiting any further instructions. By the treaty he concluded, China gave up many rights; though it is true that Russia promised to give back Yili Town.

When the gist of the treaty became known, the first to react were the critique officials. They accused Chonghou of shortcomings and even treason. The empress dowagers were irate, too. They stripped him of his title of Imperial Representative and discussed with the Secretarial officials how he should be dealt with. The Russian envoy came to the Foreign Affairs Yamen to protest, saying that it would be an insult to Russia if China punished the Imperial Representative who had signed the treaty. The head official explained that the government was punishing him for failing to wait for any orders, having come back on his own decision — nothing to do with the signing of the treaty. The Russian envoy could not protest on those grounds, and so he left.

Critique Official Zhang Zhitong wrote a report suggesting that, first, Chonghou should be executed for treachery; second, that the treaty should be declared null and void since the Qing Government had not approved it; and third, to make war preparations to defend the territory, in case Russia should declare war. Many courtiers supported his suggestion. Someone even said, "If war is inevitable, better to start now, while we have many experienced generals on hand, battle-hardened from the combats with rebels." The consensus was: "Execute Chonghou, and if Russia wants to fight, let's fight."

To appease their naive fury, the Secretarial Bureau told the Judicial Ministry to detain Chonghou. (Chonghou had confined himself at home since he had returned to the capital, hoping that things would quiet down and he might be let off lightly.) His servants went about the city, hunting for any news for him. When the message came that he was to be jailed, he put on a prisoner's uniform which he had had made. He also knew that, if war did break out, he would be executed — to encourage the people to fight. That's politics. When he was put in prison, his butler bribed the jailors so that his master would be well treated.

The Secretarial Bureau held a series of meetings with the cabinet members and Critique Official Zhang. Yixin enumerated the reasons why the government should not go to war against Russia. "Our guns and cannons are neither as effective nor as numerous as the Russians'. We haven't got enough provisions and money to support another war. We haven't sounded out the generals and soldiers — what if they are not prepared to fight?"

The belligerent polemics abated a little. The only feasible course, at present, was to send another imperial representative to St. Petersburg to renegotiate certain articles of the treaty. Now, that would be a challenge, indeed. Then they made several decisions: the government could delay taking back Yili Town, and Chonghou could be given a stay of execution, for now, as a friendly gesture to Russia. But why, if it comes to that, should Russia care about one more Chinese official, dead or alive?

War preparations went forward. General Governor Zuo left Gansu Province for Xinjiang, closer to Russia. News came to the ears of the empress dowagers that Zuo had taken a coffin with him. They were greatly moved and openly extolled him for loyalty and bravery.

After a great deal of bargaining, the first treaty was rescinded and a new treaty was signed, by which the Qing Government gave up fewer rights — but more money. Russia was asking to be repaid for their expenses in maintaining Yili Town. Well, that sounded reasonable to West Empress Dowager. In the first treaty, the fee was five million silver rubles; in the new treaty, it was increased to nine million silver rubles (equivalent to five million taels of silver). A lot of money. But as long as West Empress Dowager was happy, everyone was happy. The new imperial representative was praised for completing the difficult task. He was the eldest son of the late Elder Zeng. The event having been settled to the satisfaction of the empress dowagers, Chonghou was pardoned and released.

CHAPTER 30

West Empress Dowager had been ailing for some time, but she still participated in the policy discussions with the courtiers. Then her illness took a turn for the worse. On March 12, 1880, East Empress Dowager was left to handle state affairs alone (with the help of Yixin and other courtiers, of course). Now, West Empress Dowager really felt ill: wouldn't East Empress Dowager seize power, as soon as she was weakened, this once?

The court doctor said that her sickness was due merely to the strain of over work and suggested that she should have a complete rest until she recuperated entirely. With anxiety compounding her illness, she did not recover for four months. Medicine had no effect. No one could persuade her to relax. Then they thought of Big Princess, a widow now and living in exclusion in her own residence. She was called to the Forbidden City to see West Empress Dowager, and she stayed there to look after her day and night. It was said that Big Princess spoke so convincingly that West Empress Dowager always listened to her.

On July 13, a notice went out across the empire: "Doctors Wanted." In the emperor's name. The governor of Zhejiang Province recommended a famous Doctor Xi. By coincidence, two other governors also recommended Doctor Xi. He was dispatched to the capital, to the Forbidden City, to the presence of West Empress Dowager, in her chamber. She was lying in bed. First, Doctor Xi kowtowed before the bed, then he knelt close by to feel her pulse. He had been taught all the rituals beforehand. After taking her pulse, he asked permission to look at the tongue of West Empress Dowager. Then he was allowed to stand up, and he courteously backed away from the bed. Nearing the door, he turned round and walked out of the chamber. He was led into another room to write out his prescription, which was then checked by the courtiers in the Secretarial Bureau and even sent to West Empress Dowager herself to be approved; then a eunuch took it to the pharmaceuticals storage room in the Forbidden City where a specialist prepared the medicine.

Doctor Xi was an educated man. He had passed the second government exam and had come to the capital for the final test. At that time, the southern provinces were engulfed in war. He could not go back to Wuxi City. He had stayed on, in the capital, to prepare for the next exam. He had had plenty of time and so he had begun to study medicine, on his own. He had bought an official title but had never actually been given a post. The government found it convenient to plug a few holes in the budget by selling more titles than could be justified by the number of positions that existed. Everyone who bought a title had to either wait for a vacancy, or accelerate the process by paying more. Xi had no more money to spare, and so he waited. In the meantime, he practiced medicine and developed great proficiency. After war ended in the south, Doctor Xi had gone back and filled a vacancy there.

Now, he came to the capital as a doctor. First, he met the imperial doctor, who interviewed him closely, as though to test his medical knowledge. Doctor Xi answered all the questions with deliberation, and at last the imperial doctor could think of no more questions to ask. Doctor Xi more knowledgeable than the imperial doctor. When Doctor Xi asked him what illness afflicted West Empress Dowager, he could not say anything definite. In fact, he would not even give a general diagnosis.

Sometimes West Empress Dowager would refuse to take the medicine if she didn't trust in the expertise of the doctor. But now, West Empress Dowager took her medicine for 43 days, because she trusted Doctor Xi. She was soon convalescent and could once again attend to her official duties.

A rumor went around that West Empress Dowager had had a miscarriage, which the imperial doctor had misdiagnosed. If a doctor could not diagnose correctly, how could he prescribe the right medicine? That was why the sickness of West Empress Dowager had lasted so long. Doctor Xi diagnosed it, all right, but he did not say what was wrong. Instead, he prescribed the right medicine under the pretext of a disease that might have somewhat similar symptoms. In any event, having cured West Empress Dowager, he was given a very good position near the capital. Next time West Empress Dowager was sick, he could come on short notice.

* * *

Official Yan was an ugly man, short and thin. His eyes were uneven, one a bit higher than the other. The creases over his eyes were slanting, but he was an upright official. Tough, too. Never intimidated by unreasonable superiors. At that time, he was the Financial Official in Hubei Province, directly under the governor. The governor developed a passion for his young page, a handsome youth with fair skin. As the boy grew up, the governor endowed him with official titles, until he became a deputy general and head of the governor's bodyguards. The deputy general often bullied people and took bribes. Official Yan was on the lookout for a chance to see justice served. Waiting.

One day, the deputy general burst into a house and raped and killed a girl in the family. The father sued him in Yan's yamen. Now Yan had a reason to arrest the miscreant. Off he went to the governor's yamen, with his guards. The governor hid the deputy general. Official Yan asked to see the governor, but the governor feigned illness and declined to receive him. One of the governor's body-guards said to Yan, "When the Governor recovers, he will come to see Your Excellency." Did the governor really think he could fob off Yan with such a flimsy answer? Was Yan the type to walk away and leave the governor time to save his protégé's hide? Yan said, "The Governor will surely recover some day. I'd better wait here until then."

He ordered his guards to fetch some bedding and other necessary items from his own yamen and he stayed in the reception hall for three days, managing his own official business from there. Awkward. The governor asked the Judicial Official and his own private advisors to persuade Yan to leave, but Yan insisted that he must execute the deputy general for murdering the girl — before he could leave. The governor was finally constrained to come out and see him. The governor knelt before him to implore him to spare the life of the deputy general. Now, the governor was Yan's immediate boss, and someone observed that it was not appropriate to allow the governor to kneel before him. Yan helped him to his feet and promised to spare the life of the young man — on one condition. The governor had little choice; he had to agree. "What's the condition?" he asked.

"He must be deported to his home village and the governor can never hire him again," said Yan. He consented, and sent for the deputy general, who kowtowed to Yan for sparing his life. Yan ordered his guards to give the man forty lashes before exiling him from the province. The governor, who was not wicked so much as weak, did not hate Yan for this and never thought of revenge. On the contrary, he commended him to West Empress Dowager; and Yan was appointed governor of Shandong Province.

CHAPTER 31

At festival time, according to tradition, the emperor would give food or other gifts to the imperial relatives and close courtiers; the eunuchs would run the errands. But according to tradition, the eunuchs could not go out by the front gate of the Forbidden City unless they had a note from the Eunuch Administration. Actually, they could go out through the side gates. Young Eunuch Li was sent to the residence of Prince Yihuan, West Empress Dowager's brother-in-law and the natural father of the present emperor, Guangxu. Young Eunuch Li walked towards the front gate, carrying some food in a container.

"Stop!" a gate guard shouted.

"What's the matter?" asked Eunuch Li.

"Don't you know the rule?" The guard looked him up and down.

"What rule?" Eunuch Li asked indifferently.

"Is this the gate you think you can go through?" The guard held out his hand for a note. In his opinion, the eunuch should have produced the note long since.

"Why can't I? West Buddha is sending me on a mission." (By that time, the venerable empress dowagers were sometimes called Buddha.)

"Whatever the reason, you can't go through this gate unless you have a note."

"What note?" Young Eunuch Li feigned ignorance. "I don't have a note. If you want a note, go to West Buddha for one." Quite a few of the eunuchs (if not everyone) who worked for West Empress Dowager adopted the insolent posture of imperial representatives who deferred to no one. The bickering was so loud that the head gate guard heard it and came out of the guardhouse. This was a delicate situation. If the guards allowed eunuchs to exit through the front gate without a note, they would be accused of negligence. Yet, if Young Eunuch Li had been sent by West Empress Dowager, he didn't want to offend him. The head guard brought the discussion back to a civil tone and advised Li to go back and get a note; but he refused. He threw the food container on the ground, and ran back to West Empress Dowager and reported that the guards had beaten him. When West Empress Dowager was told that the front guards wouldn't let Young Eunuch Li go out, and had upset the food container, she was infuriated and ordered the Judicial Ministry to arrest the guards and put them to death.

In the Judicial Ministry there were eight middle-ranking officials who were well versed in the law. They were conscientious and acted by the book. Their colleagues called them the Eight Saints. This case fell under their jurisdiction. When the minister told them what West Empress Dowager had instructed, one of them said, "If Empress Dowager wants to execute them, Empress Dowager can execute them directly. However, if it becomes a case in the Judicial Ministry, we must judge it according to the law."

"What will be the verdict, in your opinion?"

"Not guilty." The minister was in a bind. How could he report that to West Empress Dowager? Another of the Eight Saints said, "In this case, we must not only try the guards, but also try the eunuch." Another of the Eight told a story from the Han Dynasty (almost 2000 years ago): someone stole a jade ornament from the mausoleum of the emperor's ancestors. By the law of the Han Dynasty, such a crime brought the sentence of death, but the reigning emperor was not content with that and wanted to execute the culprit's whole household. This was the severest punishment available in any dynasty. The supreme judge asked the emperor what punishment the emperor could inflict on a traitor, if the severest penalty was imposed on a mere thief. Forced to reflect on the matter, the emperor conceded the point. Good. The minister could tell West Empress Dowager the story when he saw her again.

But the next time he was summoned to the presence of West Empress Dowager, she gave him no chance to speak but berated him in a diatribe that went on until she felt tired and bade him to go. In her view, the guards' offense was in resisting the order of the empress dowagers, and that merited the death penalty. Indeed, by obstructing Young Eunuch Li, the guards had obstructed the fulfillment of an order from West Empress Dowager. But there was no law against that. The minister sentenced the guards to be banished from the capital; but West Empress Dowager was not satisfied. The minister had to delay the judgment of the case.

Now, another surprising event took place. An intruder had been found wandering near to West Empress Dowager's quarters. A middle-aged man. A grave breach of security. What if this stranger were an assassin? He was detained in the Judicial Ministry's jail. He looked simple-minded. Not much use to try to torture a confession out of him. How could they find out what had happened? A Judicial Ministry official went to his cell and treated him as a guest, offering him food and drink, and then talked with him as if they were old friends. The simpleton said that a eunuch who lived next door to him had taken him into that big place and left him to roam around by himself. The minister reported this to Yixin. Yixin ordered him to get to the bottom of it; this was a strange event and could not be left unexplored. What next? The eunuch was identified and taken into custody and questioned. After a bit of the customary persuasion, he confessed everything: young Eunuch Li had persuaded him to bring in his neighbor, to give the impression that the gate guards habitually neglected their duties. Now, Eunuch Li was hauled in. The Judicial Ministry's verdict was to expel the guards from their post, to exile the eunuchs and to hang the retarded man.

When this was reported to West Empress Dowager, she insisted that the guards be punished more severely. The Eight Saints researched the relevant articles in the law books and copied them down, delivering them to West Empress Dowager. She was unable to insist then on the death sentence; but she still wanted a stricter penalty. The guards were exiled to a remote province in the cold north. This became known publicly and many critique officials thought it not fair. Reports came in. One report reasoned, "What is this case about? The premise of this case is not that the guards may not ask eunuchs to show that they have written permission to exit. The premise is that the guards should perform their jobs properly in the Forbidden City. Now, it appears that the guards should not ask to see such a note from the eunuchs. As a result, a mentally handicapped man was brought in by a eunuch and no guard dared to stop him. If this is the standard of security that the verdict is intended to communicate, then why station guards at the gates? To the eunuchs, it seems we have no guards at all, though guards do stand there. How can the guards keep the Forbidden City safe? The eunuchs should be disciplined. The punishment of exile is generally reserved for a real crime. If the guards received such a sentence for doing their duty, what will people say when they read the verdict? This Critique Official thinks that the Judicial Ministry has erred; this cannot have been the intention of Empress Dowagers. This Critique Official begs that Empress Dowagers correct this mistake, so that people know that they are always fair and just." The verdict was overturned, and the guards were only dismissed from their posts.

CHAPTER 32

Zaizhen, son of Yixin, had become quite a dandy. Before the demise of Emperor Tongzhi, he had had to go into the Forbidden City to study together with the emperor. Now Emperor Tongzhi was gone and Zaizhen was relieved of that duty. Now, he was free to while away his days in the teahouse, in the restaurant, in the theater, even in the whorehouse. He had a few concubines but he had set them up in separate households, away from his main residence (which was his father's, not really his). In old China, many generations lived together. Zaizhen didn't dare to bring his concubines into his father's residence, because he had not bothered to get his father's consent to those arrangements. He therefore bought or rented a house for each of them. Some of the concubines had children with him; Yixin disowned them as his grandchildren. What a complication that would be! If Yixin recognized them, honorary titles would have to be conferred on the males and they would have to be accorded all sorts of other privileges. If not, they could expect nothing.

One of Zaizhen's concubines had been the wife of a duke. She was known as Lady Kui. Duke Kui was a spineless sap. Lady Kui ruled their household. She controlled everything. The duke lived a life of idleness and, mostly, tried to stay out of his wife's way. Lady Kui was young and beautiful; she liked to promenade in public places, mixing with the throngs and enjoying the admiring gaze of young men. One market day there was a gathering in the square before a temple. Lady Kui joined the crowd, attended by her maid. After worshipping the Buddha in the temple, she strolled among the vendors to peruse their goods. The vendors carried their wares in baskets or boxes; some would spread out their goods on a piece of cloth on the ground. Lady Kui, feeling weary at noontime, went into a teahouse for a snack. While she was sitting there sipping tea, a young man came in with an entourage of servants. Handsome. In his early twenties, and apparently born with a silver spoon in the mouth. He sat at a table, sweeping his eyes across all the female faces until his gaze froze on the visage of Lady Kui. She coyly averted her face to avoid his stare.

"Your Ladyship." Suddenly, she heard herself accosted. She turned to see a servant smiling and bowing to her. "His Esquire (indicating his master, the young man) invites Your Ladyship to that table."

Lady Kui was surprised, and resented the impudence. "I am not acquainted with His Esquire." She said it with scorn, and turned away once more.

After a while, the young man left, with his servants. But his image still lingered in Lady Kui's mind's eye. When the waiter came to replenish her teapot with boiled water, she asked about him. "Does Your Ladyship mean His Esquire? Everyone knows Esquire Zaizhen."

"The son of Prince Yixin?" Lady Kui wanted to make sure.

"None other." The waiter smiled his reply. Now that, Lady Kui thought, that was the man a woman should marry. She despised her husband; he was a useless man in every sense of the word. Although he was a duke, he lacked the power and wealth one might hope would go with that title; in fact, one would hope for more from even a marquis, an earl, a viscount or a baron.

When she stepped out of the teahouse, the servant who had addressed her earlier stepped forth, saying, "His Esquire has left a coach here to take Your Ladyship home." When she declined, the servant slung himself down on his knees and kowtowed before her, blocking her way. The servant begged, "Have mercy on me, Your Ladyship. If Your Ladyship won't ride home in the coach, His Esquire will fire me. I have a family of five to feed. So have pity on me, Your Lady-ship." He kept kowtowing until she conceded. Lady Kui had a tender heart; she didn't want his family to suffer.

But she asked, "Do you know where I live?"

"Oh yes," the servant replied. "Your Ladyship lives in Duke Kui's residence."

So they know all about me, she thought. The coachman was holding the door open for her. The servant crawled on the ground before the coach door, to serve as a stepping-stone. Lady Kui duly lofted herself into the coach, her tiny foot lightly digging into the man's spine. Her maid followed. The coachman shut the door. The servant rode with the coachman, up front. The coach rumbled forward. Lady Kui sat back comfortably and closed her eyes. The maid perched at her side, only half sitting on the seat: as a rule, a maid would never have the temerity to sit with her mistress. But she could not stand up in the coach, either. This unrestful position, then, was the posture adopted by inferiors when occasion required them to be seated.

When Lady Kui felt the coach come to a halt, she opened her eyes. Hm. Not the house of Kui. The servant came to open the door, and Lady Kui asked, "What place is this?" The servant replied, "Your Ladyship will know, when Your Lady-ship goes in." She was curious and in she went, dutifully followed by her maid. A good chaperone? Esquire Zaizhen was there to welcome her. This rather confi-dent courtship was hard to refuse, and she stayed the night. Thus, Lady Kui became a concubine of Esquire Zaizhen.

Duke Kui was waiting for his wife to come home. He waited all day, and he waited all night, but to no avail. This had never happened before. His wife must have run into trouble. The next day, he reported to the local yamen that his wife was missing. The wife of a duke was not like the wife of an ordinary person. The local yamen made it a missing-person case. But for three months, no trace of his wife's whereabouts could be detected. She had evaporated like a wisp of steam.

Just as Duke Kui was about to give her up for dead, she was spotted in a theater — together with Esquire Zaizhen. They were noticed by a patrol officer. He didn't dare to report to the yamen; he didn't want an enemy like Esquire Zaizhen. But it was not good for his yamen if the missing-person case could not be closed, either, so he went to see Zaizhen in person. Of course, he could not expect to be received by the Esquire himself. The head servant received him. He discussed with the head servant how to close the case without making a ripple into a tsunami.

Now Esquire Zaizhen was afraid — he would get into quite a mess if his father learned of this. He suggested to Lady Kui that she should go home to settle things with her husband, and then come back.

"Do you want to get rid of me?" She flared up. "Not so easy."

"Oh no, no, no, no. I need you. You know that," Zaizhen reassured her.

In her heart, Lady Kui agreed that she could not continue to hide like a criminal. They made a plan. Zaizhen promised to secure a good position for her husband as a condition of coming to a settlement. He gave her 1,000 taels in a silver note. Lady Kui appeared at her former home, the next day, to the surprise of everyone in Duke Kui's residence. She seemed suddenly descended from heaven, she seemed to materialize out of the mists like a fairy godmother. Lady Kui went to the private chambers and Duke Kui followed in, and shut the door behind him.

"Where have you been all this time? I have been so worried," said the husband.

"It's all your fault. I was confined by someone," the wife complained.

"And who is that someone?" Who would be so bold as to kidnap a duke's wife?

"Someone powerful. We are no match for him."

"Tell me who he is, first, and then we will decide what we can or cannot do."

"Esquire Zaizhen!"

"Son of Prince Yixin?"

"Who else could pull off such a feat?"

"Why did he do it?" Discretion is the better part of valor; feigned ignorance may be the better part of survival.

"Now tell me," his wife interjected. "Do you want to go to jail, or you want to be a mandarin?"

"I am not sure I understand." The husband understood quite well; but he was now facing rather unpleasant truths, and it takes a while to swallow such news. He was not a man accustomed to bold decisions and quick action.

"He knows everything you have done, how you have bent the law. He has plenty of evidence."

"What does he want?" Blackmail always has a purpose.

"He wants me. If you let him have me, he'll get you a position. Here is a 1,000-tael note to show his good faith." Pretty persuasive. "If you refuse to oblige, he is prepared to give the evidence to the Manchu Clan Affairs Administration."

Duke Kui had understood all along that his wife had never loved him; now, during the three months she had been with Esquire Zaizhen, they must surely have lived as man and wife. He couldn't really take back a wife that had strayed, whoever her suitor might be. Under the circumstances, the best course was to settle; let her go, and let Zaizhen pay him off. Lady Kui knew her husband well; she knew he would not find the courage or mental acuity to withstand the pressure. She hadn't even told Esquire Zaizhen of any illegal activities. No need. Duke Kui sent a report to the yamen, withdrawing his case, for the reason that his wife had turned up unharmed.

Meanwhile, Duke Kui had a younger brother (whom we will call Brother Kui). He was a gambler and a villain, capable of anything. A gambler always needs money. Brother Kui often went to see Duke Kui; the duke was an easy touch. When the duke didn't have any cash on hand, Brother Kui would take whatever he could lay his hands on and sell the goods. A real headache.

Brother Kui would seize every chance to pick up money. Finding out what had happened to Lady Kui, he spied a grand opportunity to squeeze a considerable sum out of Esquire Zaizhen. He meditated on the details. He would need the cooperation of his elder brother, the duke. But Duke Kui was far too timid to entertain any such talk. He wouldn't even listen. He could not afford to offend Prince Yixin (even to settle a score with the Prince's son). Brother Kui's scheme could not work without Duke Kui, the concerned party. Then he got another idea.

Why not twist Lady Kui's arm? But he didn't know where she was living at the time. He hung around in the public places where the lady had been a frequent visitor, and eventually his quest was achieved. He found her in a theater, one day; but he didn't go up to her then and there. He followed her and learned where she was living. Then he found a day when she was at home and when Esquire Zaizhen was not. He knocked at the door and said to the guard who opened it that he was the brother of Lady Kui, with an important matter to discuss. The guard didn't suspect anything, and let him in. Lady Kui was very much surprised to see her erstwhile brother-in-law. They chatted briefly; then he asked to borrow some money. His wife was sick and needed to see a doctor. Tender as she was, Lady Kui gave him a small loan.

From that day on, Brother Kui would visit Lady Kui quite often, and every time he left with a bit of money. Lady Kui's patience came to an end, however. This could not go on. One day when Brother Kui came again, the guard wouldn't let him in. He tried to force his way in, but the guard threw him out. He lay on the ground, crying, "Help! Help! They're killing me!" What if the patrol officers had heard him? Trouble all around. Two more guards rushed out of the house and took him inside. They didn't let him see Lady Kui, but tied him up in the stable and gave him a good thrashing. Then they let him go.

Brother Kui felt quite insulted. What treatment! Now he wanted revenge as well as more money. First, he went to see a doctor and asked him to write him a certificate about his wounds, for possible future use. Then he asked someone to write a statement for him about everything that had occurred so far, including what had happened to Lady Kui. He took the statement to Yixin's residence. The butler received him and accepted his statement. When Brother Kui left, the butler read the statement and was frightened. This was too incendiary to pass on to Yixin. He sent it to Esquire Zaizhen, who just put it aside and forgot about it.

Brother Kui waited for two weeks. When he realized that no one was coming to settle up with him, he had another statement written and took it to the head of the Manchu Clan Affairs Administration. The head gave the statement to Yixin. Ah. Now the fat was in the fire. Yixin ordered his butler to find his son. Esquire Zaizhen had to go. He knelt before his father, who enumerated his wrongdoings. Then Yixin told the butler to take his son to the Manchu Clan Affairs Administration. He would punish his son according to the law, never mind family sentiment. Really? And have a black mark entered into the official records, documenting the son's transgressions? The butler begged Yixin to spare his son this time. But Yixin insisted. All the household came to beseech him, on their knees, even Esquire Zaizhen's wife, Yixin's daughter-in-law. She should have been more upset than anyone, jealous, and happy to see her husband be punished. But she was a kind woman and a doting wife. Yixin softened a little. The butler, who had worked in the family since Yixin was young, seized the opportunity and said that if the son were taken to the Manchu Clan Affairs Administration, West Empress Dowager would surely come to hear of it. Why anger her? Endanger her health? She was not completely recovered yet. Then he suggested that the son could be confined in his study until he mended his ways. Yixin agreed, but added that the windows must be secured from outside and the door locked from outside too.

The butler often went to see the son, who asked him to let him out. The butler would not comply, for fear that Yixin would take stricter measures. He advised the son to send Lady Kui back home to her husband, so that perhaps his father might go easy on him. The son was eager to get out. He wrote a letter to Lady Kui without a second thought. He said that it would be better for both of them if she should return to her husband for the time being, and he swore that when he got out she could come back to him. They would find some secluded place to live together forever and ever. The butler took the letter to Lady Kui and advised her to abide by Esquire Zaizhen's request, adding that Prince Yixin would never agree to their relationship, since it involved Duke Kui.

Now Lady Kui found herself between the devil and the deep blue sea. How could she go back to her husband, since they had made a settlement? She could never do that. She had nowhere to go except to the god of hell. The next day, the maid entered her bedroom and let out a shriek. Guards and servants rushed in. Lady Kui had hanged herself. They reported it to the butler, who didn't dare to let Yixin know. Better to settle it secretly. He went to see Duke Kui and told him that his wife had hanged herself. Duke Kui was stunned, but a while later he said, "It's best for everybody." They negotiated. The butler promised to make (and pay for) all the arrangements for Lady Kui's funeral and burial. Then he gave the husband 10,000 taels of silver for his discretion. Not complete discretion, however, as a close friend later joked with Kui that he had sold his wife's body, for 10,000 taels.

CHAPTER 33

Since the treaty between Russia and China had been signed, Yili Town would soon be returned to Qing Government. The secretaries were considering whom to tap to take over the town and guard it. General Governor Zuo recommended General Zhang, who was already in Xinjiang Province.

General Zhang was born in Zhejiang Province. He was often seen in casinos, where he had earned a living in his youth. Once, an elder relative scolded him for his idleness and even boxed his ears in public. Humiliated, he left home and went to Henan Province where his uncle-in-law was the mayor of Gushi Town. He lived in the mayor's yamen and had some pocket money, too. He was illiterate, having no education at all, but he was tall and good-looking, with a muscular build. The mayor despised him and could find no work that he would entrust to the youth, who therefore idled away his time. He had a cousin, the mayor's daughter, who was nicknamed "Lady-scholar." The cousins had never seen each other.

At that time, Henan Province was one of the areas where the Nian Army was still roaming about. One day, a horrible rumor spread that the Nian Army was on its way to attack the town. A small town had no army for its own defense. People were in a panic. The mayor hastily posted a notice to recruit young men. Three hundred young people came to register, but none among them was a capable leader. The mayor put up another notice, promising that whoever could lead those 300 young men to defeat the Nian Army would marry his daughter. No one dared volunteer, despite the tantalizing prospect: the Nian Army outnumbered them tenfold, twentyfold or even a hundredfold. Someone joked with Zhang that he should try. Ha. Why not? He tore down the notice and went to see his uncle-in-law. Three hundred men were not enough to sit and safeguard the town, he said; better to ambush the Nian Army. Reasonable. Feasible, even. The mayor agreed. Zhang led the young men out of the town and laid an ambush where the Nian Army as sure to pass. The gates of the town were closed. The townsfolk stood behind the battlements. They would beat drums and wave banners when the combat began, to give the impression that a larger force was ready to come out and join the battle.

The Nian Army reached the town at nightfall. They camped outside, intending to lay siege starting the next day. They expected to make short work of it. But at midnight, Zhang and his young fighters assaulted the camp, and the army, taken completely by surprise, panicked. In the dark, they could not even estimate the number of attackers. They heard the cries of war in every direction, and the drumbeats of approaching reinforcements. Banners were brandished in the wind. By a stroke of coincidence, just as the battle was at its peak, a government army detachment came to the rescue. The Nian Army fled. So Zhang was offered a title, and he married his lovely and talented cousin. Then he was made the mayor of the town. No one knew that he could not read and write because his wife read all the documents and wrote all the reports for him. He was gradu-ally promoted to be the Financial Official of Henan Province. His illiteracy came out in the open, at last: Critique Official Liu revealed the fact to West Empress Dowager in a report. There was a rule that illiterate people could not be officials — but they could be made officers. So he became a general. General Zhang was ashamed of his illiteracy and asked his wife to tutor him. After a few years, he was no longer illiterate. Quite an achievement. When he learned that Critique Official Liu had committed serious offenses and had been deprived of his title; with no title and no post, of course, he lived now in destitution. General Zhang wrote him a letter, with a silver note of 1,000 taels enclosed. But he used a seal on the letter, bearing the word "Illiterate." The empress dowagers were delighted to hear the story and placed him in charge of Yili Town.

* * *

There were more policemen in Henan Province than in any other province, because there were more robbers and thieves in Henan. There had been a drought there and people were starving. Who is willing to be starved to death? Disasters, natural or not, always engender outlaws. Nothing amazing in that. More amazing was that some policemen had two personalities, transmuting into thieves at night. Many thefts and burglaries, therefore, could never be solved. But they were careful not to do such things in their own jurisdiction.

Once, a rich merchant was robbed on the way home, and he reported it to the yamen of the town where he lived. As a matter of course, the case had no outcome. The merchant hired a private investigator. The chief suspect turned out to be a policeman called Hu, who lived in Zhenping Town, quite a distance away. The merchant filed a lawsuit against Policeman Hu in the governor's yamen. The governor told the judicial official to detain Policeman Hu. An order of arrest came into the hands of the mayor of Zhenping Town. Mayor Ma was a scholar, having passed three government tests, but he was a bookworm, and hardly knew how to try a case. In fact, few mayors were familiar with law. Every yamen relied on advisors, particularly a financial advisor and a judicial advisor.

Mayor Ma wanted to issue a warrant to take Policeman Hu into custody, but first he consulted with the judicial advisor, by the name of Mao, who said that he didn't know where Policeman Hu was at present. Mayor Ma wondered, "How can that be? Is he not on duty in this yamen?" Mayor Ma had been assigned this post only a few days before. He knew nothing about the town. Judicial

Advisor Mao began to clue him in: Policeman Hu had probably registered there as a policeman but was never on duty. He might even be a gangster. Judicial Advisor Mao asked to be allowed time to do a little research before proceeding. He went to look through some documents, and then he went back into his own office and consulted his notebook. Hu had become a policeman on the recommendation of another policeman called Liu. Judicial Advisor Mao sent for Policeman Liu.

When Liu came into his room, Mao said to him, "Now, you are in hot water."

What kind of hot water?

"You recommended Policeman Hu. The governor wants Mayor Ma to bring him in, for robbery." This was really going to be difficult. Hu was the leader of the gangsters in this town. Liu might be able to bring in Hu, but his followers would promptly assassinate Liu. But he could not turn down the assignment, either. He went to see his false friend, the false policeman, real gang leader Hu. Policeman Liu queried him sternly and let him see the warrant. Hu took Policeman Liu to a back room and they laid out a scheme. Hu sent a large sum of money to Judicial Advisor Mao, to probe his reaction. If Mao declined, he would think of some other way; and if Mao accepted, everything would be easy. Mao took the bribe.

A new prisoner was brought into the jail, a boy of fifteen. Policeman Liu asked him, "Who are you?"

"Wang," said the boy.

Policeman Liu slapped him on the cheek. "Now, who are you?"

"Hu." The boy was on the verge of crying.

"So, remember, you are Hu, now," Policeman Liu warned him. The boy had worked in the kitchen of the ringleader Hu. He was brought before Hu and Policeman Liu. He was told that Policeman Liu would take him to jail.

"Why? I didn't do anything wrong!" the boy protested, timidly.

"No. You didn't do anything wrong," Hu confirmed. But, he said, he wanted to make a deal with him — or his parents would be killed. He had to accept. He was put into prison under the name of Hu. They assured him that he would not be sentenced to death, that he would only be imprisoned for a few years; and after he was released, he could get a wife and a large sum of money, enough to live comfortably for the rest of his life. The boy believed them, and accepted the conditions.

To show that they would keep their promise, Policeman Liu treated the boy nicely. When Judicial Advisor Mao found out that it was a youth who had been substituted for the ringleader Hu, he was afraid that Mayor Ma would find out — he was really just a boy. Policeman Liu suggested that they should persuade Mayor Ma to interrogate the boy early in the morning, when it was still dark, so that he would not find out. They could light only a couple of candles, and tell the mayor that Hu was a runt. So Mao went to see the mayor and reported to him that the dubious policeman Hu was now under arrest. The mayor was delighted to hear it, because any case sent over by the governor had to be dealt with promptly. If he couldn't get the man the governor wanted, he would lose his post. Judicial Advisor Mao added that, as Hu was a ringleader, it was best to question him secretly. The mayor agreed. The room for the interrogation was dim. Mayor Ma couldn't see clearly, but he didn't care.

"Your name?" The mayor asked the boy.

"Hu."

"How old are you?" That was the routine question.

"Twenty-one." The prisoner didn't look like a twenty-one year old. The mayor glanced at Judicial Advisor Mao, who was standing at his side. Mao whispered into his ear that the prisoner's growth was stunted. Mayor Ma believed him; he didn't even stop to wonder how a weakling could be a gangsters' ringleader. (And if he had asked, Mao was prepared to reply that the prisoner was proficient in the martial arts. The mayor was hardly likely to ask the suspect to perform, as proof.) Then the boy recited the statement of confession, which had been prepared for him: that his parents were old and starving and he had no other means to support them, that he had robbed a wealthy man so that he could buy food for them.

"Did you do it alone?" asked the Mayor. This question was not in the prepared statement. Hm. The boy didn't know how to reply, and hesitated. When the mayor pressed, the boy told the truth — that there had been four other people with him. Certainly, the four men had committed the robbery. The boy had stood on the side, looking after their things. They were gangsters, under Hu. They had gone through the village where the boy was living with his parents. They were always seeking young boys who could be trained as fresh recruits. They talked to the boy's parents, who feared for their lives; they were in no position to say "no" to such people. The gangsters had given the parents fifteen taels and taken the boy from them. On the way back to their town, they had committed the crime in question.

The mayor wanted to have the four gangsters hauled in, too. Judicial Advisor Mao observed that the crime hadn't happened in his jurisdiction, and that no one had requested that he arrest them. His assignment from the governor was to get Hu, and to send Hu to the higher government. Nothing more. (There was a secret motto, in officialdom: do exactly as ordered, and no more, because in going one step too far, you might very well step on the wrong toes.)

Therefore, the mayor gave his verdict, which was the death sentence. Hu was a ringleader and had committed many crimes. The mayor duly wrote a report and packed the prisoner off to the judicial official at the province level, who routinely upheld the verdict — since the boy was now steadfast in adhering to the text of his confession. He didn't even know that he had been given the death penalty. That little fact had been kept from him, lest he start making trouble. And when all the documents were delivered to the Judicial Ministry, the minister approved the death sentence.

When a confirmation of the approval arrived in the governor's yamen, a new official was ordered to oversee the execution of the boy prisoner. By now, the boy realized that he was about to be beheaded, and he started screaming that it was all a mistake, they had the wrong man, this wasn't right, he'd only been saying what they told him to say. . . The new official was shocked, and he reported to the judicial official; but the latter insisted on immediate execution. The new official was not about to take any chances: the penalty for executing the wrong person was severe, if it was ever found out. So he took the prisoner to the governor's yamen and reported to the governor, who agreed that this sounded like a very serious affair. They interrogated the prisoner again. Now, the boy told everything.

The governor had a good idea: better get the boy's father in to verify the story. But the governor knew that if the real Hu got wind of this, he would send someone to kill the father; for security, he dispatched one of his own guards to call on the mayor of the town in the jurisdiction where the father's village was found. The mayor went to the village himself, and asked around — who was the father, Wang? He tracked him down, and took him back to the town. The father brought with him the 15 taels of silver, as evidence. From the mayor's place, the father was escorted to the governor's yamen by 20 soldiers. They reckoned that when father met son, everything should be clear; but the judicial official persuaded the governor to uphold the original verdict because, as he said, the boy must have been an accomplice at least, and should be executed too. They never mentioned Hu, the main suspect, again. More reports to the imperial city. Official Zhao in the Judicial Ministry sensed that something was wrong, and insisted that the case should be judged under his own eyes. All concerned parties were brought to the capital. After cross-examination, the details of the case became clear. The real Hu was apprehended and executed. Policeman Liu was jailed for obstruction of the law. Judicial Advisor Mao was expelled. Mayor Ma was removed from office and banished to a remote province. The governor and the judicial official were both dismissed. And the boy was declared "not guilty," and went home with his father.

CHAPTER 34

East Empress Dowager was always honest and candid with West Empress Dowager, as she thought that they were in the same boat. West Empress Dowager, for her part, always felt a twinge of pique whenever she saw East Empress Dowager, because East Empress Dowager, as the former queen, was deemed to be a little higher in status than West Empress Dowager, the former imperial concubine. If East Empress Dowager said "no," she could not say "yes"; and vice versa. This had happened, for instance, when East Empress Dowager wanted to execute Little An, her favorite eunuch.

One day East Empress Dowager found a folded piece of paper at the bottom of her jewelry box. She had forgotten what it was, so she picked it up and unfolded it. Ha! Emperor Xianfeng's will, empowering her to execute West Empress Dowager, should she do anything to imperil the empire. A lot of water over the dam, since the emperor had died. West Empress Dowager hadn't done anything wrong, East Empress Dowager thought. What's the use of keeping such a document any longer? How nice it would be to show this will to West Empress Dowager and then burn it, right before her eyes; how much West Empress Dowager would appreciate such a gesture. Perhaps it would help make her kind and nice to other people, as she was to her.

East Empress Dowager pocketed the fateful document and went to see her counterpart. After a suitable little speech, she presented the will, held it up to the candle, and let it catch. What a touching display of trust. West Empress Dowager was certainly impressed by this heartfelt gesture, or, at least, by the naivety it expressed. She thanked East Empress Dowager profusely for her good-will, and kept her resentment to herself. Why would she resent this? Because it showed that her husband had distrusted her? Because she was embarrassed by East Empress Dowager's generosity? No. In her opinion, this was humiliating. She always tried to forget the difference in status between East Empress

Dowager and herself, but the notion that East Empress Dowager had been given such a document reminded her of it rather forcefully. And she was not a person who forgave easily.

On April 7, 1881, East Empress Dowager suddenly fell ill. It did not seem very grave, at first, when Doctor Xi went to examine her. Just a cold. After taking some medicine, East Empress Dowager felt better and went for a stroll in the garden. While she was leaning on the railings to watch the goldfish in the pond, a eunuch came up, bearing a small container. West Empress Dowager had sent her a snack, prepared just for her. She opened the container and saw a rosy-colored steamed sweet cake. Her favorite! It looked so inviting that she immediately helped herself to a little bite. But despite the fresh air and pleasant surroundings, she soon felt an acute headache. Her limbs cramped up. Her head eunuch went to report to West Empress Dowager, but she was napping and Head Eunuch Li said that she could not be disturbed. By the time the doctors were summoned, East Empress Dowager was already dead. She died at the age of 45. The two empress dowagers had worked together for twenty years, from 1861 to 1881.

According to the rules, the demise of an empress dowager should be announced immediately and her next-of-kin notified. But her death was publicized only the next day. West Empress Dowager had been sick for a long time so when the message went out that Empress Dowager had died, the courtiers all thought that it was she. When it was made clear that it was East Empress Dowager who had died, the courtiers were stunned. East Empress Dowager had always enjoyed a hale constitution. Rumors spread far and wide. Had West Empress Dowager poisoned her? During their long and mutually beneficial cooperation, there had been a few events that might have set the two empress dowagers at odds. For one, East Empress Dowager had insisted on having Little An executed. And later, when West Empress Dowager's new favorite Eunuch Li was having some fun, wrestling with other eunuchs, and East Empress Dowager passed by on a sedan chair, Li had ignored her; East Empress Dowager found this disrespectful, and wanted to have Li beaten — but West Empress Dowager had disagreed, and they quarreled. Furthermore, West Empress Dowager liked to watch operas and she had a favorite actor who often came to visit her in her private living quarters. It was said that East Empress Dowager once caught West Empress Dowager lying with the actor on her bed: highly indecent behavior for an empress dowager. East Empress Dowager criticized her, and West Empress Dowager had to express her regret and vow that she would never do such things again. She even had the actor put to death. That surely rankled still. And most recently, there was the episode with the shocking document that East Empress Dowager had produced. If East Empress Dowager had told any others about that will, West Empress Dowager would be greatly embarrassed. She already felt humble before East Empress Dowager. She could no longer bear such humiliation.

And then, how many unknown, unsuspected irritations had added up over the years? A palace is always full of secrets.

CHAPTER 35

Esquire Yang lived in Yuhang Town of Zhejiang Province. He had passed two government tests and had been given an honorary title; but he didn't apply for an official post. His family was rich. He enjoyed studying herbal medicine, and sometimes he served the neighborhood as a doctor. Across the street from his house there was a tofu shop, run by a husband and wife who made bean curd. The wife was beautiful and had the nickname, Cabbage. Fair and juicy. Esquire Yang and the husband and wife were well acquainted, since they were close neighbors. Liu, the mayor of the town, had an indolent son whose only interests were women and fun. No studying for him; no serious endeavor at all. But he was young and handsome. He devoted most of his creative energies to chasing women, or visiting with prostitutes.

One day the son happened to pass the tofu shop and saw the wife, Cabbage, who was selling bean curd to the customers. He halted before the shop, fixing his eyes on her face. When other customers left, he was still there, spellbound

"How can I help you, Customer?"

Roused from his daydreaming, he stepped forward, pretending that he wanted to buy from her. But instead of saying how much bean curd he wanted, he introduced himself, saying, "I am the mayor's son." Often, when people heard that, they would stand in awe of him. That was just the effect he wished.
Cabbage was awed, too. She apologized for not being aware of his identity and then she begged to know how much bean curd he wanted.

But he only asked, flirtingly, "How old are you, little Beauty?" Cabbage lowered her eyes and coyly smiled. The son asked, "Are you married?"

Cabbage replied this time, "Yes, I am." She hoped that he would leave, now.

"If you marry me, you'll live comfortably and happily all your life." He knew that that was impossible. His Mayor father would never assent to his marrying with the left hand. He only said it as a temptation. Anything, to get close to her.

Then the husband showed up, and he had to leave.

From then on, the mayor's son often came to the shop, but he never bought any bean curd. When the husband was out, he flirted with Cabbage, teased her, importuned her, even threatened her. Some women are vain by nature. The son would bring her cosmetics and expensive clothes. At first Cabbage refused to accept anything from him, but he would just leave the things behind in the shop and scurry away. Cabbage had to hide these gifts that were forced upon her, making sure her husband would not see them. By degrees, she came to accept the attentions of this handsome young man, the son of the mayor. And she gave in to his pleadings.

Now, the son didn't keep their adultery a secret, as he should have done. He didn't care if people knew it. Who dared to offend the son of the mayor? The husband soon came to hear of it, but what could he do? He could not sue the son in his father's yamen. The son, however, was jealous of the husband and wished to get rid of him.

One chilly day, the husband was taken ill. Cabbage went across the street to Esquire Yang and asked him to come over to see her husband. Esquire Yang followed her into the bedroom in the back of the shop. Yang considered that the husband must have simply caught cold, and he prescribed some medical herbs and minerals, and left. Cabbage got ready to go and buy the medicine, but suddenly the son arrived. Hearing that the husband was sick and that she was on her way to the drugstore, he offered to go in her stead. Off he went, and duly purchased all the medicines on the prescription. Then, as if suddenly remembering an errand of his own, he asked for a small packet of arsenic, "to poison the mice in my house." Back at the tofu shop, he gave all the small packets to Cabbage, and quickly departed. At first, Cabbage thought there was one extra packet, but she decided that she must have misremembered and that all these powders must have been on Yang's list. She put everything together in a pot to simmer. When the medicine was ready, she poured it into a bowl; after it cooled a little, she helped her husband to sip it. He drank it down. Before long, the husband cried out in pain and began to thrash around on the bed. Cabbage did not know what to do; she just watched. In the next moment, blood came out from his nose and mouth. Poisoned! Cabbage suddenly remembered the extra little packet, but it was too late to mention it now. In such a case, the wife must report to the government. A coroner came, and detected a trace of arsenic. He reported it to the mayor. The wife was arrested as a suspect.

The mayor's son hadn't thought of that. Things were getting out of hand. He went to the jail to visit Cabbage, who blamed him.

"It's no use to blame me," he said. "There is no evidence against me. I have come to rescue you."

"How?"

"You are only a suspect. If you can name someone else as the one who poisoned your husband, you will be released." The son had become quite attached to Cabbage and wanted to save her life. He knew that they must find a scapegoat, or the case couldn't be closed.

"But there isn't anyone," she sobbed.

"Who wrote you the prescription?"

"Esquire Yang." The son knew him — in fact, he hated him, for his learning. The mayor often drew unflattering comparisons between his son and Yang, and scolded him for neglecting his studies. So the son said, "Yang's the one."

"No, he's a nice man. I can't involve him in this."

"Then, you will die." The law was very simple: Anyone who kills must be executed.

"Please, do it for me," said the son. "When you are released, we'll go some-where else and live together. Besides, Yang won't be executed — he has an honorary title. At the worst, he will be deprived of his title. This time." Cabbage knew nothing of the law, and believed him. By this time, she had begun to love this man, and she was eager to believe in his vision of a life together. Especially now that her husband had died.

A few days later, Cabbage was brought before the mayor for questioning. "How did you murder your husband?"

"I didn't murder my husband. There's been a mistake," she replied, on her knees.

"If you didn't do it, then who did?" The mayor sounded fierce.

"I don't know. Not me." Her voice was so low that the mayor barely heard her. He ordered the jailors to slap her face twenty times. Cabbage cried, "No. I have something to say." So the mayor bid the jailors to wait.

"When my husband became sick, I asked Esquire Yang to make a diagnosis. And he wrote the prescription."

"Where is the prescription now?"

"At home." The mayor ordered Cabbage to be put back in the cell, and he sent one of his men to her home. The shop was closed up and the door had been locked up by the police. The mayor's agent man found a policeman to open the door for him. He went in and searched the place and found the prescription on the table in the bedroom.

At the second interrogation, the mayor asked, "Arsenic is not on the prescription. Why did you say Yang poisoned your husband?"

"He wouldn't have written 'arsenic' on the prescription, but he got the medicine for me from the drugstore." She clung to the belief that Esquire Yang would not be executed, even if he were convicted in this sordid tale, because he had an honorary title. Is a title a strong enough amulet to defy death? She had misgivings, but she did not see that she had much choice. Human beings are selfish. To save their own skin, they are usually quite capable of exposing the skin of others.

Esquire Yang didn't suspect a thing when the police came to his house. He thought that some mistake had been made and he would soon be back home after some explanation. But when Yang was taken into the yamen, the mayor didn't ask him any questions. He just told Yang to write a statement, confessing to what Cabbage had said. Of course, Yang would not comply. The mayor told the jailors to bring Cabbage in as a witness. He made her repeat what she had said: not one word more, not one word less.

Yang shouted, "Why are you framing me?"

But Cabbage was whisked back to her cell as soon as she finished speaking. Yang was tortured. He would not admit that he was guilty of the crime. He was tortured more than once; his knees were broken. He had to write and sign the statement of confession in the hope that when he appealed to the higher government this wrong would be righted. He and Cabbage were sentenced to death and the mayor sent a report for approval by the Judicial Ministry, stating that the motive behind the crime was that the husband had found out their adultery. Yang appealed. The higher government sustained the original verdict: the mayor had bribed them from time to time. Yang then appealed to the governor, who did the same, for the same reason.

Yang had an older sister. The sister had been a wet nurse in the household of a prince. When the bad news reached her, she went to beg her former mistress, the wife of the prince, to spare the life of her brother. The wife spoke to the prince about it. The prince told the elder sister to file in an appeal with the Judicial Ministry, and in the meantime he undertook to speak with the minister.

The sister got someone to write it up for her, since, like most women in old China, she couldn't read or write. She hid the written statement in the innermost pocket of her clothes and went to the Judicial Ministry yamen. She would have to throw herself on that fateful piece of wood with nails sticking out. She dressed herself in the thickest garments she could find, and set out. When she reached the yamen, she beat the drum at the entrance. Then she shut her eyes and cast herself on the sharp nails, holding her head high so that her face would not be injured. The spikes penetrated her thick clothes and scratched her skin. Some blood oozed out, but other than that, she was fine. Two guards helped her to her feet. Then she took out the appeal from her inner pocket and gave it to a policeman, who took it in to the minister.

After a period of time, the minister summoned the sister in. This meant that he had accepted her appeal. The sister knelt before the minister and said, "My brother is a scholar. He could never kill anyone, not even a hen." The minister kept his own counsel, as he was not yet familiar with the details of the case. He dismissed the sister and ordered all the individuals involved in the case to be brought from the town to the capital, to the Judicial Ministry yamen.

The town was in a far southern province. It took more than a month for the concerned parties to travel the long distance to the capital. When the minister questioned Cabbage, she was consistent with what she had said. The son of the mayor had warned her that if she changed anything in her confession, the consequence would be dire. He hadn't explained how dire; but Cabbage hadn't doubted it. She really liked him and wanted him to live. The minister had a meeting with his consultants. They knew that if Cabbage insisted on what she had confessed, they couldn't change the verdict. They had no reason to do so. They had to find a way out. They thought and thought. Finally, one of the councilors said he had an idea.

In a small room of the Judicial Ministry building stood a square table. Two people sat opposite each other. One was Cabbage and the other was Yang. They had been brought together in this room by the jailors, who told them that the minister was giving them dinner because they would be executed the next day. They were offered this chance to bid an eternal adieu to each other. There were four dishes on the table, and even wine. Yang was in despair; how unfair this all was. He hadn't murdered anybody. Cabbage hung her head low, ashamed of herself for framing Yang. At first, both of them were silent. Neither one cared to speak. To break the awkwardness, Yang began, "Well, Cabbage, let's drink farewell, then. We may meet in the next life."

Cabbage could think of nothing to say, so still she said nothing. She realized now that she had been taken in by the mayor's son. Perhaps he had never loved her at all. But why had he wanted her husband out of the way? "Cabbage," Yang went on, "We will die tomorrow. Can you tell me the truth so that I won't die in ignorance?"

Cabbage thought — what was the use, now, even if she told the truth. They would be executed the next day, all the same. So she made no answer, still hanging her head low.

Yang was a couple of years older than she. They had grown up together in the same neighborhood. They used to play together. Then Yang reached the age to be tutored, and he was generous in transferring his new knowledge to her, teaching her how to read and write. Because her family was not rich, Yang's father would not consent to their marrying; so she was married to the late husband.

"Do you remember when we read the story 'West Chamber' together?"

How could she forget? She recalled many scenes from their childhood and adolescence. She almost buried her chin in her chest.

"Cabbage, speak to me, please. Let me hear your voice once more before I die." Yang was practically begging her. Her tears dripped on her lap.

"Don't cry, Cabbage. Talk to me. We have only tonight to live," Yang said, softly.

Cabbage sobbed out the words, "I'm so sorry."

"No need to say sorry," Yang sighed.

After a while, Cabbage asked bashfully, "Do you hate me?"

"No. Why should I hate you? Everyone will die sooner or later," Yang said philosophically.

"Because I framed you." At last, she had said it.

"So, you did frame me?" Yang said without any surprise. Cabbage nodded.

"Now, tell me the truth, please."

"What's the use, now?"

"At least I should know the truth, before I die."

After further prodding from Yang, Cabbage told him everything. Yang sighed and laughed and began to eat and drink. Presently, a jailor came into their room, holding a stack of paper in his hand. He told Cabbage to sign on the bottom of the last page. Cabbage didn't know what that meant, but she signed anyway. Why should she care what papers she signed? She was about to die. Nothing mattered anymore.

The next day, both of them were brought before the minister. They thought the minister would send them to the execution grounds. But the minister asked Cabbage, "Why didn't you tell the truth in the local government? Or, at least, in the governor's yamen?" Cabbage was confused. She was at a loss to understand what the minister had just asked. She still did not realize the ruse they had used to draw the truth out of her. The minister himself had hidden in the next room, with some of his councilors. They had overheard every word murmured between Yang and Cabbage. And a scribe had written down all that Cabbage had confessed to Yang.

The minister issued an order to fetch the mayor, the mayor's son, and the owner of the drugstore who had sold the arsenic to the son. When the drugstore owner pointed to the mayor's son, not to Yang, as the man who had come to him to buy the arsenic, the son could no longer deny his crime. The verdict was overthrown and the son was executed. The mayor was removed from his office and exiled to a remote province. Cabbage and Yang were proved not guilty, and were released. Yang went back to his home in the southern provinces, with permanently crippled knees.

The case was closed. Many officials in that southern province were demoted or dismissed from their posts altogether because they had misjudged a case and jeopardized two innocent lives. The minister wrote a report to West Empress Dowager. She was interested in the case and curious to see what Cabbage looked like; she summoned Cabbage to her presence. Under ordinary circumstances, only courtiers above a certain rank could be presented to an empress dowager. Cabbage was a special case. After the interview, Cabbage became a nun.

CHAPTER 36

General Governor Zuo finished his task in the northwestern provinces and was summoned to the capital. First, he was given the title of a Prime Minister. Then he was appointed to be a secretary. Every day he went on duty in the office of the Secretarial Bureau. The other secretaries held him in a certain esteem, due to his fame; but he was not a modest man. He boasted constantly of his military victories in the northwestern provinces. By degrees, he lost the respect of his colleagues. They came to wish for his retirement after all, he was already 70, though still in a comparatively good health.

The division of the garrison of the Forbidden City had an infamous reputation for poor discipline and poor battle-readiness. When Zuo had arrived in the capital, he had brought with him a division of his own troops. He offered them to Prince Yihuan, who was in charge of the garrison division, as trainers to drill the weak division. Yihuan took this offer as a show of disdain and declined, of course. Then Secretary Zuo proposed to send his men to repair the dikes of the Yongding River, near the capital. The Secretarial Bureau consented to his proposal.

After the demise of East Empress Dowager, West Empress Dowager had begun to establish her sole and total authority. Governor Li of Zhidi Province had been the Two River General Governor, and he still had some influence in the Yangtze River area. How could she erase his roots there? Better make Zuo the Two River General Governor, because Zuo always opposed whatever Governor Li did. Off Zuo went to the south of the Yangtze River.

The head of the Two River Army Supplies General Bureau was Governor Li's brother-in-law. Li had appointed his family member during his tenure as Two River General Governor. His brother-in-law always showed himself avid for power. He didn't know anything about war, but he bragged that he would be a good general if he ever were given a chance to command an army. Meanwhile, he neglected what duties he had. He let all the defensive devices along the Yangtze River fall into disrepair. When the officers in charge reported the situation, he ignored the report and didn't have them fixed. Upon receiving notification of this, West Empress Dowager had him removed from office.

Governor Zuo's guards were all generals, and all were faithful to him. Once, Zuo sent one of his generals to the financial official, whose position was second in rank under the governor. The financial official felt that his rank was above that of a guard from the governor's yamen, and when the guard failed to show proper respect, he went to complain to Zuo. Zuo told the guard to apologize to the financial official. The financial official was relieved that the governor had saved his face. However, as he was taking his leave, the guards all lined up to give him a farewell salute — and they were all dressed in the uniform of a general, whose rank was higher than that of the financial official. Now, the financial official was really embarrassed. This was a frequently-told joke about Zuo.

* * *

Governor Yan was summoned to the capital. He was a man of integrity, and he never accepted bribes. He did everything by the book. The Internal Revenue Ministry was rife with malpractice and abuse of law, so West Empress Dowager decided to appoint Yan the minister there in the hope that he would be able to instigate some reforms. On the day of the interview, West Empress Dowager told Minister Yan that if he had any problems, he could report directly to her and that she would always support him in his performance of his duties. Minister Yan was grateful for her trust and vowed to do his best to meet her expectations.

Yan's eldest son was an official in the capital. To save the government money, Yan lodged with his son; otherwise the government would be obliged to provide him with his own residence. Minister Yan was well known for his stringency. All the officials in the Internal Revenue Ministry warned each other to be extra careful. The very next day, Yan showed up at his yamen and set about checking all the general ledgers. Usually, a new minister would rest a few days at home after receiving his new appointment. And when he did go to his yamen, he would take time to familiarize himself with everything before really tackling his routine obligations. Not Minister Yan. He sat with his Chinese abacus and started right away to go through all the entries, both revenue and expenditure, to see that they were correct.

There were two offices in the Internal Revenue Ministry. The South Office dealt only with the finances of the Manchu Clan, which was not so significant. The North Office managed all the fiscal business throughout the country. As this was an important branch, the officials working there were from the Manchu Clan. But it was known that officials of the Manchu Clan were not so well versed in math and calculation as officials of the Han Clan; the real work was actually done by clerks, who might be Han Chinese. What was the use of having officials, then? Minister Yan suggested to West Empress Dowager that officials appointed to that office should better be chosen from the Han Clan.

When Minister Yan sent for the head of the North Office and asked him how many taels were in the silver warehouse to that date, he was told that they hadn't counted recently. What an answer! No one would count the taels every day, and no one was expected to. There was a logbook to write down everything coming in and going out, and to record the totals each day. The official's response showed that he had no idea of even his most fundamental duties. Minister Yan sent for the clerk responsible for this recordkeeping — but he was on sick leave. Yan called in an aide of the head official. The aide was responsible for internal revenue. When Minister Yan questioned him on receipts, he presented a stack of revenue books and set them on the table before Yan, stating that everything Yan wanted to know was in them. Did he mean that Minister Yan should look into these books himself, to get the answers he wanted? So far, so bad. Patiently, Yan said, "Just tell me." The aide acknowledged that he did not know how to use an abacus, so he could not do the arithmetic. Yan mildly said, "You are fired," and the aide departed.

The Internal Revenue Ministry had also three warehouses to store silver and other valuables. The Stationery Warehouse held paper, ink bars, brushes, and materials to be used as pigments: minerals, sandalwood, yellow wax, vermilion and green stones to be ground into powder as color material in painting. The Satin Warehouse stored scrolls of satin, silk and brocade which were stocked as rewards for courtiers. Silver, collected from all the provinces, was kept in the Silver Warehouse.

Theft was common, despite the sentinels at each warehouse — especially the silver warehouse. Who could get into the silver warehouse? Apparently, whenever silver came in from the provinces, temporary carriers were hired to carry it into the warehouse. The carriers were stripped naked every time they went in or came out, so that they could not hide silver pieces in their clothing. Where can a naked man hide silver coins? These men practiced with pebbles, at home, until they were skillful enough to stash away a few silver pieces (a piece was worth 10 taels) as they left the warehouse at the end of they day. It was said that the most talented could hold eight pieces at a time. That was eighty taels. And just one tael of silver was worth 1,000 brass coins, while a piece of bean curd cost only a couple of coins in those days.

These warehouses were situated at three different locations. Minister Yan wanted to have a look. He went to the Stationery Warehouse first. The official in charge accompanied him on his rounds. He had intended to match the entries in the logbook with actual goods in storage, but when he stepped inside the gate of the warehouse, he was stunned. It was a complete mess. The floor was covered with a thick layer of colorful dust and scraps. There were specks of minerals and fragments of paper mixed with lint. Yan stopped in his tracks, reluctant to tread on the carpet of goods, but the official went right in, crunching everything under his feet. Yan followed. Scrolls of paper were yellowing and piles of writing materials were tumbling from shelves.

Yan asked, "Has anyone come to inspect here, before?"

"Oh, yes. But they only checked that the windows are secure and the roof doesn't leak."

A mouse scampered by. The official shrugged. Yan turned and left. He didn't have the slightest notion how to get this place cleaned up, and save all the goods that were supposed to be preserved there.

Next he went to the Satin Warehouse, inside of which rows after rows of racks held scrolls of precious fabrics, all smothered with dust. At least it looked better than the Stationery Warehouse. Yan contemplated sending a clerk over to count the scrolls to see whether they matched the numbers in the logbook.

The Silver Warehouse was the last location he visited. He wanted to check the scales there, because he had heard that the weights used on the scales were not at all standard: when silver pieces came in, the warehouse clerks would use heavier weights, so that more taels were needed. If, say, 100 taels were to be logged in, but the weights were heavier than standard, then 100 taels might only weigh 90 taels and so 10 extra would have to be placed on the scales to reach the right weight. And when silver pieces were given out, lighter weights were used, so that only 90 taels might read as 100. Yan had the weights calibrated. They were not standard. He had the weights confiscated and the officials arrested. Quite a few incompetent officials suffered an unexpected career change.

* * *

The critique officials had plenty of material to write about. The style most admired among the average courtiers was the humorous or ironic style. Once, a Manchu nobleman opened a casino. Collecting some gaming debts, he had a gambler beaten to death. The corpse was left exposed for three days and no one dared to bury it. A critique official sent in a report, saying, "It is wholly reasonable and rightful for a nobleman to kill a common gambler; this Critique Official would not have the audacity to protest it. But, thinking of our kind-hearted ancestors who always showed mercy even to birds and animals, this Critique Official can't help feeling that leaving a body exposed for days on the spot where it was killed, pecked by famished vultures, is not what our ancestors would expect of us. This Critique Official begs to have the local government inter the body in a proper manner, so that people will know that Empress Dowager is kind, even to the dead." This tongue-in-cheek report forbore to speak of murder, but it cost the nobleman his title.

Another report named two courtiers, stating that the first one "had no other merits than that he accepts no bribes," and the other courtier "had no other merits than that he does accept bribes." In other words, one courtier was useless, though free from corruption; the second courtier was useless, but could be influenced. The former found himself demoted, and the latter was fired.

Another funny report was a self-criticism from a deputy minister. This deputy minister was known as a man of gallantry. He had been twice sent to the southern provinces as an examiner to supervise the local government test. When the testing was over, the examiners were permitted to relax for a few days before they should report back to the capital. The first time he was in Zhejiang Province, and he rented a pleasure boat on the Fuchun River to do a little sightseeing. There was always a girl or two on that sort of boat to wait on the patrons. On the boat, people usually wore no shoes. In this case, the girl was also barefooted and he could see that her feet were not bound. Many Westerners think that all the women in old China had their feet bound, that is, tightly wrapped in cloths since early infancy to keep them from growing. The binding of feet was prevalent during the Ming Dynasty and the Qing Dynasty (1368 to 1911), although the practice may have originated a little earlier. But only Han girls, in the upper classes, had their feet bound; Manchu girls and the other minorities never did it. Han girls of lower background never did it either, for they had to be able to work and help their families. How could they work with tiny, painful feet? (Some ancient scholars depicted the women standing on their little stumps, swaying like the wands of the weeping willow in a breeze.) Now, this deputy minister was a Manchu and he preferred a woman with natural feet. Besides, girls in the southern provinces were known to be gentle and delicate, while girls in the north were buxom and robust. Many men in the north liked southern girls for a change. The deputy minister was very much taken with the boat girl and wanted to buy her as his concubine. But he could not take the girl with him to the capital, because a courtier performing an imperial errand was expected to focus on what he was assigned to do. Nothing else. Purchasing a girl as a concubine — pursuing his own very personal interests — would be disrespectful to the emperor and would leave an indelible blot on his reputation. He therefore paid the family up front, and told them to bring the girl to his residence in the capital a month later. But the girl was never delivered. He couldn't report it to any yamen, of course. He felt like a fool, cheated out of his money. And he was still lonely.

The second time he was sent south as an examiner, he went to Fujian Province. After the test was over, he detoured to the Fuchun River again, in hopes that he might come across the girl he had paid for. No such luck. However, he met another girl on another pleasure boat. She was tall and fair skinned, with only a smattering of freckles across the bridge of her nose. Love at first sight. He bought her. And this time he took her along, afraid of losing once again. However, he knew that any critique official who found out about this would write a report. And he didn't want to hide his beloved, like stolen merchandise. Better to go ahead and criticize himself, before anyone else did.

His report went like this. "This deputy minister had five brothers, who all died, leaving no sons to carry on their lineage. This deputy minister has only two sons, and two sons are not enough to be adopted by five brothers' families to continue the lineage. Therefore, this deputy minister has bought a girl of 18 on his way back from performing his official duties. This deputy minister being known to be honest and upright, it would not be fair that, when other courtiers have faults, this deputy minister should report on them, yet when this deputy minister has faults himself, he should not report. Thus, this deputy minister begs to be punished accordingly."

West Empress Dowager had never read such a report before, in all her twenty years of rule. She gave it to the secretaries for discussion. One of the secretaries had a grudge against the deputy minister and proposed removing him from his post; others, who had no specific link to him, neither friendly nor unfriendly, agreed. The deputy minister lost his title and his position, but he didn't care a bit; he moved out of the capital to live in a secluded place with his new love. Happy ever after?

* * *

Governor Ding of Sichuan Province had a clean reputation. He never accepted gifts or any money except his salary, which was 11,000 taels of silver annually, less than 1,000 taels a month. All the governors and mayors and other officials employed private advisors to help them handle their affairs. They paid them out of their own pockets. 1,000 taels monthly was really not sufficient for a governor. To eek out his monthly cash flow, he tossed some old clothes into a trunk and sealed it with the mark of the governor. The trunk went to a pawn-shop, for 200 taels. Ordinarily, the owner or the manager would look at the items to see if they were worth the amount of money requested. The pawner and pawnee could bargain. But this trunk was sealed and the owner could not evaluate its contents. He had to trust the governor. The trunk came to the pawnshop toward the end of every month, and the money was repaid at the beginning of every month and the trunk would be taken back. Year in and year out the monthly cycle went on, routinely, until Governor Ding was promoted to another location.

Once, Governor Ding went back to his homeland on a visit. While he was traveling through another province, the governor of that province gave him a 3,000 tael silver note, saying that if Ding didn't deign to accept it, he would be offended. Governor Ding had to accept it; but on his journey back, he went through that province again and returned the 3,000 taels to the governor.

It was not easy to be a good governor or a good mayor. If one's policies were beneficial to the common people, they would certainly be unfavorable to the wealthy. Ding, while he was lauded by most people, offended the landowners and merchants. They wrote a little ditty about him, called "Four Heavens and Earths." It went like this: "The name of Your Excellency shocks Heaven and Earth. The arrival of Your Excellency gladdens Heaven and Earth. The policy of Your Excellency darkens Heaven and Earth. At the departure of Your Excellency, we thank Heaven and Earth."

CHAPTER 37

Back in 1862, France and China were at war over the Vietnam issue. Vietnam had always been under China's protection. That summer, Vietnam was forced to sign a treaty with France, stating that Vietnam was now under French protection. During next five years, the French Navy arrived and gradually occupied the southern part of Vietnam. In 1873, France invaded the north. The Vietnamese government sent General Liu to resist. Liu was a Chinese and had fought in the Peaceful Army. When the Peaceful Army had failed, he escaped into Vietnam, bringing his troops with him. They were called the "Black Banner Army," and a black banner announced their arrival wherever they went. The Black Banner Army set off to fight the French, and killed the French general. Thus, the following year France and Vietnam signed a new treaty, in Saigon. The Qing Government remained neutral, at that time, because they were busy disputing with Japan over Taiwan.

When France encroached on the north of Vietnam once again, China stepped in. Many courtiers favored going to war. Prince Yihuan was also inclined in that direction, but Prince Yixin took the view that China was in no condition to take on France and that it would be better to negotiate. With opinion thus divided, no policy could be chosen. West Empress Dowager finally decided to prepare for war even while seeking peace talks; but by then, certain military options had already been lost. A great number of French soldiers had already landed in Vietnam and they were attacking the Black Banner Army. If the Qing Government had been more decisive and sent its army into Vietnam to reinforce the Black Banner Army, they might have been able to occupy all the strategically important locations before the French army had consolidated its hold; and the final victory might have belonged to China.

The Qing Government promised to provide the Black Banner Army with ammunition and provisions through Guangxi Province, but the Guangxi governor withheld much of the materiel. How could the Black Banner Army resist the French? They were beaten, this time. Then the Qing Government sent some detachments into Vietnam as reinforcements, but the detachments that were selected were not able to give each other strategic support when the situation required. The result was that they, too, were overpowered. News reached the capital that some occupied towns in Vietnam had been lost, and the courtiers made angry comments. One critique official wrote a report indicating that the secretaries should be blamed.

West Empress Dowager blamed Yixin and removed him from all his offices. She then changed all the members of the Secretarial Bureau and put Yihuan, her brother-in-law and the biological father of the present emperor, in charge; but Yihuan was not as smart as Yixin. The situation could only go from bad to worse, even though the Qing Government army and the Black Banner Army did win some battles, later, in Vietnam.

French warships were cruising near the coast of Fujian Province with the intention of landing there. Someone suggested that the Chinese South Sea Navy could take the initiative and sink the French warships, but those who wanted peace talks, including Governor Li of Zhidi Province, were opposed to that. China was not in a strong condition. Then the French warships began to attack what navy China had, and sank four warships. West Empress Dowager was enraged; no choice but to declare war, now. Since China could not fight France on the sea, they planned to allow the French soldiers to land and then ambush them. But no French soldiers came ashore.

The French navy went on to attack Taiwan. China didn't have any warships there but the general who guarded Taiwan sank some boats and blocked the entry into the Fresh Water Harbor. 1,000 French soldiers landed on Taiwan and fought with the Chinese soldiers, but they were outnumbered. The French were driven back to sea, to their ships. So China won battles on land, and

France at sea. No war can go on forever; and after much negotiation, a treaty was signed between the Qing Government and France.

* * *

After Sushun was executed, Yihuan had been appointed as head of the imperial bodyguards, the special division, with Ronglu as his assistant. Yihuan had plenty of ambition but not much brains. When Yixin had been in charge, Yihuan had envied him. Now, as Yihuan took charge of state affairs, Yixin commented to a friend, "You know the saying. When you see someone else shouldering a burden, you don't know how heavy it is." In just a few months, Yihuan came to feel the weight on his own shoulders, but there was no one he could shift it to.

One day Yihuan went to see Yixin and said, "I really envy you your leisure, no responsibilities."

"How can that be?" Yixin smiled at him.

"Could you help me?" Yihuan really needed a capable person to share his duties. But what could Yixin say? It was up to West Empress Dowager, not Yixin himself. He had been forced to retire — just when the empire needed him. Yihuan hinted to West Empress Dowager that she should allow Yixin to resume some of the responsibilities. But West Empress Dowager stood fast. Her decision was not based on any doubt of Yixin's abilities, but on the fact that she had many plans in mind that Yixin would block.

West Empress Dowager would never forget that when she had wanted to rebuild the Round-Bright Garden many courtiers, headed by Yixin, had vehemently objected. Despite all her enthusiasm, she could not break through their opposition. Now Yixin was out of the way, and so were many of his supporters. If she wanted work done on gardens and pavilions now, no one would thwart her. But where was the money for it? The cost was too high, as she knew very well. Finally, she decided to repair the buildings at the Three Lakes and make that area an imperial garden. She would name it the Garden of Good Health and Harmony. But still, where would they get the money?

Someone suggested to Li, her head eunuch, that they use part of the money that had been requisitioned to build up the navy. Good idea. The Sino-French War had resulted in the loss of Vietnam, which became a French protectorate. That had been enough to inspire West Empress Dowager and the Secretarial Bureau to take the decision to build a strong navy; money was collected via customs duties and the salt tax and also from "contributions" from all the provinces. However, since that war was already over, West Empress Dowager thought that there was no particular urgency in the naval arena. History proved that she was mistaken in her sense of priorities, and China's modest fleet was defeated again, in 1894, by Japan.

However, before that happened, West Empress Dowager ordered the formation of a Navy Yamen, and she made Yihuan its head. Yihuan could never say "no" to West Empress Dowager, and so the bulk of the expenses for constructing the garden came from the Navy Yamen. The rest was siphoned ff from the young emperor's upcoming wedding account. Why didn't West Empress Dowager order the Internal Revenue Ministry to construct her garden? That ministry would appear to be a reasonable source for such expenditures. But Minister Yan would refuse the funds. He would have to have been replaced, and for no apparent reason. That would draw attention to what was going on. West Empress Dowager still wanted to maintain her good public image. The landscaping project went forward, in secret.

The Imperial Household Department was put in charge of it. They were also building a stage, right close to where West Empress Dowager lived. It was supposed to be finished before her birthday. Three days short of the deadline West Empress Dowager went to have a look, thinking that surely the construction would be in place by then; but it was not completed. Some of the officials pleaded that they would have everything in place before her birthday, but West Empress Dowager was petulant and fined them each 3,000 taels.

The silver was to be handed over by a certain date. One official did not possess that much ready cash, and West Empress Dowager sent a eunuch to scold him. This was a custom in the Qing Dynasty. If a courtier did something wrong or angered the emperor, the emperor would send a eunuch to his residence to scold him. The courtier had to prostrate himself before the eunuch, listening to whatever he said. The eunuch was there as the emperor's representative, so the courtier had to receive the eunuch on his knees. The eunuch was to begin simply by pointing out whatever errors the courtier had committed, and in the name of the emperor to insist that the courtier should not make the same mistakes again. But eunuchs often had particularly bad tempers and carried a large load of resentment, and the reproach could be expected to devolve into a stream of vituperation, even foul words. It also depended on the mood of the eunuch. If he had just been reprimanded or frustrated in some way, himself, he would take it out on the courtier. This was particularly humiliating to the courtier, because eunuchs were not considered complete human beings. If a courtier could not stand to be berated by a eunuch, he would have to bribe him to stop. On the day in question, the eunuch was not in a happy frame of mind and the courtier had no money with which to bribe him. He called the courtier every name he could think of. The courtier blushed purple and tears trickled down his cheeks. At the end of this elevating rite, the courtier still had to thank West Empress Dowager for sending the eunuch to scold him.

* * *

The reconstruction of The Garden of Good Health and Harmony was completed in 1895, and it served as one of several summer palaces. It remains the best-maintained imperial garden in China's capital, housing a collection of fine buildings and displaying a variety of gardening styles as well. The total area is over 700 square acres.

It was first called the Garden of Clear Ripples, but all the buildings were burnt down by Great Britain and France, and their allies, in 1860. Reconstruction started 25 years later, in 1885, and took ten years to complete. The design gives prominence to Longevity Hill and Kunming Lake. Many scenic highlights were built in imitation of those on West Lake in Hangzhou City, Zhejiang Province. In a sense, it is a miniature West Lake.

The Eastern Palace Gate is the main entrance to the Garden of Good Health and Harmony. The opening in the center was for use by the emperor and empress dowager exclusively. Two side openings were provided for princes and courtiers. Eunuchs and soldiers used auxiliary gates to the south and north. The legend "The Garden of Good Health and Harmony" in Chinese characters in front of the gate was written by Emperor Guangxu himself, and the stone slab in front of the gate bears a relief carving of two dragons playing with a pearl — a symbol of imperial authority.

"Be Diligent in Administration Hall" was renamed during the reign of Emperor Guangxu, and is now known as "Benevolence and Longevity Hall." There, West Empress Dowager and Emperor Guangxu received courtiers.[1]

---

1. The corridor is about 2200 feet long, extending from a moon gate in the east to Shizhang Pavilion in the west. All 273 sections are decorated with paintings, with more than 8000 landscapes, florals and human figures.

Dispersing Clouds Hall is one of the main buildings on Longevity Hill; it was specially built for West Empress Dowager to receive her birthday greetings. Crimson pillars and a roof of golden-glazed tiles blaze on sunny days.

Buddha Fragrance Pavilion stands on a stone terrace on the sheer slope of Longevity Hill, overlooking Kunming Lake. Looking south from Longevity Hill, the Seventeen-Arch Bridge[1] and Nanhu Island appear to float on the Lake.

A *faux* business street was laid out along the Rear Lake in The Garden of Good Health and Harmony. Called Suzhou Street, it imitated the style of a typical marketplace along a river in the south of China. Whenever West Empress Dowager and Emperor Guangxu went there, the eunuchs and palace maids would entertain them by playing the roles of shop assistants, hawkers and customers. West Empress Dowager, always happy for a bit of theater, enjoyed the place very much.

* * *

Governor Li of Zhidi Province had a maxim: "Learn from foreigners to conquer foreigners." West Empress Dowager liked that.

One day, he suggested that they print and issue banknotes. That way, he reasoned, one tael of silver could be used as two. Sounds great! But how would it work? He explained it this way: if there were five million taels of silver in circulation, and if the government released banknotes worth five million taels, the two together would make ten million taels: The currency was doubled. The property of the government was doubled, too, according to this logic. Better than borrowing — no interest to pay.

The suggestion came to the attention of Prince Yihuan, who latched onto it fervently. First, they would have to open some banks. Sensing that people would be uncomfortable with a foreign name, they called the banks "silver shops." No argument, so far. However, considering that West Empress Dowager was sure to look upon the silver shops as her personal treasure chests, Governor Li insisted that the general manager must be a foreigner — thinking that a foreign manager would be more able to resist any unreasonable demands from West Empress

---

1. The Seventeen-Arch Bridge, shaped like a rainbow, is 25 feet wide and 450 feet long; it links the East Causeway with Nanhu Island on the Kunming Lake. The two-tiered Marble Boat, over 100 feet long, was made of huge stone blocks in 1755. The immovable vessel symbolizes the steadfast rule of the Qing Dynasty.

Dowager. But the Internal Revenue Minister of the Manchu Clan, father-in-law of the late Emperor Tongzhi, opposed placing a foreigner in charge of the silver shops. What if the foreigner took all the silver off to his own country? Like hiring a wolf to guard the sheep. He went to see Prince Yihuan, and threatened to resign. That plan was aborted.

Governor Li's second suggestion was to build a railroad in Shandong Province, along the river. But many conservative courtiers opposed that, too. If the dike broke, the river would flood the railroad. And while transportation by rail was faster than by ship, thus helping commerce, this would render many workers redundant and they would become outlaws. Furthermore, while the train would be a convenient way to convey soldiers here and there during a war, a rail line is easy to disrupt. What was the use, then? And it would be impossible to guard the line from end to end. Besides, suppose the intended railroad line cut through some graveyards, as was bound to happen. The corpses would be dug up, disrupting the *fengshui* (something like geomancy: in this context, the theory is that the location of the graves and their orientation will affect the fortune of the family). This last point was the strongest; how could they bring such calamity to the populace?

Prince Yihuan could still remember when the first railroad was in China, in 1865. It had been built by a British merchant, outside the capital, as an example, only a quarter mile long. When the train began to whistle and rumble, the crowds who had come to watch flew into a panic, crying "Monster! Monster!" The government had ordered the whole thing taken apart and removed. The second railroad was built by a British company in 1877, and it ran from Shanghai to the outlet of the Wangpu River, with freight carriages and passenger cars mixed. Business had been good, though there was still some resistance. Unfortunately, a pedestrian was run over. This occasioned mass protests and demonstrations. The Foreign Affairs Yamen had had to intervene, purchasing the railroad from the British company for 285,000 taels of silver. Then the government had ripped up the rails and sunk everything in the sea. The third railroad was constructed in 1881 near Tangshan Town, to serve the coal mine. It was some five miles long. Only, the freight cars were not drawn by a locomotive, but by horses and donkeys. A laughing stock among the foreigners.

Chapter 38

In 1886, Emperor Guangxu was sixteen. Time for West Empress Dowager to let him rule. She certainly was not willing to do so, but she had to, at least in name. When she made a declaration to that effect Yihuan, the emperor's father, begged her on his knees to postpone the change until the emperor was twenty years old and more mature. (By tradition, when an adopted emperor came of age the natural father had to retire from any office and leave the political stage entirely, to prevent him from becoming an over-emperor and interfering with the administration of state affairs.)

The other courtiers also implored West Empress Dowager to postpone it for a couple of years. But West Empress Dowager persisted in her decision. Yihuan and several courtiers sent in a written petition requesting that, when the emperor came into power, he must still seek the opinion of West Empress Dowager before making any decisions or appointing any officials and officers. West Empress Dowager was glad to accept that, for it allowed her to hand over the reins of power only symbolically. The emperor was less favorably impressed; but it was not up to him.

On February 15, 1887, the power-returning ceremony was held. The emperor got up early. At 4:00 AM, accompanied by officials, he went to the place where the portraits of the ancestors were hung and he kowtowed to them. At 8:30, he went to see West Empress Dowager and kowtowed before her. At 9:00, he sat on the throne and all the courtiers kowtowed to him. His natural father was not present, of course. Then a statement was issued to the whole empire and a feast of celebration was given in the Forbidden City.

* * *

The emperor was 17 now. It was high time for him to get married. West Empress Dowager would take care of everything, as his adoptive mother. On January 20, 1888, she issued an order that the preparations should begin. On February 28, she ordered the Internal Revenue Ministry to pull together five million taels of silver. On June 17, she announced her decision that the emperor's wedding would take place in February of the next year, and that after that she would let the emperor have full and complete power, making decisions all by himself. Formal statement was made to that effect on July 27. On September 3, she set the wedding day for February 26, 1889, and the selection of girls began in late September, 1888.

A first field of 96 candidates was quickly winnowed down to 31. On September 24, the girls hovered, waiting, before West Empress Dowager and the emperor. The process started late in the evening so that West Empress Dowager could view the girls by candlelight; it went on until early morning. Two of the girls were her nieces, which was against tradition. And one of them was 21 years old — well over the traditional age. But everyone was far more concerned with conforming to her will than with conforming to tradition; and West Empress Dowager was only concerned with traditions that suited her interests. Sixteen girls were left after the first sifting, including the nieces and two other pairs of sisters. Four days later, eight of the remaining sixteen were selected. These eight girls were now housed in the Forbidden City, to allow for close observation of their comportment. Three were eventually sent home; one of them was the younger niece of West Empress Dowager. The other niece remained. The emperor would choose his queen and two concubines from the five surviving candidates.

The five girls were the older niece and the two pairs of sisters. One pair were daughters of the governor of Jiangxi Province; the other pair were daughters of a courtier in the capital. These were the only candidates who had learned to write poetry. The eldest daughter of that same governor had been the late Emperor Tongzhi's imperial concubine, and was now an imperial widow — this was the one that West Empress Dowager had liked best and had wanted her natural son to choose as queen, but the headstrong boy had had the gall to select another girl — bringing ruin to them all. Now, West Empress Dowager selected the governor's other two daughters, but this time her goal was to have her niece, not the governor's daughter, become queen. The daughters stayed for the night with their sister, the imperial widow. She complained about having lived in seclusion and solitude, even while Emperor Tongzhi had been alive. A concubine in this predicament was called a "widow with husband alive." The sisters understood that being selected might not be such a boon as anticipated. The eldest sister smiled: "It is easier not to be selected than to be selected." She advised them to wear blue, because West Empress Dowager didn't like that color, and to act a bit listless — but not so much as to be obvious. West Empress Dowager preferred young ladies with a little life in them.

On November 8, the five girls were lined up before West Empress Dowager and the emperor. The niece stood foremost, although she should stand behind the others, by tradition. The younger candidates ought to have stood in the front. The governor's daughters were stationed near the emperor, a little behind the niece. They were beautiful girls, while the niece was rather ordinary. West Empress Dowager had often had that niece come and live for a few days in the Forbidden City, to play with the emperor when they were both children. She had hoped to engender a relationship that would grow from that of playmates to lifemates, but in fact the emperor had never liked his cousin.

When the emperor was instructed to give the symbol, a *ruyi* of jade, to whichever girl he wanted to be his queen, he walked towards one of the governor's daughters. "Emperor!", West Empress Dowager hissed, a little too loud for the occasion and not without some irritation. The emperor was startled and turned his head. She gestured toward her niece, with her mouth. He shrunk a little, deflated on this joyous occasion, but had to obey. He by-passed the beautiful duo and handed the *ruyi* to the niece, who went down on her knees to receive it.

West Empress Dowager didn't let the emperor choose the concubines, either. She chose for him the daughters of the courtier. The elder girl was fifteen and the younger thirteen, and they were now called Concubine Jin and Concubine Zhen. The other two girls, lovely and desirable as they were, were returned to their parents. If they had stayed on as concubines, why would the emperor give the least attention to the chosen queen?

After the selection Big Princess chided West Empress Dowager, saying that if she had desired her niece to be the queen, she ought to have told the emperor so directly, so that his public gesture would be as she had wished. Such an awkward situation could have been avoided. West Empress Dowager admitted that it had partly been her fault.

On December 4, 1888, the emperor sent wedding gifts to the queen's family. The father of the lady in question was West Empress Dowager's brother, and held the title of duke. He was a worthless man, as devoted to opium as he had been in his youth. Now, he wanted to hold a banquet at his home. He wanted to invite all the princes and courtiers, but was afraid that many of them would not come because they despised him. Even with his daughter selected as future queen, his station was elevated just so much. Could he ask West Empress Dowager to lean on them? West Empress Dowager advised him to invite the courtiers only, not the princes, because princes were higher in rank than a duke; and West Empress Dowager said that it would not be suitable for her to issue an order. Her brother had to settle for that.

On February 24, 1889, Concubines Jin and Zhen were carried into the Forbidden City in sedan chairs, but they were not to see the emperor at this time. February 26 was the wedding date, set so long in advance. The queen was brought into the Forbidden City in a magnificently-decorated imperial palanquin, and a series of rituals began for the imperial couple. Finally, having honored all the traditions for this particular event, they were escorted into their bed chamber. The emperor was so exhausted that he promptly fell asleep. The next day, the emperor was expected to host a feast of celebration, but he was not feeling well at all. A eunuch was sent to announce that the feast had been called off. A bad omen. And it made the queen's family look bad. The queen's family was West Empress Dowager's family. She went to see if the emperor was really sick. He did look bad, so she did nothing but urge him to get over it quickly. The celebration went on, in any case, until March 9.

Celebrations in the Forbidden City always involved opera performances. There was an imperial cast for all occasions but after East Empress Dowager's demise, West Empress Dowager often brought in actors from outside the Forbidden City for a change of pace. This time a new actor from Shanghai was debuting. West Empress Dowager was so fascinated by his performance that she decided to interview him afterwards. This was a man who had enjoyed operas as a child and had been studying since he was very young. Then he had defended his country, fighting the Peaceful Army. He had been promoted to the officers' ranks. When the war was over he had returned to Shanghai, where he sometimes acted as a guest performer in one theater or another. As a rule, an officer should not perform in public and he was criticized for that. He decided to give up his officer's title and became an actor by profession. In fact, he became a famous actor. Hearing that West Empress Dowager wished to speak with him, he was flattered; but he sighed and observed, "When I risked my life to fight the Peaceful Army, no one gave me such an honor, but now that I am only an actor, Empress Dowager wants to interview me." Eunuch Li said to him, "You should know that there are many officers like you, but there is only one actor like you. You should be pleased." The actor then assumed a pleasant attitude and went to see West Empress Dowager. She wanted to re-instate his title but he refused, saying that it was unsuitable for an actor to have an official title. So West Empress Dowager gave him more substantial gifts in recognition of the pleasure he gave.

The imperial nuptials cost more than 4,000 taels of gold and more than 4,800,000 taels of silver. It was the most expensive imperial wedding in Qing Dynasty.

The emperor treated the queen with due respect, but he didn't love her. He liked Concubine Zhen best because she was so young and so naïve that she often did or said funny things, which amused the emperor. But funny things often went against the palace rules.

The emperor and Concubine Zhen had a lot of things to talk about. The emperor told Concubine Zhen something that had once happened in the Forbidden City: The emperor's natural father, Yihuan, was the seventh son of the late Emperor Xianfeng. Prince Cun was the fifth son, the emperor's uncle, now deceased. "He was a funny man," said the emperor. "Once, Empress Dowager was listening to some girls who had been called in from outside the Forbidden City to entertain her by singing folk tunes. Against tradition, of course. Fifth Uncle went to see Empress Dowager, and as he strode into the room, he whistled the same tunes. Thus Empress Dowager became aware of criticism making the rounds, and she sent the singing girls away. Another time, when Fifth Uncle wanted to present a special fish to Empress Dowager, a eunuch refused to perform the task unless Fifth Uncle gave him some money. An old custom, but Fifth Uncle never liked it. The next time Empress Dowager wanted to see Fifth Uncle, he brought a fish himself and offered it to Empress Dowager in person. When she asked why he hadn't had a eunuch do it, Fifth Uncle told her; and the eunuch got a beating."

Concubine Zhen could write poetry. She had read many books, especially history books. She told the emperor a story from the Song Dynasty. One of the emperors had no son of his own and wanted to select his successor and heir from the sons of his imperial relatives. They ought to be good boys, under seven years old. Ten lads were selected, but after the preliminary selection only two were left, one lean and the other plump. The emperor was about to choose the plump one, because in those days well-rounded meant well-fed, and in the view of the Chinese people, fat meant fortunate. But just then a cat wandered by. The fat boy had a naughty streak, and he kicked the cat unconsciously, out of habit, while the lean one stood quietly by. The emperor decided on the lean boy. The emperor had later explained that the cat hadn't done anything to deserve the kick; and if the fat boy kicked an innocent cat, he would have killed innocent people when he had become the emperor. So, historians reported that the fat boy had kicked away his throne, not just the cat.

* * *

Governor Li of Zhidi Province had established a fleet of 25 ships. West Empress Dowager thought that that gave him quite enough power, and she set up the Navy Yamen and placed the overburdened Prince Yihuan as its head. Governor Li's fleet was, naturally, under the command of the Navy Yamen. West Empress Dowager wished to have a clear idea of the status and capabilities of the fleet. She sent Yihuan to inspect it, with her Head Eunuch Li as his attendant. This contravened once again the rule laid down by the ancestors that eunuchs were not permitted to go outside the capital; but since the demise of East Empress Dowager and the removal of Prince Yixin, no one had been bold enough to oppose her decisions. Some blamed Yihuan for going along with all this. Yihuan could not admit that he was afraid of West Empress Dowager, so he said, "It's my fault. I asked Eunuch Li to accompany me there." He didn't want to think that West Empress Dowager didn't trust him.

Then Ronglu came to visit him. Ronglu had not been in a good health recently and he was no longer officially in service. Ronglu consoled Yihuan. "Since we have spent so much money on the navy, Empress Dowager wants to know what condition it is in now and how well it can fight. That's why Empress Dowager sends Li with Your Highness." But he could not explain why it was Eunuch Li who was supposed to report to West Empress Dowager about the navy when that should have been Yihuan's role. Ronglu would never let slip a negative word about West Empress Dowager. He was always faithful to her. There was even a rumor that sometimes when Ronglu was summoned to the Forbidden City, he met privately, very privately, with her. But that was only a rumor.

Head Eunuch Li was cleverer than Little An. He played down his role and was content to act as though he were just Yihuan's attendant. They traveled as long as necessary and reached the place where the fleet was at anchor. Yihuan went on board the flagship with his entourage. He stayed in the captain's suite while the fleet was pulled out to the sea to put on a mock battle. Cruising on the vast expanse of waves, the fleet formed a line forward, then maneuvered into a wide front, and then shifted into the shape of a vise. Some old junks were floating at a distance, as targets. At a signal from the flagship, the cannons boomed. In a flash of fire and thunder, the old junks exploded into a rain of fragments. Nothing was left but driftwood dotting the distant blue water. Prince

Yihuan slowly clapped his hands a few times, as if he was watching an opera. The naval officers around him were exhilarated at his approbation.

At the dinner party celebrating this success, Head Eunuch Li sat with the navy officers. He told them a story about how champagne was treated in the Forbidden City. The French envoy had presented several bottles to West Empress Dowager as gifts. On a festival day, West Empress Dowager ordered a eunuch to open a bottle of champagne. The noise the bottle made as it was opened startled West Empress Dowager, and the champagne gushed out, soaking the clothes of Big Princess, who was standing to the side to have a look. The eunuch got a beating, though it was not really his fault. One of the officers wondered whether West Empress Dowager drank champagne anymore after that. Eunuch Li said that someone got an idea that, before opening the bottle, a hole should be punched into the cork stopper to let out the gas.

* * *

Ex-Governor Tang had been in the Judicial Ministry's jail for two years. He had withdrawn from Vietnam during the Sino-French war, without first asking the central government for approval. The verdict was death. In feudal China, prisoners under the death sentence were executed once a year, in autumn. Prisoners who had been courtiers received somewhat different treatment from other prisoners. On execution day, all those sentenced to death would be taken to the execution grounds but only those whose names were crossed out in red, on the death list, were actually executed. Others were taken back to the jail to try their luck the next year. The emperor, now West Empress Dowager, decided whose names would be crossed out. Sometimes a pardon order would be issued for a certain person. The pardoned ones were usually exiled to a remote province. Tang was an able man and quite a few courtiers had thrown in a good word for him, saying that it would be a pity to execute such a talented man for such a petty crime. His name had remained on the death list for two years. Tang had two sons. Through one channel or another, his elder son contacted Head Eunuch Li and begged for his father's life. Having been offered a suitable bribe, Li promised to try.

Since the miscarriage of the banknote scheme, other suggestions had been made for boosting the treasury. One of them was to mint more brass coins, which could also increase the currency. West Empress Dowager accepted the suggestion. But first, where was the copper? The copper mines were mostly in

Yunnan Province, where Tang had been the governor. He knew every aspect of copper mining. So this time, on execution day, he was pardoned and sent to Yunnan Province to supervise the new project.

CHAPTER 39

Now let us have a look at West Empress Dowager's everyday life. West Empress Dowager had some hobbies or, at least, if not hobbies, then habits.

She lived a quite routine but busy life. She got up early. After the process of hair dressing and being changed from sleeping garb into formal dress, she had her breakfast. After that (indeed, after every meal), she would take a "constitutional," a walk, as was the custom in those days, to promote digestion. Then she went to see the courtiers. If no urgent affairs needed her attention, she would retire to her living quarters.

Every day except on holidays she would read reports (and sometimes when emergencies were reported, she read on holidays too) and make decisions accordingly, or hold special court to discuss the problems with her courtiers.

Every day, she had a nap after lunch. Then she would sometimes play mahjong. Big Princess was often her partner, and she would choose two other players from among the wives of her highest-ranking courtiers. Wives of courtiers were often invited into the Forbidden City on festival days. Whoever flattered her best would win her preference and join her in playing mahjong. Of course, everyone who played with her would intentionally lose; but they tried to lose tactfully, discreetly. Such pretence might require considerable practice, and talent as well. But "losing" in this game could benefit their husbands, who would quickly move ahead.

It was also said that she occasionally played Xiang Chess. Whereas in the Western version the playing pieces are positioned in the spaces, in Chinese chess they are placed on the intersections where the lines cross each other. In the Chinese version, the pieces known in the West as "knights" are called "horses," and the rooks are called "chariots." There are two cannons for each side, five pawns and two scholars, and two prime ministers for the red side and two elephants for the blue side with the same function. Blue has a general and Red has a marshal; the capture of either one ends the game.

Anyone who played chess with her had better realize that all of life is a chess match, too. West Empress Dowager was not a good loser. Winning proved that she was wiser than her opponent. A story, probably apocryphal, has it that once she was playing chess with a eunuch and he warned her that she was about to lose a chessman: "Your slave will kill Old Buddha's horse." She suddenly flared up and said, "And I will kill your family." And the eunuch and his family were all killed. Whether this anecdote was true or not, her temper was, indeed, unpredictable.

She also liked to read. Classical Chinese novels such as *Three Kingdoms, The Beach, The Red Chamber Dream, The Journey to the West,* would have been on her list, and she read history books, too, by which she learned from the experiences of other sovereigns how to rule the country. Only, she did not learn how to improve conditions for her people — she learned, principally, how to keep herself in power. She often had old eunuchs tell her stories from history.

She practiced calligraphy. She liked to write, with a long brush, big Chinese characters like "Blessing" and "Longevity." She had the characters made into scrolls and she gave them to her favorite courtiers, who would treasure them as gifts of honor. She learned something about painting, but she never completed a painting: she would sketch out a kind of outline and the palace painters would fill in the details and colors, then sign her name to it.

But her favorite pastime was watching Peking operas. She organized some of the younger eunuchs into an opera cast and wrote scenarios for them, with the help of another courtier's wife who was versed in writing and poetry. She would look at the scripts while the actors were singing, so that she could follow the words they sang. Operas were performed regularly on her birthdays and the birthdays of the emperor and his queen, on festivals, and on the first and fifteenth days of every month of the lunar calendar — at any opportunity. The biggest stage, the Imperial Theater, had three stories and is the largest of its kind in China today. It is 65 feet high. Under the ground floor a few dry wells were dug, to allow for special effects — an actor in a ghost costume could appear out of nowhere, and other characters might simply vanish. A winch could lower performers and props from the second floor down to the ground floor through a hole in the ceiling; performers could appear on the three floors at the same time.

Second best, she liked to have her photograph taken. It was said that at first she had distrusted photography, because (and this is a common belief among "primitive" people) she thought the photograph must have taken the person's spirit as well as his image; that could not be good. But later, as gradually so many foreign things were introduced into the Forbidden City and as she got used to them — and especially after so many of her acquaintances had been photographed, with no apparent harm being done — she began to have her picture taken, too. She enjoyed looking at her own image. The photographs she liked best were those in which she was attired in a Buddha's costume.

She took up the study of English as late as 1900, when she was well into her sixties. Upon her return from her brief retreat to Xi An City during the war, she had to receive the wives and daughters of the foreign envoys in an effort to shore up relations with foreign governments. The Foreign Affairs Ministry wrote down for her some English sentences that she could say to them, but since she could not speak the language correctly, she set about learning English from the wives and daughters of her courtiers who had served as envoys in foreign countries for several years. She liked to keep busy.

She also liked to be bathed. She had a silver kidney-shaped tub; but she did not sit in it. When the water was the right temperature, she would sit on a low chair close by, attended by four maids, with another four maids as their assistants. They washed her upper torso first, in an elaborate process of gently patting and stroking with warm, damp towels. The maids who rubbed her chest had to be careful to hold their breath, as they could be punished for exhaling in her face. Then they would daub some perfume on her, with cotton pads, and cover her with a kind of nightgown. Then came the lower torso.

A different tub was used for the second part of the job — why use one, when you can afford two? West Empress Dowager considered that the upper torso was like the master and the lower torso was like the servant; how could master and servant share the same implement?

When the bath was over, two maids remained to wash her face and hands and, especially, to do her nails. They used the warm, damp towels, and then rolled a short round stick of jade on the skin of her face to massage it and "to iron out the wrinkles," as they would say. Then came the nails. She only grew her nails about an inch long on her thumbs, ring fingers and little fingers; the others were far longer. First, the maids would steep her nails in warm water in jade bowls. Then they brushed them clean, and straightened the long nails, which were apt to curve. They filed the nails, where needed, applied polish, and then put a case made of yellow brocade on the long nails to protect them. That was the last event, before she went to bed. It was said that she always had white, soft, smooth skin, and looked much younger than her real age.

As noted earlier, she paid particular attention to her long, gleaming black hair. Before the eunuch Li Lianying came along, no one had ever been able to do her hair to her satisfaction. She tried one eunuch after another, but could never find one with the talent — or, as Li Lianying proved, the necessary training — to meet her expectations. If the way to a man's heart is through his stomach, he found a way to her heart through her hair. For this, he was made the general head eunuch in the Forbidden City.

West Empress Dowager was very fastidious about food. The imperial kitchen provided for the entire imperial household in the Forbidden City, but she had her own private kitchen as well, called West Kitchen. Each cook there was in charge of a certain sort of food: there was a vegetable chef and a pasty chef, some who specialized in various kinds of snacks, and some who only focused on delicacies like shark's fin, sea cucumber and abalone. West Kitchen could provide more than 4,000 different dishes.

Breakfast was generally at six in the morning, lunch at noon, and dinner at six in the evening. And snacks — at any time. Food was carried from the kitchen to her dining place in warm boxes with tight lids, with pewter containers at the bottom to hold hot water. It is said that there were always 100 dishes served at her main meals; and it was said that the cost of one such meal could feed a family of four for a year.

When dinner was served, one young eunuch carried one food box on his right shoulder, and all the other eunuchs would follow in a row. Some of the senior eunuchs would take the dishes from the boxes and lay them one by one on the big, oblong table. When she looked at a dish, a eunuch would get it and place it before her. But before she tasted it, head Eunuch Li would dip a pair of silver chopsticks into the food — if the silver chopsticks turned black, that would show that there was poison in the dish. (Not much protection, but better than nothing, with so much poison going around.) Of course, she could not eat 100 dishes. She often ordered some of them sent to a certain favorite courtier or given to Head Eunuch Li, which was considered an honor.

PART THREE
TUMBLING DOWN

CHAPTER 40

Every dynasty has corruption, and in China as elsewhere the corruption of one dynasty eventually would bring about its downfall and the advent of a new one. Embezzlement, bribery and selling of government positions were the most common abuses. In the late Qing Dynasty, the positions being sold had fixed prices which were open secrets. Before the emperor came of age and the reins of power were ostensibly handed over to him, all the courtiers were appointed by West Empress Dowager. These courtiers still felt loyal to her, even after the emperor took over. They were called the Empress Dowager's Party.

When Emperor Guangxu came into power, he wanted to rout out the corruption. There were quite a few honorable courtiers who abhorred corruption and supported him. They were called the emperor's Party. The former comprised most of the governors and those courtiers who were experienced in government administration — they held all the power. The latter consisted for the most part of young and inexperienced courtiers, who did not have much power.

While the emperor was racking his brains to find ways to reduce corruption, his beloved Concubine Zhen was racking her brains to find ways to get more income. By tradition, the queen received 1,000 taels of silver every year from the government, but a concubine received only 300.

Concubine Zhen was just an adolescent, with no experience in the outside world. Her head eunuch prompted her to ask the emperor to appoint a certain person as an official of a certain rank, so that she could exact a commission for it.

But her head eunuch had gotten the idea from West Empress Dowager's Head Eunuch, Li.

Li had made a fortune on bribes for the sale of official positions. He was too cautious to ask West Empress Dowager outright to make the appointments. He merely asked certain members of the Secretarial Bureau to suggest to West Empress Dowager a certain person as suitable to fill such and such a position. In return, Li would throw in a few good words for them in his conversations with West Empress Dowager. She relied on him as her eyes and ears, and used him as her spy to detect anything she wanted to know. After West Empress Dowager had dinner and before she went to bed, she would summon Li and have him tell her whatever he had learned during the day. Story time, as Li would say. He picked up a lot of hearsay. He could not investigate how much truth was in the gossip. If she really wanted to know the truth, Li would send another eunuch to nose around. And that was how Concubine Zhen's doings came into her ears.

* * *

Although West Empress Dowager had handed over the rulership to Emperor Guangxu, she still controlled him, and, eager to build up more wealth, she began to sell the official titles and posts on a large scale. Head Eunuch Li acted as a go-between, and so he also pocketed his share of bribes — but he didn't dare to let West Empress Dowager know that he was making money on her deals. The emperor could not refuse whomever West Empress Dowager wanted to appoint to a vacant position, although he did observe that some of the officials were not fit for the positions they were given. The emperor knew that Head Eunuch Li was a go-between on his adoptive mother's side; but who was the go-between providing the clients? Li could not be slipping out of the Forbidden City all the time; and he could not very well have put up an advertisement. Where was the missing link? Eventually, the emperor learned that a Taoist named Gao often came to see Head Eunuch Li.

There was a Taoist temple, White Cloud Temple, in a western suburb of the capital, where the Taoists worshipped a statue of Taoist Qiu. Qiu had lived in the Ming Dynasty and had castrated himself in the interests of perfecting a certain style of kungfu. As a result, the eunuchs thought of him as their protective god and came to worship him. Gao was the head Taoist of that temple.

Gao was born in Shandong Province and had been a shop apprentice there. Once, he pocketed some money and the shop owner came after him; he fled to a

Taoist temple and joined their ranks. Somehow, the shop owner had learned that he was hiding in the temple and sent someone there to catch him, but he escaped to the capital, into the White Cloud Temple. Through years of flattery and other efforts, he had slowly climbed the ladder to the top rung as head Taoist. Since Head Eunuch Li, like the other eunuchs, often came to the temple, they struck up a friendship and became sworn brothers.

Whenever Taoist Gao came into the capital, he always lodged in a certain inn. He had his own room there. Once, while he was staying at the inn, a man came to see him. The man was a wood merchant by the name of Yuming, and he was recommended by someone working in the Imperial Household Department. Merchant Yuming supplied wood to the Household whenever there were repairs or constructions in the Forbidden City. He was very rich, and recently had earned another fortune on the repair work in the Garden of Good Health and Harmony. Someone had hinted to him that the head of the Department of Salt and Tea Tax Collection in Sichuan Province had been accused of corruption and that the position would soon be vacant. Now, that was a fat position, involving great sums of money. Sichuan Province yields tea and halite (rock salt), which were sold to Tibet, Yunnan Province, Guizhou Province, Hunan Province and Hubei Province for huge profits. Yuming felt that such a position was a worthy follow up to his success in the capital, so he offered 100,000 taels of silver for the post. Taoist Gao promised to get the post for him, but said he must contact Head Eunuch Li first. Merchant Yuming gave him the note for 100,000 taels. But Head Eunuch Li was busy these days and Taoist Gao could not find him.

The merchant was anxious and feared that the vacancy would be given to someone else. He also knew that Concubine Zhen was now the emperor's favorite. If Concubine Zhen could ask the emperor to give the vacancy to a certain person, as a favor, the emperor would not refuse. And it was more direct, because any order of appointment was issued by the emperor anyway. So, through another clerk in the Imperial Household Department, he got in touch with Wang, Concubine Zhen's head eunuch. Eunuch Wang had always envied Eunuch Li for his easy access to money. Here was the chance for him to show that he could make easy money, too. 100,000 taels was a good start. If only he could persuade Concubine Zhen. Eunuch Wang knew that she needed money to give to her parents. Her father was a mandarin, but he was not rich enough to easily bear the expenses his position called for. If her father went to visit any superiors or princes, as etiquette required, he had to tip the doorkeepers or they would not report to their masters that he had come and was waiting to be received. And if his superiors never learned that he had come to pay his respects, they would think that he was neglectful and would begin to dislike him. Then he could never get a promotion. Of course, he could mention that their doorkeepers had required payment, or they wouldn't let him in. But this was a long-established custom and no one was inclined to combat it.

Eunuch Wang and the merchant struck up a bargain: the eunuch would get him the post within 25 days and the merchant would pay him 100,000 taels of silver. If the eunuch couldn't do it within that period of time, the deal was off. At the earliest opportunity, Eunuch Wang mentioned to Concubine Zhen that she could get 100,000 taels just for putting a word in the emperor's ear. Concubine Zhen looked doubtful. She was only thirteen, but she had a sense that meddling in state affairs would bring the wrath of West Empress Dowager upon her. But Eunuch Wang persuaded her, saying that West Empress Dowager sold posts for money, herself. This gave Concubine Zhen a little encouragement. "Who wants the position?" she asked timidly. Eunuch Wang presented her with a slip of paper with a name on it. Concubine Zhen glanced at the name. Of course she didn't recognize it. She told him to leave the paper on the table. "Is the post worth so much money?" she wondered.

"Oh, yes. It is one of the juiciest positions in the country."

"I'll think about it." She dismissed him.

The emperor finished his daily routine and came to see her, as usual. After some pleasant conversation, the emperor noticed the paper on the table and asked what it was. Concubine Zhen replied nonchalantly that this man wanted to have such and such position, and had begged her to say a few good words for him to the emperor — but that she knew that she should not interfere with the appointment of government officials, and so she had not promised him anything. Young she was, but clever, too. This was the ploy known as "Retreat before advancing." The emperor was enamored of Concubine Zhen and was always looking for a way to please her. So he picked up the paper and put it into his pocket.

Taoist Gao learned about this, through his private grapevine, and resented it. When he finally reached Head Eunuch Li, he told him what had happened. Li was infuriated that Concubine Zhen had cut in on a deal that should have been his. However, since West Empress Dowager always consulted Eunuch Li whenever she was unsure which way to go, they would still have the last word.

Soon she read the Personnel Ministry's report that the former head of the Department of Salt and Tea Tax Collection in Sichuan Province had embezzled

400,000 taels of silver within two years, and she said to Eunuch Li, "I never knew this position was worth so much money." Eunuch Li remarked casually that that must be why he had heard that someone was willing to pay 100,000 taels for the position. West Empress Dowager wanted to know who that was, but Eunuch Li answered evasively, and suggested that Old Buddha should keep an eye out for the name. Therefore, when the emperor sent in the appointment order for West Empress Dowager's approval, she put it aside in favor of Eunuch Li's unnamed candidate.

When the appointment was thus sidelined, Eunuch Wang knew that it was Li's doing. After 25 days, his deal was off. Then and only then Eunuch Li reported to West Empress Dowager that that was the very man who was offering 100,000 taels. West Empress Dowager was elated, and granted the appointment.

Now, according to ceremonial requirements, there had to be an interview with the official who was being appointed to a high position outside the capital. The date for the interview was set. When Eunuch Wang reported the whole tale to Concubine Zhen, she was outraged. Might as well scuttle the whole affair, in that case. She implied to the emperor that she had learned that this man was only a merchant, basically illiterate, not fit for the post after all. The emperor was surprised, but he didn't have the heart to blame her — she hadn't really asked him to give the man the position. It was he who had tried to do her a favor. Therefore, during the interview, the emperor asked the merchant to write up a short resume of his life. But the merchant could not even write his own name. The post was given to someone else. Li got nothing; the merchant lost his 100,000 taels to Taoist Gao, and he didn't dare to demand its return.

* * *

At first, when Imperial Concubine Zhen had come into the Forbidden City, West Empress Dowager had treated her just like the other members of the imperial family. She hadn't especially liked her, but she hadn't disliked her, either. Later, as it became clear how much the emperor preferred her over the queen, and as Concubine Zhen started to infringe palace rules, and things started to sour.

Concubine Zhen was young, bold and carefree. Once, she asked the emperor to allow her to ride on a palanquin carried by eight eunuchs. That was certainly against the rules, because by tradition only the empress dowager, the emperor and the queen could sit on such a palanquin. When West Empress Dowager learned of this, she didn't believe it. Then one day she actually came across Concubine Zhen riding on one, just like that. She was outraged, ordered the palanquin to be broken into pieces, and got Concubine Zhen a severe scolding.

Concubine Zhen liked to have her photos taken. Her cousin got her a camera. She had her picture taken, dressed in the emperor's formal clothes embroidered with dragons. This was also against the rules. When the queen got her hands on one of the pictures, she showed it to West Empress Dowager. This was beyond all bounds. Time to punish Concubine Zhen for all her accumulating offenses — in addition to the acceptance of bribes. The punishment was severe: Concubine Zhen was shut up, alone, in a deserted building. This was toward the end of the year 1894. The country was at war with Japan, and was about to lose Korea. Difficult times all around.

CHAPTER 41

Vying for power happens at every level, in every location. It happened in Korea, then. The Qing Government sent troops to maintain law and order there. Japan had always coveted Korea — and this provided Japan with a pretext. So on July 23, 1894, Japan sent her army into Korea, seized the king and occupied the palace. Thus began the conflict between the Qing Government troops and the Japanese army. At first, gods of battle favored the Qing Government, but then Japan sent reinforcements, and the Qing troops were vanquished on July 28. On August 1, under pressure from the public and the media, West Empress Dowager declared war against Japan. But the Chinese armies in Korea were defeated after only one battle. The commanders were all fools, the historians said. Maybe there were other factors, as well.

Now the whole nation turned its attention to the navy. Nearly ten years before, when the Sino-French war ended in 1885, it had been agreed that China needed a strong navy. On June 21 of that year, West Empress Dowager had met with the courtiers and decided to build a fleet. Fortunes were spent buying warships from foreign countries. By 1888, the Navy had 25 ships of different sorts and sizes.

On September 17, 1894, the fleet was tested. While the Chinese ships were on the way back to Luda Harbor, the Japanese fleet suddenly appeared. Small and unprepared, the Chinese fleet pluckily set forth to meet the challenge, and a maritime campaign took place on the Yellow Sea near the coast of China. Most of the newly-built fleet was destroyed. Then, the Japanese army crossed the Korean boundary into Chinese territory. On October 24, another Japanese detachment landed, on Liaodong Peninsula, and on November 22, they occupied Luda. On December 29, the Japanese army set foot on Shandong Peninsula. By December 31, 35,000 Japanese soldiers had landed and detoured to the back of Weihaiwei Town. On February 2, 1895, they took the town and captured the remaining ten ships. In early March of 1895, the Japanese army occupied the Liaodong Penin-sula. The Qing Government had no hope of recovering the lost territory and so, in a very weak negotiating position, they were constrained to sue for peace. On April 17, 1895, a treaty was signed in Japan.

After this resounding defeat, the courtiers who lacked the nerve to blame West Empress Dowager set the blame on Governor Li. It was Governor Li who had built the fleet. It was Governor Li who had commanded it. He had always been against war, and now his long-boasted fleet had been sunk to the bottom of the sea. Even West Empress Dowager was stunned at the news, and resented Governor Li for all the money he had spent on his fleet. Besides, she needed a scapegoat. Governor Li was relieved of his duties. But people all over the country knew that West Empress Dowager had diverted funds that had originally been requisitioned to strengthen the navy, and considered that in building her Garden of Good Health and Harmony it was she who had caused the navy to be defeated.

Losing the Sino-Japanese War forced the Chinese people as well as the government to confront a harsh reality. Japan was only a small country, far smaller than China: how had this happened? China was desperately behind, desperately weak, both financially and militarily. Debates erupted in newspa-pers and on the street. One sole conclusion was drawn: "We need reform. Like Japan."

The emperor wanted reform. West Empress Dowager wanted reform, too, if only so that she could trounce the foreign invaders and take revenge. She therefore agreed to the emperor's reform notion, in general, though the conserva-tive courtiers opposed it. Prince Yihuan, the emperor's father, had died by now, so finally Yixin, his uncle, was allowed a second chance. Too late — he, too, died before long. On his deathbed, he advised the emperor to carry out his reforms, step by step, and to do nothing against tradition — although it is not at all clear that he was able to suggest how those two contradictory goals might be achieved.

The emperor appointed a group of officials to design a detailed reform plan. His former tutor Weng, now a secretary, gave the emperor his full support. Official Kang drafted all the reform decrees for the emperor. Kang's disciple, Official Liang, and Official Tan were also instrumental. On June 11, 1898, the emperor issued a statement to declare the beginning of reform. Then, over the next 100 days, he issued a series of orders, 180 or so altogether.

The orders involved (1) selecting supporters of reform as government officials; (2) abandoning the old examination system for the selection of officials and the development of a modern education system; (3) changes to the government administration system and the elimination of national corruption; (4) permission for the open expression of opinions by the people at large; (5) rewards for inventions and incentives for the development of trade, agriculture and industry; (6) the rebuilding of a navy.

Looks good on paper. However, most of the governors hesitated to implement any of the changes; they were waiting to see which way the wind blew. Was West Empress Dowager really in favor of reform? Most of the emperor's orders were not carried out. Only one thing was successful: a university was established in the capital.

On June 16, 1898, West Empress Dowager forced the emperor to issue some orders of appointments and removals. Perhaps most important was the appointment of Ronglu as the Governor of Zhidi Province (the capital was in this province) and as head of the newly-trained armies.

Ronglu had been idle for years, partly because of his poor health. He had enjoyed very few promotions, considering his abilities. Presumably, West Empress Dowager had been leery of attracting cries of favoritism, since she was suspected already of having a special relationship with him. Finally, the time had come when Ronglu's fate could take a turn for the better. Prince Yihuan was taken ill, was bed-ridden, was partially paralyzed. West Empress Dowager had to call upon Prince Yixin again; and Prince Yixin knew that Ronglu was both talented and prudent. He suggested appointing Ronglu as the commander of the garrison division to guard the capital. West Empress Dowager had no objection, of course. The next year Ronglu was named Military Minister. Then he became a prime minister. West Empress Dowager, by now a mature politician, had studied the chessboard well. And when young Emperor Guangxu, influenced by new concepts, wanted reforms "like Japan," she entrusted the military forces to Ronglu.

The other order was to remove Courtier Weng, who had been the emperor's tutor, from his office as secretary of state and expel him back to his hometown. Thus the emperor lost his most important ally.

Then a statement was issued indicating that West Empress Dowager and the emperor would go to Tianjin City to watch the military parade. A rumor spread: West Empress Dowager was going to force the emperor to abdicate while they were there.

On August 30, the emperor made a public decision to merge six government bureaus, whose responsibilities were fulfilled by corresponding ministries. Better for efficiency, but worse for the officials who would lose their posts. Many old courtiers implored West Empress Dowager to stop him, but she demurred. She wanted to see how far the emperor would go.

The emperor became impatient when most of the officials refused to carry out his orders. On September 4, he decided to retire six mandarins in the Etiquette Ministry and he appointed his own officials the next day. A new administration?

On September 7, the emperor removed two courtiers from the Foreign Affairs Yamen. Furthermore, he sought to appoint two foreigners to be his advisors, one an English priest and the other a Japanese dignitary, an ex-prime-minister in the cabinet of Japan. Conservative courtiers were in a panic, saying that foreigners would soon control the Qing Government. West Empress Dowager shared their qualms, but decided to wait a bit longer. Let him hang himself.

On September 14, when the emperor went to see West Empress Dowager, she rebuked him sharply for his recklessness. An open rupture.

The emperor's supporters knew that without any military forces under his control, the reform movement would fail. Why not send for Yuan Shikai? He was training his army in the Western style near Tianjin City. His army was called the New Army. The next time Yuan came to the capital, the emperor received him and gave him a secret order, in writing: bring the New Army to Peking, surround the Garden of Good Health and Harmony, and confine West Empress Dowager. Yuan knew that most of the courtiers and all the governors supported West Empress Dowager. If he wanted to keep his position, never mind win a promotion, he must side with West Empress Dowager and betray the young man. Emperor or not, he was a political novice, inexperienced, and more ambitious than clever.

When Yuan returned to Tianjin City, he tipped off Ronglu, who immediately took the night train back to Peking and went to see West Empress Dowager. (So the railway did have its uses.) He showed her the emperor's secret written order, which Yuan had given him.

On September 19, West Empress Dowager cornered the emperor on an island in the middle of a lake in the Forbidden City. The island was connected to the other parts of the Forbidden City only by a small footbridge. A pretty tight cage. No fire, either, for heat, and very little food: the emperor was treated very badly. He was declared to have fallen ill, seriously ill. The imperial doctors' prognoses were proclaimed abroad every day to reinforce the message: the emperor was really in a bad way. But people thought it was not his health that was in jeopardy. The newspapers conjectured that the doctors' proclamation were only a preliminary step towards deposing the emperor.

The new officials whom the emperor had appointed were all dismissed from their posts. Official Kang, who had been the most active and enthusiastic in the reforms, escaped on board a British ship to Japan. Official Liang, Kang's disciple, fled into the Japanese legation and then was escorted to Japan, too. Another new official, Tan, had to stay and face his fate — because if he ran away, the government would go after his father, instead.

Official Tan had a sworn brother Wang, a helpful sort and proficient in the martial arts, nicknamed Big Sword. He worked as a contract bodyguard or property guard, or both — if a rich man or a rich family wanted to travel a long way with valuable luggage, Wang could be hired for protection against robbers.

When Wang learned that Official Tan was in trouble, he went to have a word with him. Not publicly: he went at night, jumped over the wall from a side street, then snuck into his study. They discussed how they could spring the emperor from his trap and spirit him away to the southern provinces. Once the emperor was out of West Empress Dowager's clutches, everything would be fine. According to their plan, as soon as they got the emperor out of the Forbidden City, they would hide him either in some foreign legation or smuggle him into one of the foreign colonies in Tianjin City. Then they would escort him by foreign ship to the southern provinces. In their minds, wherever the emperor was, the power was. The emperor could issue orders from anywhere. And courtiers and governors were duty bound to carry out his orders. Good theory.

Wang took the matter into his hands. He knew some eunuchs in the Forbidden City. He found one and invited him to a restaurant where they ate, drank and conversed merrily. Eunuchs liked to brag about life in the Forbidden

City. Wang showed great interest in the eunuch's tales. Wine makes people talk, and so does a good listener. The eunuch even drew a sketchy map of the Forbidden City to satisfy Wang's curiosity. The next night, Wang went to the Forbidden City. He slung up a hook, which held fast on a battlement. He nimbly climbed up and jumped over the city wall. In black clothes. But either the map was not quite accurate or Wang didn't remember the details, for he could not find the place where the emperor was confined. He had to beat a retreat before dawn and try again another night.

On September 23, a ceremony was held. West Empress Dowager took power once again, officially. Then she issued orders to annul all the emperor's decisions and she restored almost everything that he had changed. She said that she would go on with the reforms, but more gradually.

Then came an order to arrest all the emperor's supporters. Two of them had escaped abroad. Seven were imprisoned. Six were publicly beheaded on September 28, including Official Tan; the last one was exiled to Xinjiang, the farthest of all the provinces. And this was called the "One Hundred Day Reform" in the history of China.

West Empress Dowager summoned all the senior courtiers to her presence. The emperor was there, too. West Empress Dowager accused the emperor, saying that she had agreed to the reforms but with the caveat that traditions not be broken; the emperor had gone too far. Then she asked the emperor what he would have done if Yuan had brought in his New Army: "Did you wish to kill me?" she demanded. The emperor just sat there, glumly. Nothing to say, when the game is up.

But West Empress Dowager hated Official Kang most of all, because it was he who had drafted the decrees. When she asked if Kang was under arrest yet, they answered, "Escaped." One of the courtiers suggested that whoever had tipped him off should be arrested." West Empress Dowager glanced at the emperor and said, "It's Emperor who wrote to advise him to do so." Now, no one had anything more to say.

Kang's place had been ransacked and all the documents found there were presented to West Empress Dowager. Among them was a letter from the emperor, ordering him to go to Shanghai to publish a newspaper. This was a coded sentence. And so Kang had fled.

Some historians said that if the emperor had implemented his changes one at a time, allowing the reactions to flare up and cool down rather than bombarding the country with reforms, the history of China might have been different. Russian rulers have always taken the approach that one cannot cross a chasm by small steps, and they wrenched their country out of medieval obscurity through sweeping reforms. But then, they did not have an empress dowager at the helm.

CHAPTER 42

While West Empress Dowager was pondering how to depose Emperor Guangxu, the newspapers in Shanghai printed all sorts of conjectures. One official, head of the Telegram Bureau in Shanghai, sensed what was coming and drafted a petition. He gathered 1,231 signatures, including many famous scholars, and telegraphed it to the Foreign Affairs Yamen. The officials there could not conceal it and sent it on to the Secretarial Bureau. Ronglu, now the head secretary of the Bureau, took it to West Empress Dowager, who in turn asked Ronglu how to deal with it. Ronglu said that the best way to quench such a rumor was to let them know that the emperor was still the emperor. So they made a public statement in the name of West Empress Dowager that a celebration would be held the next year for the emperor's 30th birthday. Of course, they didn't have money for such a ceremony, as West Empress Dowager had used every possible resource to build her garden. The next day the emperor made another public declaration: since the government was experiencing financial constraints, he would prefer to forgo the celebration, with all due thanks to his adoptive mother. This demonstrated that he was still the emperor; it depicted a thoughtful mother and a responsible son — a harmonious family.

The next rumor had it that the emperor had escaped from the Forbidden City and was traveling south, in disguise. Seven men came to lodge at the temple grounds just outside Qizhen Town, in Hubei Province. One, elegantly dressed, looked like the master, a nobleman. Another looked like his butler. Four men looked like servants or bodyguards, and the last one looked like a cook. He even had some utensils. They paid a 50-tael deposit and rented an independent housing unit in the back. The master kept to himself, staying in his room most of the time. The butler was busy, in and out, in and out. The four servants waited on the master. The cook went out every morning to shop for food, then came back and did the cooking. The monk whose duty was to receive visitors found this group suspicious, and reported to the local yamen. Police were sent in to keep an eye on them; they even followed the butler and the cook for a few days, but nothing unusual happened. Still, the group was mysterious. The mayor finally sent his aide to pay a call on the group, to see what he could find out. The men spoke the Peking dialect and seemed to come from the capital; the butler and the servants acted like they were serving a prince, and the master was the right age. The servants met the mayor's aide, and he, being of low rank, could not insist on speaking with the master directly.

Whatever their mission, the servants were discreet, and answered his questions evasively.

Finally, the aide said, "Then, your master must be an imperial envoy, in disguise."

"You may surmise whatever you will."

The mayor sent for one of his advisors. He reckoned that, before any imperial envoy left the capital, the message would appear in the official newsletter from the capital. Since no such message had appeared in the most recent newsletter, the man in question must not be an imperial envoy. Besides, generally speaking, an imperial envoy would be much older. Then he asked himself, in a stage whisper, "If the rumor is true, could this be the emperor, making an escape to the south?" The mayor was horrified. If that was the case, this was a very subtle, very delicate, very dangerous matter. What should they do? How could they know if the rumor was true or false? The mayor decided to visit the master himself, but the advisor had a better idea.

One day when the cook went to the marketplace, someone picked a fight with him and he was taken to the local yamen for questioning. The cook did not know his master's true identity, but supposedly shared some telltale traits that seemed to coincide with the emperor's known foibles.

"My master is afraid of thunder. During a thunderstorm, the butler and the servants are always with him." The real emperor was known to be afraid of thunder. . .

Still, they could not be sure who the master was. The mayor finally went to see him, with some policemen, all dressed like civilians. If he was an impostor, they could take him into custody right away. If he really was the fleeing emperor, they would pretend that they didn't know anything about a runaway emperor and go back to make further plans. But, what if they still could not decide?

This time, since the mayor himself came, the master received him.

"Where are you from?" the mayor inquired, like a routine patrol asking a lodger in an inn.

"The capital." The young man's voice was low, as if he had a sore throat. The butler stood beside the master all the time.

"In which yamen do you work?"

"The Imperial Household Department."

"You have any official business down here?"

"Yes."

"What's your business?"

"Confidential matter." He cast a look at the butler.

"Will you go further south?"

"Yes."

"Do you have any official traveling documents?"

"Confidential."

What else could the mayor say? He returned to his yamen for consultation, and suggested that he was an impostor.

"An impostor for what?" the aide asked.

"He didn't say he's the emperor. How could he be an impostor?" said the advisor.

"I'll take full responsibility, if anything happens to show I am wrong." The mayor persisted; the others had to go along. They laid out their plan in detail. They would invite him to stay in the yamen — by force, if necessary. He must be under their control first. Then the mayor would report to the governor. If it turned out that he was really the emperor, they could say that they had wanted to protect him. If not, he would be popped into jail.

Thus, the whole little band of travelers was taken into custody and transferred to the governor's yamen at Wuchang City. The governor had had an interview with West Empress Dowager and the emperor, so he should be able to recognize the emperor. Not so easy: during the interview he had been prostrate and had not dared to look up. As a last resort, they sent someone to the capital to sniff out the emperor's status. The man the governor sent was smart. He went to the teahouses where the eunuchs would gather after work. He wiggled into their confidence, plying them with food and drink, and eventually gleaned an assurance that the emperor was still penned up in the Forbidden City.

Back the messenger went, and the governor accused Yang, the master, of impersonating the emperor. Yang noted that he had never said that he was the emperor; that was the mayor's idea. He pleaded innocence. But no: he was guilty anyway. The governor knew that such a case would please West Empress Dowager, and that, after all, was what really mattered. All seven were executed.

They would have died eventually, anyway — even if they lived to the age of 100. Why not let them die a little earlier, to please West Empress Dowager?

CHAPTER 43

Once the emperor was confined on the island, the temptation to depose him became irresistible. A public call for recommendations of physicians was interpreted as a sign that the emperor would soon be forced to abdicate. The French Envoy came to the Foreign Affairs Yamen to recommend a French doctor, but an official there said that they were not entitled to make any decision on the matter, either affirmative or negative. They would have to report to West Empress Dowager, and the answer would be given after three days. Three days later, the French envoy came once more. The answer was negative: the imperial family placed their faith in herbal medicine. The British Envoy came, too. They confessed that their governments were worried about the emperor's health and felt they must send someone to have a look at him (in other words, to see if he were still breathing). West Empress Dowager called a meeting with the court-iers. One of them remarked that it was not polite to refuse the visit of a French doctor — just a neighborly visit when one is concerned for the health of another neighbor. But West Empress Dowager didn't want her foreign neighbors to be concerned for the health of the emperor. At last, she was persuaded to accept that a French doctor could come to see the emperor, accompanied by two princes.

But West Empress Dowager was still pondering how to depose the emperor. Who could succeed to the throne, this time? Not an adult, certainly. And no suitable little boys came to mind. Besides, many courtiers were set against this, and now even foreign countries were starting to interfere. She hated the foreigners all the more.

Ronglu felt that deposing the emperor and changing the succession now would disrupt things severely and could occasion a foreign intervention (not to mention the opposition of the governors and the people); but he was too wise to display his opposition openly. Two prime ministers had submitted a report to West Empress Dowager to propose the deposal of the emperor. West Empress Dowager told them to show the report to Ronglu and ask his opinion. Ronglu reached out to hold the document, but failed to grasp it securely, and allowed it to slip into the brazier. It flared up immediately and was burned to ashes. The two prime ministers were furious; they marched back to West Empress Dowager and accused Ronglu of disrespect to West Empress Dowager. Would West Empress Dowager punish him for it? No. And now, in consultation with his advisors, Ronglu decided that the best move at present would be simply to propose a successor to the emperor — since it was always better to be prepared for any mishap that might come along.

Ronglu reminded West Empress Dowager that the foreign governments had declared that they would not accept a new emperor in place of the current one, and persuaded her that it would be better to bide her time, adopt some boy as a son of the late Emperor Tongzhi, and make him a potential successor. West Empress Dowager thought it feasible, and settled on the son of Prince Zaiyi, who had married her niece. The boy was fifteen at the time. He didn't like to read; he liked to play and fight. Not ideal characteristics for a ruler. But West Empress Dowager didn't know this. The eunuchs and imperial maids took a dislike to him immediately. His face was unappealing, with thick lips and the upper lip curving upward. Not a face that anyone would consider imperial. But he was West Empress Dowager's relative.

When his son (who was now called Big Brother) was selected as the potential successor, Prince Zaiyi became powerful. Now, if anything happened to the emperor, his son would inherit the throne. But the meddling foreigners threatened his sweet dream. He hated them. He wanted to drive all of them out of China. He waited for a chance.

In the Opium War in 1840, the foreign fleets had broken open the golden gate to China, and many priests had come to build churches and preach to the Chinese people. Quite a few Chinese people had accepted the Western god. But the traditional religions in China were Taoism and Buddhism, and far more people believed in them. Religious differences are usually fertile grounds for conflict, even war. In China, those who adopted the Western god were seen as sacrilegious and many people, including priests, were killed and churches burned to ashes. Diplomatic problems ensued.

In Shandong Province, there was a group called the Yihetuan, or the Society of Righteousness and Harmony. Europeans called them the "Boxers," because they practiced a special kind of martial art. They claimed to have magic powers: they were impervious to bullets. They hated foreigners and believers in foreign gods. They took a violent approach to clearing them out, and the foreigners took exception to that, every time. After several foreign diplomatic protests, the Chinese government had to begin to arrest and even execute members of the

Yihetuan, which was growing fast. Under foreign pressure, West Empress Dowager appointed Yuan Shikai Governor of Shandong Province. Arriving there on December 25, 1899, he turned his guns on the Yihetuan, who were armed with swords, spears, and hoes. Yuan captured some of them and gunned them down in public, disproving their claims. The bullets very clearly penetrated their bodies. The rest of the group was forced to flee in spring, 1900, into Zhidi Province — closer to the capital.

Then one of them had a bright idea. They put up a banner, saying "Help the Qing Dynasty to Wipe Out Foreigners." The slogan struck home, and their numbers swelled. Indeed, quite a few courtiers were inclined to pacify the Yihetuan. Prince Zaiyi thought it might be handy to use them to drive out the foreigners so that West Empress Dowager could force the emperor to abdicate, paving his own son's way to the throne. West Empress Dowager wanted to use the Yihetuan to expel the foreigners, too, so that she could be rid of their interference.

The Yihetuan, bolstered by Prince Zaiyi and some other courtiers, became bolder and wilder. In revenge for Yuan's massacre, they began to ambush small groups from the government army. They pulled down telegram cables and chopped up the posts. They dug up rails to disable the railway. All these actions were reported to West Empress Dowager, who ordered Ronglu to send troops to protect the railroad and the telegraph system. Ronglu had already been made a secretary, but he still controlled the army in the capital area. Secretaries could not, ordinarily, command armies, but Ronglu did. No one had had more power than Ronglu in all the days of Qing Dynasty. Whom else could West Empress Dowager trust? Ronglu would never betray her.

The Yihetuan assailed the division that was guarding the railroad. The army killed some and dispersed the rest. But in Tianjin City, anyone who dared to criticize the Yihetuan was killed. When they were walking the streets, even the mayor had to step aside and let them pass. The whole city was out of control. The governor of Zhidi Province believed in their magical power and treated them as his noble guests. He even allowed their leader to ride in his own official palanquin. That being the case, the policemen did not dare to interfere with whatever they were doing. The Yihetuan were eventually allowed into the capital itself, and their leaders took up lodging in Prince Zaiyi's residence. The situation was deteriorating rapidly and chaos was spreading.

Gradually, West Empress Dowager began to find that she didn't like the boy. He was naughty and refused to study. He had brought in two dogs, and was constantly playing with them. Once, she went to see the current emperor, and saw that his upper lip was a little swollen. Now, Prince Zaiyi had always cursed the emperor behind his back, wishing him to die; his son had heard his father say it so many times that he developed a hatred for the emperor, whom he ought to have revered as his uncle. The young fellow had gone to see the emperor and provoked him that day; the emperor told him to leave him alone, and turned his back. At that, the boy had rushed at the emperor and knocked him over. Even under the circumstances, that was too much. West Empress Dowager was irate and summoned the boy to her presence, and she told her eunuchs to give him a good whipping on the buttocks.

When Prince Zaiyi heard about that, he feared that West Empress Dowager might start to rethink the succession. Someone advised him to ensure his son's future. And the most decisive step would be to remove the emperor entirely, so that his son could take over the throne immediately. An idea with a certain allure. One day, Prince Zaiyi took some members of the Yihetuan into the Forbidden City. The guards didn't dare to stop them. Prince Zaiyi led them to where West Empress Dowager generally received the courtiers. He didn't know the way to the place where the emperor lived. He asked to see West Empress Dowager, who came out to see him. The members of Yihetuan made threats and demanded that West Empress Dowager give up the emperor. But Ronglu had many bodyguards stationed there to protect West Empress Dowager; they dashed out and seized all the intruders, and executed them as robbers. Prince Zaiyi had to leave the Forbidden City without his goal fulfilled.

On May 20, 1900, all the foreign envoys in Peking held a meeting, and the next day they sent a notice to the Qing Government, requesting that the leaders of Yihetuan and their accomplices be executed and that the officials who refused to arrest members of the Yihetuan be punished. They added that, if nothing was done within five days, they would find themselves obliged to send more soldiers into the capital to protect their legations. But by that time the government had lost control of the Yihetuan. Many Chinese soldiers sympathized with them, and even joined them.

On May 31, more foreign soldiers did come into the capital to safeguard their legations. The Yihetuan set out to lay siege to the largest cathedral in the capital, the North Cathedral, but they met with strong resistance. The clergyman and his assistants, helped by many new Chinese Christians, defended the building. Everyone was expecting the leader of the Yihetuan to use his magic powers, but he said that he had been with his wife the night before, and that had

214

weakened his power. Maybe tomorrow. But he didn't come the next day either, leaving others to continue the attack. The city was in an uproar.

When West Empress Dowager heard all this, she gave a written order to Prince Zaiyi to put down the Yihetuan for once and for all. Too late. He just crumpled up the order and stuffed it into his pocket. Another prince was at his residence at the time and, seeing this, he quickly returned home and told his servants to bar the door. No one would go out and no visitors would be received. They had already stockpiled enough of everything to live for several months. Many courtiers followed the example.

On June 2, foreign troops disembarked from their warships and gathered along the coast. They began an assault on Tianjin City. The general whose duty it was to defend the city told the mayor to send the Yihetuan to drive the foreign troops back to their ships. A leader of the Yihetuan came to see the general and told him to fire his cannons at the foreign troops.

"What if they return the fire?" the general asked.

"I will use my magic power to disable their cannons for six hours." When he left, it was nightfall, so the general prepared to attack the next day. But at dawn, a member of the Yihetuan came to ask the general if he had fired his cannons that night, implying that, during the night, the foreign cannons had been disabled by the Yihetuan leader's magic power. A little joke?

On June 10, the foreign troops began to march toward Peking. No trains were available — the Yihetuan had got there first, and torn up the rails. A long walk. On June 12, they marched right into an ambush and had to retreat. Foreign fleets were attacking Dagukou, a fortress on the harbor, at the same time.

From June 16 through 19, West Empress Dowager met with her courtiers to discuss whether to fight or negotiate with the foreign aggressors. Ronglu voted for sustaining what peace there was, but Prince Zaiyi insisted on war. None of the plans suited West Empress Dowager — she had set her heart on driving the foreigners out of China, but no one could assure her of success.

At this critical moment, Prince Zaiyi and his followers decided that they must do something to tip the scales in their favor. The prince sent an advisor to visit a telegram decoder. For 10,000 taels of silver, he obtained a telegram supposedly coming from the foreign governments. Usually, when a telegram came in, the operator gave it to the decoder, who rendered it into regular text and dispatched it to its intended recipient. It was mighty easy, then, to come up with a false telegram and hand it in to the Secretarial Bureau. This missive was delivered, and the decoder vanished with the money.

When West Empress Dowager read the telegram, she was scandalized. A nightmare! It listed the following demands: (1) to free the emperor and turn over the power to him; (2) to disperse the Yihetuan and, if the Qing Government could not do it alone, to allow the foreign governments to send their armies to help; (3) to consult the foreign governments as to how many troops the Qing Government would train and maintain; and invite foreign officers to drill its army; (4) to invite the foreign governments to supervise and control the collection and use of all the taxes.

Those were conditions that no sovereign power could accept, and West Empress Dowager was not about to relinquish any of her authority. So on June 19, when Dagukou fell to the foreigners, West Empress Dowager declared war. The foreign envoys were told to leave Peking in 24 hours.

On June 20, the German Envoy set out for the Foreign Affairs Yamen, but on the way he ran into a squad of Chinese patrolling soldiers and was killed. At 4:00 PM that same day, instigated by Prince Zaiyi, the Yihetuan started to assault the foreign legations in Peking. A government division under Ronglu's command went over to Prince Zaiyi and joined the Yihetuan besiegers. The general of the division had been a rebel in the northwestern provinces. He had gone over to the Qing Government and had been promoted to the rank of general. Now, Prince Zaiyi had lured him over by promising that if his son succeeded to the throne, the general would be made a governor. And since Prince Zaiyi and Ronglu both served West Empress Dowager, this was not deemed a betrayal. Ronglu could not even report this inside perfidy to West Empress Dowager, for fear that she would blame him for his inability. What could he do, if this was not betrayal?

The Yihetuan and the army division had only rifles and could not inflict much damage to the legation buildings in any case. The general went to see Ronglu, to borrow the cannons that were under his control. Of course, Ronglu flatly refused; and this, too was reported to Prince Zaiyi. When West Empress Dowager was told that Prince Zaiyi wanted to use the Yihetuan to assault the foreign legations, she hadn't said anything — which meant that she acquiesced. Prince Zaiyi had promised to seize all the legations and capture the foreigners within a short period of time. Three days went by, and he hadn't done it yet — so he complained to West Empress Dowager that Ronglu had refused to let him use the cannons. Without cannons, how could he take the legations in a short time? It was Ronglu's fault, not his. West Empress Dowager told Ronglu to lend him the cannons, but Ronglu pointed out that there was a risk of hitting the Temple of General Deng, which was very close to the foreign legations.

General Deng had been a general during the Ming Dynasty. His troops had been camped north of the Great Wall. The first emperor of Qing Dynasty liked to travel alone to inspect the terrain, for military purposes. Once he was taken captive by soldiers of Ming Dynasty and sent to General Deng. The emperor had made a favorable impression on the general, and Deng had secretly released him. Later, when Japan had invaded Korea, General Deng was sent to fight the Japanese Army and died there. The first Qing Emperor thereupon had built a temple in his memory. When the Qing Dynasty was founded, within the entire territory of China, the emperor built another temple in Peking, also called the Temple of General Deng, and every subsequent emperor would go there to worship. Hitting the temple with their own cannons would be a crime against their ancestors. A strong pretext for rejecting Prince Zaiyi's demands; West Empress Dowager agreed.

But she did want Ronglu to use his cannons to support the attack on the foreign legations. Ronglu went back and told the officer in charge of the cannon regiment to open fire. He didn't specify "on the foreign legations"; but he did indicate that the sound of the cannons had better be audible within the Forbidden City. The officer turned his cannons in the opposite direction and fired away. Ronglu always opposed the Yihetuan, but he never openly disagreed with West Empress Dowager.

The death toll was high on both sides from June 20 through 24, but Prince Zaiyi and his followers still had not got control of the legations. This shook West Empress Dowager's faith in him, for if he could not capture a few buildings, how could he drive out all the foreigners? On June 25, she ordered an end to the attack, but the Chinese soldiers and the Yihetuan still surrounded the foreign legations and they did not really stop fighting until August 14.

On July 14, the foreign unified forces seized Tianjin City. No one wanted to be the bearer of bad news. Prince Zaiyi could not foist that job off onto anyone else, though, and he had to report to West Empress Dowager. Their meeting was unpleasant. Even with the help of magic, he had failed! How could it be that Tianjin City was lost? West Empress Dowager slapped hard on the table before her, which startled the prostrate prince.

"If the foreigners come to the capital, I will put *you* before their cannons," she hissed, and dismissed him in frustration.

Ronglu went to see her the next day and reported that, after some investigation, the telegram supposed to have come from the foreign governments was proved to be a fake. There was no record of any such telegram at the station on either end — it must have been written at the order of Prince Zaiyi, who had been pressing her to declare war on the foreigners. To her great peril. Now, West Empress Dowager summoned Zaiyi.

"Do you know what 'deception' means?" She smacked the side table with her fist.

"I would never dare to trick Old Buddha!"

Zaiyi had no defense. He only knocked his forehead on the floor, begging pardon.

"You think I don't know the things you did. I understand what you want: You want to be the over-emperor when your son inherits the throne. I can tell you right now, don't have any illusions on that score."

Prince Zaiyi went home, only to find that his favorite lieutenant and his whole family had been killed by the Yihetuan. They accused him of having given them insufficient provisions. Zaiyi sent for their leader, who shrugged and said that there were traitors among them who had done it. "Traitors" was just a pretence they used to elude criticism from other courtiers. That the leader would say it to him was beyond belief. He had invited wolves into his own sheepfold.

But he was more afraid of the courtiers who opposed him than of the Yihetuan who betrayed him. First, he accused three courtiers of treason and had them jailed. Two courtiers wrote a report to West Empress Dowager, declaring that Prince Zaiyi should be held responsible for all that had happened, but Zaiyi said that they were guilty of treachery and begged West Empress Dowager to execute them. And West Empress Dowager did order them executed. Prince Zaiyi insisted that the three courtiers already imprisoned should also be executed, and again West Empress Dowager went along.

On August 4, the foreign troops left Tianjin City. They marched towards Peking. Outside the city, Chinese troops led by Ex-Governor Li Binheng lay in wait. Ex-Governor Li had originally argued against declaring war on the foreigners, but when the foreign troops had attacked Tianjin City, he recruited a division and marched to rescue the capital. West Empress Dowager was impressed, and interviewed him, and presented him with an imperial sword — a very high honor. An imperial sword conferred authority in and of itself. A man with an imperial sword could execute anyone who disobeyed his orders, without first seeking the emperor's approval. However, when the foreigners approached,

Li Binheng's newly-recruited soldiers ran away at the sound of the cannons and guns. He used the imperial sword to cut his own throat. Now, the foreign troops marched onward without facing any resistance. On August 14, the allied troops entered Peking and strutted into the Forbidden City, from which West Empress Dowager had recently fled.

CHAPTER 44

Concubine Zhen had been locked away in an empty chamber in an old, deserted building. She had always been kind to the eunuchs and maids, and now they often came to see her and talked a little. Her sister, Concubine Jin, would send her maid with some delicious food, and while Concubine Zhen was eating, the maid told her all the news through a barred window. One day, she asked the maid to take a note to her sister. The maid hid the note in her pocket, but somehow she lost it on the way to Concubine Jin's chambers. She didn't even realize she had lost it; but when she reached her destination, she could not find the note. Now she was in a panic, and Concubine Jin was terrified, too. What did the note say? West Empress Dowager might easily put them both to death.

The note was picked up by a eunuch, who promptly delivered it to West Empress Dowager. It did not make her happy. The note said, "Get the emperor to stay for the negotiations." However, this was not the moment to address such a trifling matter. At just about this time, late in the evening of August 12, to be exact, the bad news came at last that the foreign troops would soon enter the capital. Time to go.

Prince Zaiyi dashed in and asked, "What shall we do?"

"You said that the Yihetuan could resist the foreign invasion: 'They have special magic and are bulletproof.' Fine. You go and defend Peking. If you let the foreign armies enter the capital, I will have you flayed alive." West Empress Dowager was beside herself.

But the Chinese army and the Yihetuan scattered before the foreign guns. Early the next morning, West Empress Dowager sent for the emperor, the queen and Concubine Jin. She told them her decision, and ordered the queen to take her eunuchs and have her treasures buried in the yard.

Then she had herself dressed like a peasant's wife, and the others were suitably dressed as well. Before her departure, she ordered Concubine Zhen to be brought before her. "The foreign troops will soon come into Peking. I can't take you along; there are already too many people traveling with me. They will certainly rape you, which would be a great insult to the imperial family, and especially to the emperor. I advise you to end your life before such things happen to you." West Empress Dowager spoke in a calm, serious voice.

"I am not afraid of death, but I beg Old Buddha to let the emperor stay to deal with the foreigners." If the emperor could get out of West Empress Dowager's grasp, he might still have an opportunity to seize power. But West Empress Dowager was far too clever to take such chances, and she did not appreciate this last ploy. She ordered the eunuchs to throw Concubine Zhen down a deep well. The emperor implored West Empress Dowager, on his knees, to spare her life, but she waved the eunuchs off to execute her order. Concubine Zhen, not yet 25 years old, left a long, loud shriek trailing behind her as she fell.

At this very moment an old prime minister, Xu, was hanging himself, at home. He was the most conservative courtier and had always opposed anything made in foreign countries. While the other courtiers had adopted the kerosene lantern, he still used candles. He was shortsighted, but refused to use glasses. Now the foreigners would soon reach the Forbidden City. He didn't want to see West Empress Dowager and the emperor taken captive or insulted. He decided to die for the nation. He called in his son and urged him to be a martyr, too. His son promised to die with him. They prepared two lengths of rope and set up two stools. The father put his head into one noose and the son stood at his side and comforted him. "Father, you go first. I will follow." He yanked the stool from under his father's feet and watched the poor man hanging from the ceiling; then he fled over the back wall. However, as destiny would have it, he was captured by the Japanese and held captive until a peace treaty was signed; then he was transferred to the Qing Government and executed by order of West Empress Dowager.

But now, West Empress Dowager and the emperor rode out of town on a wagon, and the queen and Concubine Jin on another wagon, followed by some courtiers on horseback. Prince Zaiyi and other princes followed. At noon, they reached a small village. Head Eunuch Li found an old man and brought him out to speak with West Empress Dowager. Or, rather, to have her speak to him. She couldn't oblige the old man to kowtow, because of her disguise, but she was still his superior.

"Have you any food?" she asked.

"All gone. The soldiers just left."

What could she say? The soldiers wanted to eat, too. Lucky they didn't kill the old man and eat him, too.

"Do you have tea? We are thirsty," Eunuch Li asked.

"This a poor place," said the old man, "Never tasted tea my whole life. We use dried date flowers." So saying, he went to boil water and poured hot water into a crude bowl with some dried date flowers.

West Empress Dowager looked at the dirty bowl, chipped at the rim, and frowned. But thirst compelled her to drink. A few hours later they arrived in a small town. The mayor received them and provided them with decent food, but not like the dainties served in the palace. At least their hunger was cured, for the moment.

Now they wanted to issue several urgent orders, but in their haste they had not brought any official seals. A written order had to have a seal on it, the seal of West Empress Dowager, the seal of the emperor, or the seal of some other authority. Every yamen had its own seal, but the emperor and the empress dowager could hardly use the seal of a township yamen. Just then another secretary caught up with them, bringing with him the seal of the Secretarial Bureau. First, they issued orders to move the troops to block the foreigners from any pursuit. Next, they discussed where to set up a temporary residence. They could not stay in this small town. The nearest city that was large enough to have a decent accommodation for the imperial family was Taiyuan City. So to Taiyuan City they made their way.

The mayor of this small town was Wu Yong. West Empress Dowager was satisfied with his service and appointed him imperial harbinger to prepare lodging and food for them. He went ahead and came into another town, but it was even smaller than his. It was deserted. Not even the mayor was there. A band of eunuchs, some bodyguards and soldiers arrived, and promptly demanded food and fodder, but there was nothing in this deserted town. An officer glared at Wu Yong, and drew his sword. Would he kill Wu? Go ahead! Wu glared at him and said, "You fled before the foreign armies, and now you want to kill me! Are you ashamed of yourself?" Recalling all the dreadful events that had happened recently, he was temporarily blinded by bitter tears. When his eyes cleared, he was alone again. Later, people said that the soldiers had been driven away by his tears: perhaps he should weep before the foreigners and drive them away, too.

When the imperial party arrived in Taiyuan City, bits of news came in. Ronglu was in Baoding City preparing for any emergency. The foreign armies had the capital under control and were waiting for the Qing Government to send a representative to negotiate. Negotiations began, even while West Empress Dowager was still on her way to Taiyuan City. One of the conditions the foreign governments insisted upon was that all the courtiers who had set the Yihetuan against the foreigners, and hence had caused the war, must be executed. Practically speaking, that would have meant beheading the entire administration. The Qing Government representatives pleaded that, under Chinese law, princes were never executed. No dice: the joint foreign troops marched on Baoding City and took that, too. West Empress Dowager was afraid that they would come after her in Taiyuan City, so she went on to Xi An City with the emperor and other imperial family members, leaving behind in Taiyuan City those princes and courtiers who were on the foreigners' list.

At last, they reached Xi An City, their final destination. It had been the capital for many dynasties, long ago. It was inland, far from Peking. Far enough, West Empress Dowager thought, to deter the invaders. Safe again, she returned to her luxurious lifestyle, although the capital was still in the hands of the foreigners. And Ronglu joined them, coming to Xi An directly from Baoding City.

On September 7, 1901, a treaty was signed and peace was restored. The Yihetuan were killed, arrested or scattered. All the courtiers who had been belligerent to the foreigners, and on whom the war was blamed, were executed — except for Prince Zaiyi, who was banished for life to Mongolia. China, shaky as it already was, was further weakened by the treaty which obliged them to pay 450 million silver dollars to the foreigners, to destroy several of their own military installations, and to turn over to foreign troops the main railway.

This was the beginning of the end — unless you consider that that had already come some time before.

* * *

There were two theaters in Xi An City. Once West Empress Dowager had set up her temporary palace there, Big Brother went to watch operas every day, escorted by a group of eunuchs, at a theater that also happened to be frequented by some of Ronglu's soldiers. Big Brother liked to beat the drum that accompanied the singing, so the owner of the theater and the leader of the troupe had to let him do it. One day, Big Brother was not beating the drum correctly and the opera singer faltered in his singing. The soldiers, who had no idea this was Big Brother, laughed at him. Contempt! He began a fight with the soldiers, and the eunuchs had to join in to protect Big Brother. No matter how much they wished to see him thrashed. If anything serious happened to Big Brother, they would be executed.

The general of the division went to Ronglu to beg pardon, but Ronglu told him not to worry — Big Brother was to blame. Ronglu would take care of it. Better to pacify soldiers, in wartime. When Big Brother complained to Ronglu about his men, Ronglu criticized Big Brother; he, in turn, took it out on the theater owner. He complained to the mayor of Xi An City, who ordered the theater to be closed. Furthermore, he declared that in wartime all the restaurants and places of entertainment should be closed.

Was that right? With so many courtiers and other wealthy people coming into the city, this was the best business season they had ever seen. The theater and restaurant owners sent in a petition and, after the necessary inducements had been offered, these places were opened once more. But fighting was prohibited.

In the meantime Mayor Wu Yong, whom West Empress Dowager had sent off on various business matters, came back with a report of success. West Empress Dowager was happy with him. Seeing that the moment was favorable, he added that while passing through Canton City, he had met Governor Zhang, and Zhang had recommended advising West Empress Dowager to expel Big Brother. It was in his interests that his father, Prince Zaiyi, had brought such catastrophe upon the country. Besides, the boy was wholly unsuitable for the position, as he lacked the mind for it. West Empress Dowager already disliked the boy and other courtiers had counseled her to get rid of him, for the same reasons. So the boy was deprived of the title and packed off to live with his father in the Mongolian district.

CHAPTER 45

West Empress Dowager and the emperor set out to return to the capital. On the occasion of such a voyage, all the roads were expected to be repaired, with no pits; and yellow sand must be strewn on the road surface. Even at such a time, the routine was observed. Local governments had to organize people to do the work. And for the return trip West Empress Dowager, the emperor, the queen and Concubine Jin all rode in palanquins — no more bumping wagons for them. When they reached Kaifeng City, which had been the capital of the Song

Dynasty, West Empress Dowager received a report saying that the foreign troops had withdrawn from the capital after the treaty was signed, and that the foreign envoys would come to meet her when she arrived in the capital. She was relieved to hear that the foreign envoys were still observing protocol — who knows what attitude they might have taken, after the war broke out.

From the Kaifeng City they were ferried across to the north side of the Yellow River, and soon entered Hebei Province, where they were transferred to a special train, which took them on to the capital. This was West Empress Dowager's second train ride. The first time had been in the prototype train in the imperial West Garden, before the Purple-Light Pavilion.[1]

Now, when West Empress Dowager got off the train, she waved to the foreign envoys, who had come to welcome her; then she was carried in a palanquin into the Forbidden City. Once she had returned to her chamber, those who had remained in the Forbidden City, the imperial household, the maids and eunuchs, all came to pay their respects to her. Except one: Imperial Concubine Dowager Yu (the concubine of the late Emperor Tongzhi, West Empress Dowager's son, not of the present Emperor Guangxu). In the absence of West Empress Dowager, she had taken charge of everything in the Forbidden City.

She was summoned to see West Empress Dowager later, alone. "The buried treasures are still there," she said. "And now, I must return these to their rightful owners." A eunuch knelt a little behind her, bearing several objects wrapped in yellow brocade: the imperial seals. One belonged to West Empress Dowager, and was made of white jade. One was the emperor's, carved from an emerald of the finest quality. The third was the queen's, cast in gold. What if these seals had been stolen? Concubine Dowager Yu really deserved a reward, and in this case words were the reward of highest value. "I have always appreciated that you are a good and thoughtful lady." West Empress Dowager had rarely praised anyone so clearly and sincerely.

* * *

---

1. The foreign businessman who wanted to build railroads in China thought to win her over to his project by offering West Empress Dowager a sample mini-train as a gift; the rails only ran a short distance, with a couple of train cars on them. However, for reasons of safety, West Empress Dowager would not allow the locomotive to draw the mini-train. Instead she ordered eunuchs to push and pull the carriage she sat in. This became a great joke among the foreigners.

It was said that after she had ordered Concubine Zhen drowned in the well, West Empress Dowager often had ghastly dreams of her. And it was said that maids and eunuchs often encountered something like a shadow wafting through the air near the place where Concubine Zhen had lived.

"I don't know how to report to Old Buddha . . ." Concubine Dowager Yu didn't finish the sentence.

"You can say whatever you want. I won't be offended."

"Concubine Zhen has often appeared in my dreams. She asks to be buried somewhere. She doesn't like to lie in the well. It's too cold there."

West Empress Dowager had the same impression, and she gave an order that Concubine Zhen's corpse should be lifted from the well and buried with a proper ceremony befitting her status as an imperial concubine.

"Your slave has one more thing to report to Old Buddha. Your slave has dreamt of Concubine Zhen many times. Concubine Zhen says that she needs a memorial tablet[1] so that her ghost can sit behind it, rather than floating in the air."

West Empress Dowager agreed. Circumstances had changed, and while she was still set on controlling the emperor, she would have to treat him decently again, just like before the reforms. The emperor would be meeting with the foreign envoys, according to international practice. The reforms he had launched had impressed the foreign governments and now, if he said anything about his maltreatment, they would have an excuse to insist that she relinquish her power.

"You'd better plan to attend Concubine Zhen's funeral," West Empress Dowager advised the emperor, indicating that she had never disapproved of their love for each other. "She will be buried as an imperial concubine."

But her Head Eunuch Li was sent to see the emperor when he returned to his study. West Empress Dowager didn't really want the emperor to see Concubine Zhen's ghastly corpse, which would only remind him of the horror of how she had died. But Head Eunuch Li didn't know how to dissuade the emperor from attending the funeral.

"Can you get something for me?" the emperor wistfully asked. "Something Concubine Zhen used or wore, by which I can remember her."

---

1. A small wooden tablet on which the name of the deceased was engraved. The tablet was usually placed on a table with incense and candles before it so that people could pay their respects to the deceased.

Head Eunuch Li was not sure where he could turn to look for what the emperor so desired; then he realized that very probably Concubine Jin had kept something of her sister's as a memento. He went to see her, and conveyed the emperor's wish. She rummaged in a trunk and produced a small gold box, which she gave to him. Presenting it to the emperor, he noted, "Concubine Jin suggests that it's better the emperor not attend the funeral. It's so cold outside. If the emperor should get a chill and fall ill, Concubine Zhen will be uneasy in her afterlife."

"I will accept her advice," said the emperor. And Head Eunuch Li went back to report to West Empress Dowager.

* * *

Since the German Envoy had been killed in the Yihetuan riot, the German King insisted that the Qing Government should send a prince to Germany to apologize. West Empress Dowager sent Prince Zaifeng, the present emperor's stepbrother, to Germany. As the emperor had made a good impression on the foreign governments, the German King received his stepbrother in a cordial manner and encouraged him to participate more in political activities. When Prince Zaifeng returned and reported to West Empress Dowager, she sensed that the foreign governments might support Prince Zaifeng as a successor to the emperor. She knew that Prince Zaifeng was not a particularly able man and he had no ambition whatsoever. But could he be goaded in that direction?

In old China, if the son of a family should go astray, the parents would find him a wife who could lead him back to the right path. Such a wife must be demure and proper, and must have the talent to twist the husband round her little finger. West Empress Dowager began to look for such a girl to be the wife of Prince Zaifeng.

Ronglu had had a son and a daughter. The son had died young, but the daughter was about the same age as Prince Zaifeng. She was known to be both shrewd and eloquent. Head Eunuch Li suggested that she was the right girl for Prince Zaifeng. However, Prince Zaifeng had already been engaged to another girl from a Mongolian family. West Empress Dowager ordered the engagement broken. Normally, if a boy's family broke the engagement, it was assumed that they had found some discreditable qualities or misconduct on the girl's part, and she was disgraced. Although this case was quite different, the girl found it disgrace enough, and she committed suicide by drinking poison.

Prince Zaifeng and Ronglu's daughter Funiu were soon engaged to be married. West Empress Dowager often summoned Funiu into the Forbidden City. She was a clever girl and knew how to talk sweetly. Before the wedding day, West Empress Dowager said to her, "While I think you already have everything a person could wish for, I still would like to give you something as a wedding gift." She gestured to her head eunuch to bring in her jewelry box, from her bedroom. Eunuch Li had two eunuchs present it. When the box was opened, a dazzling array of gems and gold was revealed. West Empress Dowager beckoned Funiu forward and told her to select six items, whichever she liked best. An astonishing privilege, even for a future niece-in-law.

There were four compartments in the box, for pearls, precious stones, jade and miscellaneous pieces. "Why not choose from the miscellaneous compartment first," West Empress Dowager advised her. There was a diamond ring; a diamond as big as an apricot pit. Funiu was tentatively reaching toward it when she heard someone give a little cough. She looked up at Big Princess, who was moving her head a bit from left to right. So she picked up a diamond bracelet instead. "Mmm. That is a nice piece. Try it on," West Empress Dowager instructed. The girl put it on her wrist and showed it to West Empress Dowager. "It looks pretty on you," West Empress Dowager commented. So Big Princess said, "You can keep it on." Then she was told to select six pieces. The bracelet was an extra gift — and she got six more.

Ronglu was seriously sick at the time, but the wedding was held anyway. An event like his daughter's marriage into the imperial family should have driven away the demons of sickness. But these demons had no fear, and took Ronglu away with them not long after the wedding. The news of Ronglu's death hit West Empress Dowager somewhere near her heart; this time, she actually wept.

CHAPTER 46

Although the emperor's reforms had failed, people all over the country were still anxious to move forward, and they blamed West Empress Dowager for the fiasco. The newspapers were calling for change.

West Empress Dowager publicly declared that she wanted reform, too, but step by step. First, she wanted to discard the examination system for the selection of government officials and establish new Western-style schools. Of course, this aroused the adamant opposition of the entrenched bureaucrats who owed their positions to the examination system.

West Empress Dowager also agreed to send a group of young students overseas to study in America. China needed people with new skills, including knowledge of foreign languages and lands, and the technologies for building transportation and communication infrastructures: telegraph networks, railroads, and steamboats, warships and cargo ships, and modern mining and metallurgical sciences.

But many students who went abroad picked up the Western lifestyle and customs, betraying their Chinese traditions. Some of the courtiers demanded that all the students return to China, lest their minds be further contaminated. And after endless debates, West Empress Dowager consented to having the students return. The newspapers called it a waste of money, but some of the students had already learned enough to become the earliest Chinese engineers, and went on to build railroads and ships.

In order to study political reform, West Empress Dowager sent five courtiers abroad to learn from Japan and other foreign countries. On the day they were to leave, the five courtiers arrived at the railway station one by one. Just before the train started, a middle-aged man dressed like a servant tried to board the carriage in which they were seated. The guards stopped him at the door, but just then a bomb went off, killing the man and the guards and wounding two courtiers. The carriage was destroyed. Terrified, one of the courtiers resigned from his assignment, which everyone else had envied.

It was said that this early suicide bomber was a member of the revolutionary party in Canton City, whose aim was to overthrow the Manchu Clan. They declared that the Qing Government was cheating people by sending courtiers to learn from foreign countries how to organize the election of a house of representatives, to form a congress in China. Despite the opposition, West Empress Dowager promised to go ahead. And the Japanese experience was used as a starting point.

The staunchest resistance was reserved for the reorganization of the system of officialdom. So many government officials, at every level, were afraid they would lose their jobs. But this time, West Empress Dowager supported the reform, so all opposition was futile. And no one really lost his position: some ministries changed in name only; new ministries were formed; and many officials were shuffled from one ministry to another. The Foreign Affairs Ministry replaced the Foreign Affairs Yamen, and a Civil Ministry was formed, along with a Military Ministry, the Ministry of Agriculture, Industry and Commerce, and a Communications and Transportation Ministry. Those who were placed on a waiting list for new assignments still were paid the same salary. In the old ministries, two ministers had shared the responsibility equally, one from the Manchu Clan and the other from the Han Clan. The new ministries had only one minister, who could be from either clan; but most of them came from the Manchu Clan, and the Han courtiers complained about it on the sly.

* * *

After Ronglu's death, Prince Yikuang became head of the Secretarial Bureau. He was an avaricious man. He had accumulated 600,000 taels of silver, and now he wanted to deposit it in a foreign bank. Lucky for him, his son knew the manager of a British bank, so they deposited the money there. The bank manager and the Prince's son were both fond of women and often went to the brothels; but the manager was a bigger spender and so was more warmly welcomed. The son was jealous, and once he told his bodyguards to beat up the manager. What was he thinking of?

The manager wanted revenge. He went to see a friend, a critique official. A report showed up on the West Empress Dowager's table, indicating that Prince Yikuang had deposited 600,000 taels of silver in a British bank and asking why he hadn't deposited it in one of the government-run money shops. West Empress Dowager found the question quite valid, and asked Prince Yikuang to explain himself. The prince had to disavow the story: there was no legitimate way he could have come by such a sum, and he was not about to explain its true origins. He begged West Empress Dowager to send someone to investigate, adding that, if the investigation proved that he had the money, he would donate it to the government. Of course West Empress Dowager sent a secretary of state to the bank that same day. But the secretary could not breach the bank's confidentiality policy and he had to report the setback to West Empress Dowager.

Meanwhile, Prince Yikuang tried to withdraw his money and deposit it with another foreign bank. The manager advised him that there was no point in transferring the money; the best thing to do would be to change the name on the account. Prince Yikuang handed over his account book and his personal seal; the day, the manager brought him a new account book and another seal, with a new name on it. All set.

Six months later, he needed some money and sent his butler to make a withdrawal — but he was told that the account was dry and the manager had moved on, no trace to be found. In fact, the manager had used the Prince's account book and personal seal to withdraw the money and put into his own account; then he had given Prince Yikuang a new account book with no money in it. One third of the money went to the critique officer. The rest, he took to Shanghai. So the beating the prince's son had ordered cost them 600,000 taels. Pretty costly.

CHAPTER 47

After the Sino-Japanese war, the Japanese army had stayed in place, occupying the northeastern part of China. There were three provinces involved. Russia also had its army there: they had entered during the Yihetuan riot and had stayed on ever since. Now, a declaration of war between Russia and Japan seemed inevitable.

When that day came, all the other countries with troops in China proclaimed their neutrality. Japan warned the Qing Government that China had better keep neutral, too. It sounded ridiculous that two parties should be fighting on Chinese territory and expect China to stay out of it — like two intruders brawling in someone's house, with the owner expected to stay on the sidelines. (On the other hand, would you step in, if two armed robbers were fighting in your house?) The Government was too weak at the time to prevent the war; but strict neutrality was impossible. Japan had bribed Prince Yikuang, and so the Qing Government favored Japan, allowing her to recruit the horse thieves to fight against the Russians. With secret help from the Qing Government, Japan defeated Russia in the Liaodong Peninsula.

Russia had a fleet in the harbor of Luda. Japan sank some ships at the mouth of the harbor, to block their escape. There was a low hill at the other side of the harbor. If Japan could occupy that hill, she could wipe out the Russian fleet. The fighting was focused on that objective and in due course, the Japanese captured the hill. The Russian fleet had to surrender.

The next battle centered on Liaoyang City. Russia gathered 400,000 men, and Japan 300,000. The front line meandered for hundreds of kilometers. A Japanese detachment went a roundabout way and managed to come up behind the Russian troops; by the time the Russians knew what had happened, they were already surrounded. But to surround 400,000 soldiers with only 300,000 was not easy, and the Russian troops broke out. The losses were heavy on both sides, and an unproclaimed truce followed.

Two Russian fleets came around the Cape of Good Hope from the Black Sea. When they reached the Yellow Sea, they were ambushed by a Japanese fleet and destroyed. But Russian army reinforcements made it through. This war went on and on; it seemed that no one could win it. With America playing the role of mediator, Russia and Japan finally signed a peace treaty.

The war was over, but their armies were still in place. Other foreign countries insisted on their removal and said that when the three provinces were returned to the Qing Government, there should be three governors for these provinces. Official Duan Zhigui wanted to govern Heilongjiang Province. He thought he would bribe Prince Yikuang, as head secretary of state, but someone suggested that it would be more effective to bribe the prince's son. That would be easy, because he was such a sucker for beautiful girls. And beautiful girls didn't cost much.

Theatrical troupes had begun to train actresses, and the actress Yang Cuixi was already something of a celebrity. Official Duan invited the prince's son to watch an opera starring Actress Yang; from his look, Official Duan could tell that he had fallen in love at first sight, a fly in the honey. Actress Yang had been sold to the troupe by her poor parents. Official Duan found the troupe's owner and paid him double the price, thus freeing the girl from the troupe. She had been the star of the show and the owner was reluctant to part with a lucrative player, but he didn't dare to refuse the offer of an official.

Official Duan bought a house and installed Actress Yang there. Then he invited the son to dinner. When he arrived and sat down at the table, Official Duan excused himself for a moment — actually, he left the house altogether. The son waited for Official Duan to return, but to his surprise it was the actress who next stepped into the room. And she went right up and sat in his lap! He was young and good-looking, and a nobleman besides. She smiled. He embraced her and kissed her on the cheek. She offered him a cup of wine, and let matters take their course.

Official Duan became Governor of Heilongjiang Province. But the Japanese army had not yet withdrawn. He would have to wait.

* * *

By tradition, the celebration of the emperor's (or empress dowager's) every tenth birthday called for an extra special one, especially the fiftieth year. West Empress Dowager was still put out that her 50th birthday, which should have been one of the happiest and most exciting days in her life, had coincided with the outbreak of the Sino-French war, and the celebration had been curtailed. When she turned 60, the Sino-Japanese war had interrupted the celebrations. The Russian-Japanese invasion had prevented a proper recognition of her 70th birthday, and who knew if she would make it to 80?

West Empress Dowager was quite old now, 74, and though he was only 38, the emperor was quite ill. Or was he? Word leaked out that the imperial doctors didn't think the emperor was suffering from any serious illness. However, in 1908, West Empress Dowager was really sick. Doctors diagnosed it as dysentery, which is not necessarily a terminal disease, but considering the medicine at that time and her advanced age, her case was thought hopeless.

Some courtiers even hoped that she would die, so that the emperor might step forward. Others were afraid that that might happen — for he had his enemies, too, and they might be killed. One of the latter was Yuan Shikai, who had betrayed the emperor when he gave him the secret order to kill Ronglu and bring the New Army to Peking to trap West Empress Dowager. Rumor had it that the emperor used to draw a turtle on a piece of paper, write Yuan's name on its back and then tear it to bits to vent his anger. If the emperor ever found himself in power, the first one who should fear for his life was Yuan. But Yuan could do nothing to prevent the inevitable from happening. He lived in fear and self-pity. The emperor also hated Head Eunuch Li, whom he called West Empress Dowager's running dog. And that one could do quite a lot to prevent the inevitable.

On November 14, 1908, Emperor Guangxu suddenly died. Poisoned by Eunuch Li, or by Li at the command of West Empress Dowager? The palace was always teeming with secrets and mysteries, especially when an important individual died.

Lying in sick bed herself, West Empress Dowager decided to make Fuyi the heir and successor to the throne. Fuyi was the son of her nephew Zaifeng, who was appointed Prince Regent, because Fuyi was only three years old when he was crowned. On November 15, 1908, West Empress Dowager died.

Fuyi became Emperor Xiantong. He was Emperor only for three years: in 1911, all the newly trained armies, which consisted entirely of the Han Clan and included many soldiers who were revolutionaries, rose up in mutiny and forced Emperor Xiantong to abdicate. The Qing Dynasty was finally overthrown, and the whole dynastic system along with it.

Xiantong was the last emperor of the Qing Dynasty and the last emperor of China; but it was Empress Dowager Cixi who presided over imperial China's final chapters.

Made in the USA
San Bernardino, CA
15 October 2015